PRAISE FOR ONLY IN SPAIN

"Nellie dives into her dream when she flies from selling clothes in Sydney to stomping flamenco in Spain. Hands, ... every fiber of her body…faster, wilder. The notes of the guitar 'chase each other' up her spine. ¡Ole!

"Her passion sweeps the reader in. I confess, she had me turning pages to flamenco music and dancing to the kitchen for snacks. I was with her every stomp of the way, every visit to a tapas bar. But there's more. As she says, 'Dreaming is good but living is better!' Her lust for adventure infuses this book with emotion and joy. Readers will walk away seriously thinking about how to bring excitement into their own lives. ¡Ole!"

—*Rita Golden Gelman, author of* Tales of a Female Nomad

"Reading this vivid, entertaining memoir, I could see, hear, smell, and taste the pleasures of Nellie Bennett's Spain. Willing to give up a comfortable (if conventional) life to feed her wanderlust and new-found flamenco passion, the gutsy Bennett had me shouting ¡Ole! and itching to pack my bag and join her."

—*Ann Vanderhoof, author of* An Embarrassment of Mangoes *and* The Spice Necklace

"A peripatetic Australian's account of how a flamenco dancing hobby led to high adventures in music, food, and love in Spain… Lightweight, footloose good fun."

—*Kirkus Reviews*

"Bennett's transformational adventure parlays into a fun, sparkling memoir."

—*Publisher's Weekly*

ONLY IN
SPAIN

A Foot-Stomping, Firecracker of

a Memoir about Food, Flamenco,

and Falling in Love

NELLIE BENNETT

This book is a memoir. It reflects the author's present recollections of experiences over a period of years. Some names and characteristics have been changed, some events have been compressed, and some dialogue has been re-created.

Published by Sourcebooks, Inc.

P.O. Box 4410, Naperville, Illinois 60567-4410

(630) 961-3900

Fax: (630) 961-2168

www.sourcebooks.com

Originally published in 2012 in Australia, by Allen & Unwin.

Library of Congress Cataloging-in-Publication data is on file with the publisher.

Printed and bound in the United States of America.

VP 10 9 8 7 6 5 4 3 2 1

THE SHOPGIRL

Or
You have to have it!

It was the perfect skirt. Red wild silk with layers of ruffles and a wide sash that cinched in the waist. It was the kind of skirt that makes high heels optional. You could wear it barefoot through the city with just a flower in your hair and be a gypsy princess.

I couldn't help myself. I unclipped it from the hanger and closed the fitting room door behind me. I knew I shouldn't be dreaming such a dangerous dream, but the skirt was whispering to me, "Try me...try me..."

I slipped it on over my trousers. As I tied it around my waist, I caught sight of myself in the mirror. The three lights shone down on me like spotlights. I swished the skirt, imagining I was Carmen dancing on a table in front of her bullfighter lover, lifted up onto my toes and—

Knock knock knock.

Uh-oh.

Dropping my arms, I quickly stepped out of the skirt and unlocked the door. Standing outside with her hand poised to knock again was a woman holding an armful of clothes to try on.

"Hello." I gave a bright smile and straightened my suit jacket.

"Let me take those for you." I took the clothes out of the confused customer's arms and hung them up in the fitting room. "I love this dress," I said of the black-and-white cocktail dress she'd picked up off the front display. "It looks fabulous on."

The woman looked around the fitting room for clues as to what I'd been doing in there. Her eyes dropped to the red silk skirt in my hand. "What size is that?"

"Er…" My grip tightened on it. "This one's on hold." Yeah, right. On hold for who? For me? And how exactly was I planning on buying a seven-hundred-dollar wild-silk creation with the twelve dollars and seventy-three cents I had left in my bank account until payday? "Just let me know if you need anything," I said, stepping out of the fitting room. The woman stared at me without saying a word as I closed the door on her.

I held up the skirt again. It was a dream with three tiers of ruffles. It was the kind of skirt you'd slip into before climbing out your bedroom window in the middle of the night to run away with the gypsies.

Run away with the gypsies…

If only, I thought, looking around at the customers waiting to be helped, sweaters waiting to be folded, shelves to be dusted, racks to be restocked. Of all jobs, this had to be the most ungypsy. I was a shopgirl. You may or may not know my particular shop, but they are all pretty much the same. It was a grand establishment department store. This one was in Sydney, but they are the same in every big city. It had been there in my grandmother's day, though it had a different name back then. It was the place my mother used to take me when I was little to choose a present on a special birthday, and I'd feel so grown-up when the ladies sprayed perfume on my wrist. It had always been a part of my life, and every time the doorman pulled open the door it was like coming home…

But I didn't get to go through that door anymore, with its

green-uniformed doormen and the pianist playing "Rhapsody in Blue." I had to walk an extra half block to the staff entrance. It was there, under the fluorescent lights, that I'd swipe my ID card, fix my hair, and join the line to check my bag.

Standing in line with a dozen other shopgirls, I tried to remember back to when this job had felt glamorous to me. It hadn't been so long ago. This was my first job out of high school, but my excitement at joining the workforce was quickly dulled by swipe cards and bag checks and rosters and five-minute coffee breaks.

The bag check was supposed to be a must, as apparently most in-store theft is committed by staff. Still, some of the women I worked with flouted the rule, like Vivienne from Covers, who strode past the security guards on her five-inch stiletto heels, muttering to the Howard Showers girls in her gorgeous Polish accent, "I won't leave my bag with those men. It is worth more than they make in a year. Imagine they put a scratch in it? I sue the store!" The girls sashayed past in a cloud of perfume and stepped through the open doors of the staff elevator.

But I didn't mind handing over my scruffy old bag. They could put as many scratches in it as they liked and I would never notice. I placed my bag on the counter, and the security guard gave me my ticket. And with the ticket tucked away in my pocket, I squeezed into the service elevator with ten other black-suited women to take the short ride up to Level Two—Women's Fashion.

Every morning at nine twenty-eight the elevator doors opened and I'd walk across the marble floor. First I'd wave to the girls in Burberry as they fixed their makeup, then say hello to Martene in Escada as she started up the computer. I'd call out a "Hi!" to Nathan in Moschino, who would always respond by jumping up and down and giving me an enthusiastic wave. Then I would say a professional "good morning" to silver-haired and gray-suited

Deborah in Armani. Next to Armani was our little corner, which was where I'd find Sascha, flipping through French *Vogue*.

"Darling…have a look…" Sascha pointed to the latest paparazzi pics of aspirational celebrities and their handbags. Sascha had an obsession with designer handbags. She herself had an impressive collection, and an equally impressive collection of Amex bills.

You see, retail is a dangerous profession. Once you're in it's very difficult to get out. When you spend all day behaving as though there could be nothing more natural than spending three hundred dollars on a T-shirt, you start to lose a little perspective. And when the new collections come in, you start using on yourself those same arguments that you're trained to use on your customers. "It really is an investment piece," you tell yourself, ignoring the little voice of reason that says, "What?! *Property* is an investment. *That* is a red trench coat!"

And then, of course, there's our favorite trick, the price-per-wear ratio: retail price divided by number of days worn equals daily wear price. Sascha had taught me this magic ratio. When I'd been shocked by the price of the new ostrich-skin Birkin bags, she had patiently explained to me that you have to look beyond the fifty-thousand-dollar price tag and remember that its daily wear price is only a dollar sixty-seven (if you live to be a hundred and five). By this ratio, every day you don't buy it you're actually losing money. So you buy it, and then, like Sascha, you have to work Sundays. For the next ten years.

I knew there was probably something wrong with me, but I just couldn't get excited about the idea of spending fifty thousand dollars on a handbag, especially not one that I would only end up bringing to work every day. And not when there was a whole world outside of *Vogue* magazine to explore.

I wasn't normally interested in fashion magazines, but this morning the latest *Harper's Bazaar* caught my eye. Scrawled across the cover in red letters was an invitation to "run away with the gypsies."

Standing behind the counter, I leafed through the pages, gazing at the dark, evocative shots of models posed in the moonlight in front of campfires and painted caravans. Their fabulous clothes were thrown on like rags. I took in the detail of ripped stockings under ruffled skirts, a tarnished-gold bullfighter's jacket over a tight black dress; it didn't matter to me whether the beaded bolero jacket was Valentino or Chanel, or if the silk-covered stilettos were Jimmy Choos or Louboutins. It was the idea behind the photos that spoke to me. *Run away with the gypsies…* It was the idea of escape.

This issue also featured a tribute to the magazine's iconic editor, Diana Vreeland. As part of the tribute they had revived her signature column, *Why Don't You?*, in which Vreeland used to make obscenely extravagant suggestions for improving and reinventing yourself.

Why don't you…dance flamenco in Dior stockings?

Yes! Why not? I could just see myself in an underground flamenco bar: dripping with polka dots, sipping on Spanish wine as a handsome bullfighter whispered sweet *nadas* in my ear…

And that was when the bell rang over the speakers, letting us know that the doors were now open to customers. I snapped back to reality, put the magazine away under the counter, and started up the register.

The number-one rule of retail is that the first customer of the day is always returning something. I spotted her as she stepped out of the elevator and remembered her from a week earlier: I had spent two hours with her as she tried on everything in the store before discarding it on the floor like used Kleenex. In the end she had bought one sweater off the sale rack. And I knew that sweater was what was inside the rumpled plastic bag that she held in her hands.

I took a deep breath and reminded myself of my shopgirl training—those three days when the store managers take normal, functioning people and try to brainwash them into chirpy department store lackeys. *First-Class Service Rule #1: Smile!*

Smile. Hmmm, there's an interesting concept. In retail you only really smile when your customer says the words: "I'll take one in every color." When I first started working, I was genuinely bright and friendly, but with time I'd become like the rest of the girls. We didn't spontaneously smile. It just wasn't done. Instead, we had degrees of smiling. There's the "Can I help you? I thought not" smile. The "Oh, it's you again" smile, and the "Please go away and let me finish my coffee before it gets cold" smile. I hated being like that, but it was contagious. Though with the nine-thirty returns I generally didn't even try to fight it.

The woman with the return walked past me and up to Sascha at the register. Sascha managed a tight smile and the standard response: "Not suitable then?" I watched as she took the sweater out of its bag and inspected it for sweat marks before processing the refund.

I couldn't help thinking about the absolute futility of this entire industry. Why so much effort goes into producing garments that within six months will be old and "so last season" and sent out to be incinerated. And I couldn't help wondering what I was doing with my life. It seemed to be ticking away as I gazed at the clock, waiting for my coffee break. I entertained myself by wandering around and choosing the one thing I would buy if I could afford to.

Why don't you…team a strict suit jacket with a sexy silk skirt?

That was when I found the red skirt. It had just been flown in and was the star of the new collection. I held it up to myself and imagined that I was in some glamorous nightspot, drinking red wine and dancing on tabletops…

By the time lunch came around we still hadn't made one sale. I slunk into the dusty back room and sat down on a wooden stool to eat my lunch. The room only had about as much floor space as a handkerchief, but it contained the entire autumn/winter season on racks and in boxes, stacked high above my head.

Why don't you...drink sangria instead of wine at your next summer party?

Oh yes! I imagined going to a place where lunch was a long, leisurely affair, preferably outside in the sun with a glass of sangria. Looking around me, all I could see were boxes full of white shirts and pinstriped pants. I wondered, *What if these boxes fall and I am crushed to death? Crushed to death by business suits. How tragic.*

When I stepped back out onto the floor, fixing my (polished and professional) lip gloss, Sascha was helping a woman into an alpaca coat. The customer was a tall, blond, aspirational mother, the kind you see in ads for dishwashers and home Pilates studios.

"Oh yes," she cooed as she gazed at herself in the mirror. "I have to have it." As she strolled to the register, she grabbed a mink stole off a shelf, glanced at it, then threw it at me. "Wrap this up for me too, will you?"

All in all it was a day like any other. When the six p.m. bell finally rang, my back ached from carrying armfuls of clothes to and from the fitting rooms, and I had more mascara under my eyes than on my lashes. Feeling rebellious, I scorned the staff elevator and went down the escalators with the customers. I pulled off my name tag and pretended that I too was just out for a late-afternoon shop. On the ground floor I wove between the cosmetics counters where tired makeup artists were packing up their brushes and the perfume squirters were putting away their samples. I strolled across the marble floor, ducked into security to pick up my bag, then stepped out the gilt doors into the cool evening air.

I love the bustle of the city just as the shops are closing. Customers wander past with their new purchases, chatting happily. They run across the street and jump into empty taxis, while shop assistants make a dash to reach their bus before it leaves the curb.

I saw my bus pull in but decided to let it go. I wasn't in a hurry to get home. Instead I wandered down the busy city street doing some absentminded window-shopping. My eyes lingered briefly on a Ferragamo scarf, a pair of red stilettos, a Gucci bag. A gloved hand reached into the Cartier window and plucked out the diamond-encrusted watches to take them to their nightly resting place in the safe.

At the end of the street, the glowing windows of the designer boutiques gave way to the brightly lit shop front of a travel agency. A sign in the window offered best prices to Rome, New York, Singapore, Paris. There's nothing I love more than gazing at the window of a travel agency. I love looking at the names of destinations I've never visited and imagining the adventures that could await me there. Athens, Bangkok, Madrid…

Why don't you?

THE WINDOW

Or
What's your best price on a ticket to everywhere?

Dubai, Honolulu, Marrakesh…

Perhaps not everyone window-shops for adventure, but I was raised by travelers and had a genetic predisposition for it. In our house we had almost as many maps as books, and the books reached as high as the ceiling.

Traveling had always been a part of my life. My parents were independent filmmakers and their whole marriage was one long honeymoon trip, occasionally docking in Sydney to regroup and refuel. My two younger brothers and I came along for the ride.

I had a passport before I could walk, and when I was little, one of my favorite games was to spin the globe in my father's office and jab my finger at a destination, then try to read the name. I just loved the idea of far-off places, and when I spun the globe, it was all one big swirl of possibilities.

Standing on the busy city street watching tired-eyed women in black suits rush past on their way home, I couldn't help feeling a little in awe of that child who had played with a globe of the world like it was a toy. Life was still a game to her, because she hadn't been burdened with the questions that plagued this shopgirl's waking hours:

"Is this blue or black?"

"What size is a fourteen?"

"How do you get to Menswear?"

Surely I was destined for something more than this? I'm relatively intelligent. I mean, I'm no Einstein, but on an intelligence graph I rank somewhere between Posh Spice and Stephen Hawking. Okay, more up the Posh Spice end, because graphs make me dizzy. But surely the extent of my ability wasn't holding T-shirts up to the light to determine whether they were dark navy or bluish-black?

The job was only ever meant to be temporary. I'd been hired to work through the busy Christmas season, but that was more than two years ago. I was asked to stay on because I was good at the work, and I accepted, always thinking it would only be a couple more months until something else took off in my life and I could leave the smell of plastic suit bags and the click of hangers behind.

What that something else was I didn't know. I wasn't content to just do something for the sake of doing something, though if I'd agreed to fulfill my role in the social contract then I would already have been most of the way through a law degree.

We all have a social contract, whether we're aware of it or not. It lays out the terms and conditions of our lives, how we are to behave and what is expected of us at each juncture. No courts or judges are needed to see that it's upheld; guilt and obligation work perfectly well. Simple comments like "after all your parents went through to get you a decent education" are usually enough to keep most of us in check.

My parents had been patient. They had agreed that I should take a year off after high school to think about what I wanted to do. But as a year stretched to two my father's face became increasingly pained whenever he asked the question, "Have you thought about what you want to do with your life?"

What I want to do with my life?

What I want to *do* with my *life*?

I want to be wild and daring and dance till dawn beneath a full moon. I want to hitch my caravan to a star and live each day like it's my last… But as far as I knew that wasn't a job description, so what could I say?

Maybe I'm a hopeless romantic. Maybe I'm just plain hopeless. But I wanted to live a passionate life. I wanted to feel a part of the world and be in love with the world. I wanted to live my destiny, and whatever that was, I knew it wasn't nine to five, or a house in the suburbs, or a Birkin bag. And I wasn't going to compromise. I didn't want a plan B. I didn't want anything to fall back on, because I was afraid that if I chased up a plan B, I might miss my plan A.

I'm sure I'm not the only high school graduate to have an existential crisis, but all my friends seemed to have made a smooth transition from school to university life. We met up every now and again for happy hour cocktails, and they would talk about jurisprudence and negatively geared mortgages, and I'd go home afterward knowing that however crazy I might seem, I'd made the right choice, because there must be more to life than case studies and water views.

It seemed that everywhere I looked all I could see was emptiness. There was emptiness in the excitement with which a woman bought a thousand-dollar outfit for a wedding. She'd wear it once, maybe twice, and then it would be forgotten in the back of the wardrobe. There was emptiness in the men who came in looking for a gift for their wives. They'd tell us what size and how much they wanted to spend and we would choose something and wrap it up, and the man would tuck the receipt safely away so she could come back and exchange it for what she really wanted. It seemed as though everyone was rushing and running and saving and spending and always trying to get that one last thing that would make their lives complete, whether it was Sascha's gloves in the window of Hermès or the big job a customer needed a new suit for. But I never saw anyone who was actually truly happy with what they had.

So while the other shopgirls fogged up the windows of Cartier and Tiffany, I stood gazing longingly at airfares. And for some reason I couldn't get those images of the gypsy camp out of my mind.

Why don't you…run away with the gypsies?

Why not?

THE CALL

Or
Operator, give me flamenco

In Retail Land, lunch is either before twelve or after three, or, on really busy days, not at all. I always preferred the late lunch, because if I stretched a three o'clock lunch to three thirty-five, that only left me with two hours before I could go home.

You can always tell how unhappy you are in your work by the amount of time you try to waste during the day. For example, if you're in the elevator and you accidentally on purpose press the button for every single floor just to make the ride go longer, you need a new job. And if you offer to pick up the clothes from alterations every day just for a chance to get away for five minutes, you need a new job. And if you're in the bathroom washing your hands and you lather them up with soap, then rinse them, then decide to lather them up again just to make the most of your toilet break, then you need to get out of there. Immediately.

I pondered this a few days later as I rode the escalator down into the depths of the food court. I stood slumped against the arm rail, too tired to bother putting one foot in front of the other until my feet slid onto the lower ground floor.

I usually brought my lunch to work, but there were days when I was just too disorganized, or when the sight of the pot of brown rice in the fridge made me feel that a trip to the food court would be an elegant move. On these days I went to the sandwich stand.

"Salad sandwich on rye, no butter, takeaway."

That was the guy behind the counter, not me. They knew my order. And by that I don't mean to say that this was my favorite thing to eat. I would have loved to make it a cheese and salad sandwich *with* butter, salt, and pepper. But that would not do for a vegan.

Yes, that's right, I was a card-carrying, co-op shopping, chickpea-sprouting vegan. I'd always loved dairy. I loved butter and cheese, and hot chocolate on a cold night, but I had read so many books about raw food and macrobiotics with their horror stories of how milk clogs up your system and butter clouds your chakras and how refined sugar and white flour *will kill you* someday that I stoically gave them all up. I'd been a vegan since I was fifteen; of course I'd been on and off the wagon, often succumbing to the caramel embrace of a Magnum Ego, but the thought of all those free radicals ravaging my system would keep me up at night, so it was never worth it.

There were many reasons why I'd chosen to go vegan, so even when I managed to convince myself that one bacon-and-egg roll wouldn't be the death of me, I would think of the poor little pig and all the karma demerit points I'd be clocking up if I ate it. My father was a Buddhist, and memories of the color-in karmic wheels I'd done as a child would come back to remind me that it's wrong to take a life, even if it is in the innocent form of a five-dollar breakfast special.

And there's nothing like fitting room mirrors to make you want to go on a juice fast and slit your wrists for good measure. I don't know why that is. I would have thought that stores would want customers to think they look good in the clothes they try on and that one of the easiest ways to boost sales would be to set up changing rooms with atmospheric lighting and fun house mirrors that make everyone look like Kate Moss. I was a small size two, but even so, each time I caught sight of myself in one of those mirrors, I was reminded of why I was the one who got to iron the clothes that Megan Gale would wear down the runway for Fashion Week and not the other way around. So I'd reaffirm my veganism and swear allegiance to brown rice.

The lunchroom was on Level Three, Sleepwear and Intimates. When I walked in with my sandwich, Deborah from Armani was sitting alone at a table by the bare window, lending a sense of quiet elegance to the drab room. I imagined casually pulling up a chair next to her and starting a conversation about the season's colors but didn't dare.

Retail is like high school all over again. The best table by the window overlooking the park was where the concession ladies sat. They were the sales assistants who were not employed by the department store but worked for individual designers who rented space inside the store. They made more money than regular sales girls, went to fashion parades and champagne launches, and got to wear clothes off the racks. They generally stuck together and looked at the rest of us with a mix of pity and disdain.

The girls from Young Fashion all sat together and wore the same skintight black pants and low-cut tops. They shared the long table with the Level Three women, who always looked exhausted from a day of bra fittings and ringing up endless Spanx. I looked around the room, wondering where to sit. Seeing Liz sitting by herself, flipping through the local paper, I went over. Liz ran the Australian Designers section on my floor. By "ran" it, I mean she was the one who was always running around the floor every evening at ten to six wanting to know if anyone had seen the dress that was missing from her display rack.

"How's it going on your side of the floor, hun?" she asked.

I shrugged. "We had two returns this morning and a rush at midday, but it's quieted down now."

I took a newspaper from the table and flipped to the back, the classified section. I always checked the classifieds, though I never really knew why. I suppose I was waiting to see the ad that would read: *Nellie, your destiny awaits you! Call this number NOW!* Though it didn't even need to be that specific. I also would have circled anything along the lines of *Stowaway needed for icebreaker headed to North Pole—immediate start* or *International art thieves seeking new recruits. All training provided.* Or any recruiting ad for an international association of adventurers who needed someone with my ironing expertise and unsurpassed gift-wrapping skills. But instead it was all ads for counter hands and sandwich makers and the old one that read: *Fire your boss! Work from home and make $$$!* And who actually answers those anyway?

But on this particular day something leaped off the page at me as though it was written in neon lights:

FLAMENCO DANCE.
NEW TERM BEGINNING.

Flamenco…the image of a model in a ruffled red silk dress from the *Harper's* gypsy chic shoot jumped into my mind. *Why don't I?*

"Have you ever seen flamenco dance?" I asked Liz.

Her eyes got all misty as she breathed, "Flamenco! I saw a performance in Barcelona, years ago. I was on a cruise to Italy and the boat stopped there overnight. It was in a little restaurant in the backstreets. There was just a small stage with one guitarist and a dancer in a red dress. She was so passionate!"

I tore the ad out of the paper and promised myself I would call the number when Sascha went on her break. But first I needed to make a quick trip to the ground floor.

Here's something else about me: I love stockings. Not tights, not pantyhose. Stockings. I love sheer black stockings with seams and squiggles and arrows and flowers and lace tops, and I'll pay extra for buckles and ribbons and bows.

I love stockings so much I don't dare go into the hosiery section lest I be seduced by new limited-edition wartime-revival silk stockings that come in a tissue-paper-lined box and that I absolutely *have* to buy in case I never see them again.

And that is a valid point, because it isn't so easy to buy stockings in Australia. This is the land of bikinis and spray tan. I gave up on trying to get a tan before I was thirteen. The whole Aussie beach-belle look was never going to happen for me, so the only thing to do was go continental. And often when I lamented the limited supply and exorbitant prices of the stockings on the ground floor, I wished myself to Europe, where chic ladies rush to the powder room because they've popped a suspender in a fit of excitement over a particularly good coffee.

But now that the idea of dancing flamenco in Dior stockings had been put in my head, I knew exactly the ones *Harper's* was talking about. They had been featured in all the fashion magazines that season, and there was a sale in Hosiery… That was all the persuading I needed to exchange two hours' pay for a couple of diaphanous wisps of nylon.

Then, as soon as Sascha went off for her skim cappuccino, I picked up the phone and dialed zero. A familiar woman's voice answered, "Switchboard, what number?"

I read out the number from the classified ad and waited. My heart raced as the phone rang. It was as if somehow I knew that this one phone call would change my life forever.

THE CLASS

Or
Gallardos, escobillas, remates, *oh my!*

It was the evening of my first flamenco class and I gazed up at the clock, watching the final minutes tick past. As soon as the bell rang, I pulled off my name tag and skedaddled down to the ground floor to grab my bag before the hordes of black-suited women descended on the bag check counter.

In my bag I had everything I needed for class. A bottle of water, a long skirt that I'd found at the back of my wardrobe—okay, it wasn't the red silk creation I'd been lusting after, but it would do for the first class. The one purchase I had made was a pair of black leather dance shoes the teacher had told me to buy before the class. I'd gotten them from a dancewear shop in the arcade across the street from work. I was served by a sixteen-year-old ballerina who had been demonstrating different models of pointe shoes to a young girl who was auditioning for the National Ballet Academy, and there's nothing that makes me feel clumsier than seeing girls in leotards spinning around on their tippy-toes.

I would have loved to be a ballerina, and I couldn't help feeling envious and intimidated by the shop assistant as she lazily pirouetted in pointe shoes. Ballet dancers are so über-cool, with their elastic hamstrings and perfect posture, but I couldn't even touch my toes, and just the word *plié* made me nervous.

Was flamenco going to be like ballet? Surely not. But it occurred to me that I actually didn't know anything about flamenco. Well, I knew that it was Spanish and smoldering and I'd heard once that Ava Gardner had danced it on a tabletop with no underwear on, but that was about it. I'd never been much of a dancer. In fact, I'd always had an aversion to physical activity, and the only cardio I did was my daily dash for the bus. Now that I was going off for my first-ever dance class I was afraid. What if it's too hard? What if I can't do it? What if I trip on my skirt and fall over and everyone points and laughs at me?

I had to remind myself that I was on a mission from Diana Vreeland, and that there was no time for that kind of debilitating self-doubt. But still, it wouldn't leave me alone.

✳

The flamenco studio was located in the bohemian inner west suburb of Newtown, and it seemed to belong there among the African hairdressers, Moroccan and Turkish furniture stores, Chinese bakery, and the only Viking restaurant I'd ever seen.

I took the street down alongside the railway tracks to the old converted grain silo that housed the dance school. Even before I saw the building I heard what sounded like thunder. At first I thought it must be a storm rumbling in the distance, but as I got closer I realized it was the sound of stamping feet.

As I climbed the stairs to the fifth floor, the sound of stamping got louder and louder until it felt like the whole building was shaking. I stepped in through the open doorway of the school. The walls were decorated with black-and-white photographs of a woman in a long sleek dress dancing on stage. In each picture she wore an angry glare on her face. This was the teacher, Diana.

Diana was one of the most beautiful women I had ever seen. She had pale skin and arched eyebrows, like an evil queen from a Disney movie. The evil queens are the best—not like those prissy princesses who are always off singing to the birds. The queens are glamorous and stylish and have personality, because you need personality to pull off a cape.

Standing in reception, I could see through the open doors of the dance studio as the advanced class was ending. There were three lines of dancers, all dressed in black. They twisted their bodies and curled their arms up above their heads, making shapes with their hands as though forming shadow puppets. Then, at a stamp of the teacher's foot, they let their arms fall and drilled their feet into the floor.

Most of the girls looked Spanish. They had dark hair pulled back tightly and beautiful dark eyes. And as they danced they looked so fierce and passionate, and angry.

Like, really angry.

I'd expected flamenco to be passionate, but these girls actually looked mad. One girl in the front row snarled as she threw herself into the final turn. Wow. I couldn't wait to get my shoes on and start stamping. After a day of First-Class Service Rule #1—Smile!, it was exactly what I needed.

I tore my eyes away and went into the changing room. It was full of women who'd just come from work, like me. They pulled off suit jackets and loosened their hair, and as they zipped up their long skirts, they flicked the switch from daytime to their flamenco persona.

The sound of clapping came from the studio; it seemed the advanced class was over. The changing room doors opened and the dancers streamed in. They pulled water bottles out of their bags and toweled off their faces and necks.

The girl who had made that spectacular turn stood next to me at the mirror. She put her foot up on the bench and starting unbuckling a pair of forest green dance shoes. They weren't anything like the ones I'd bought. They were made of thick suede and the sole looked like it was made out of wood. She took one off and put it down on the bench with a heavy clunking sound.

"Where did you get your shoes?" I asked her.

She had long black hair pulled up on top of her head in a tight bun and wore a pair of big hoop earrings that bobbed up and down as she spoke. "These are Gallardos. They're the best. But you have to order them from Spain. The last pair I bought were made in Japan and one of the heels broke during an *escobilla* when I was doing the *remate*."

I nodded and pretended to understand what she was talking about, while my mind raced. Gallardos? *Escobilla*? *Remate*?

I smoothed down my black skirt and stepped out of the changing room, nervous about what was ahead of me. A couple of the advanced girls were still lingering in the studio, going over the footwork and asking each other questions about "the new bit."

"Is that how you do it?"

"No, the *gólpe* is on the one."

"No, it's on the twelve."

"I thought it was a *contra*."

"No, that's the *tacón*."

Gólpe, contra, tacón? What wonderful words. All the more wonderful because I had absolutely no idea what they meant.

When Diana came back in, they scurried off to get changed. Diana took her position at the front of the room and lifted the hem of her long skirt, revealing beautiful black suede shoes. She picked up one foot and slammed it into the floor, making the mirror tremble.

Whoa.

The next twenty minutes were spent learning variations on stamping: double stamps, triple stamps, jumping stamps, ball-heel stamps.

By the end of it my thighs were burning, my hips were aching, and my feet were killing me. If I hadn't had that glimpse of the advanced class, I wouldn't have believed that this stamping could bear any resemblance to dance. It felt more like military training. And though Diana assured us that we were building up strength and technique, it was hard to see how what we were doing would one day become a dance.

When Diana gave us a five-minute break, I went to the back of the studio and leaned my elbows on the windowsill, letting the evening breeze cool me down. I could literally feel calluses forming on my feet. *If I keep this up*, I thought, *I'll never be able to wear sandals again.* Sascha would not approve.

As I looked out the window, there was something about the soft evening light on the terra-cotta rooftops that made me feel that I could be in Spain. And just as I thought that, a guitar started to play behind me. It was a run of notes that seemed to chase each other up my spine. I froze and listened for the first time in my life to a flamenco guitar.

I turned around and saw a guitarist sitting in the corner tuning up. He adjusted the bar on his fretboard and played again. I leaned there against the windowsill, completely captivated by the music. I didn't know then that the song he was playing was called a *soleá*; all I knew was that I wanted to make this music the soundtrack to my life.

Diana called us back from our break. She stood facing us and lifted her arms above her head in two perfectly curved lines. We followed her movements and circled our arms around our heads, first right, then left, then both arms together.

I saw my reflection in the mirror as I circled my arms above my head. Okay, so my skirt would never make it into the style pages of *Vogue*. My shoes weren't those made-in-Spain suede creations the advanced girls wore, and with my red hair and pale skin there was no way I would ever pass for a gypsy chick. But as the long-haired guitarist in the corner played his Spanish guitar, I couldn't help but feel fabulously exotic.

My shoulders burned and my fingers trembled as Diana coaxed us to stretch our arms out and back and up and around. If she hadn't been so intimidating, I would have dropped my arms and rubbed my poor aching muscles. But when Diana demonstrated the movements, I was stunned by the beauty of her silhouette. She twirled her wrists and circled her arms like a witch conjuring spirits.

I was so taken by the elegance of her movements that I forgot what I was doing and mixed up my arms. But I didn't care how bad I looked. I knew I'd practice every day if I could one day be half as good as her. I couldn't imagine anything more beautiful than to twist and twirl and stamp my feet to the sound of a flamenco guitar. And when your heart wants that, what can you say, but... *Well, why don't you?*

THE SHOES

Or

Trent Nathan, Trent Nathan, Trent Nathan...

From then on, I was hooked. I lived for my weekly classes and practiced every chance I got. If anyone had ever watched the Level Two security tapes, they would have seen a girl attempting to hide behind rails of clothes while doing very strange things. I was always slightly nervous that the floor manager would call me into her office and ask me to explain why I had been seen twirling around the mannequins or stamping on the carpet, but I was too addicted to stop.

As the term continued, we began to learn more and more complicated steps, tricky combinations of tapping toes and knocking heels that I practiced while standing behind the desk writing up the sales book. Then there was "running step," which I'd do as I hurried down the staff corridor after work. The jumps and the stamping were more difficult to practice discreetly. For those I needed a place where no one would hear the sound of my feet clattering on the floor, so I started practicing in the elevator. The elevator had two advantages: the trip was always short, so it forced me to work on speed, and the sprung floor meant that I didn't hurt my knees.

Then Diana taught us a new move called the hammer step. It

involved jumping up and landing with a heavy thud on one foot and stamping three times. It was repeated over and over again, right then left then right then left, so that when you got your speed up it sounded like a jackhammer—hence the name. This is an important step in flamenco and is used a lot. It's all about power and precision, and you need to build up strength in your legs to make sure that each of those stamps sounds even and is dead on the beat, especially when you're going fast. But it was a difficult one to practice without attracting attention.

One day when Sascha sent me down in the staff elevator to pick up some docket rolls from Level One, I decided to try doing ten hammer steps in a row before the doors opened. I was up to seven when suddenly the elevator stopped.

I couldn't believe it. I was stuck between floors. All my jumping around must have triggered a braking mechanism. I started to panic. There's nothing like an elevator breakdown to remind you of the fact that you are suspended in midair and that the only thing protecting you from the undiscriminating force of gravity is an old cable and some rusty brakes. The elevator jerked into motion, then stopped. "Oh God." I whispered, my heart thumping. The elevator started to descend again, and I clutched at the walls and held my breath.

The doors opened on Level One, and I stumbled out into a crowd of black-suited women. "What was all that noise?" they clucked. "It sounded like someone was hammering in there!" I slunk away to find docket rolls and decided to find somewhere else to practice.

After the first term, I moved up to intermediate level. Intermediate was a different world. A lot of the students were doing it for the third or fourth time, because Diana didn't let just anyone into her advanced class, so they knew a lot about flamenco. Some of them even made yearly trips to Spain, to places with wonderful names like Jerez and Granada and Andalusia.

Most of the girls in my new class were Spanish, or came from Spanish families, or had some kind of story that involved Spanish ancestry, like that they were descended from Spanish shepherds who came out as free settlers. I went through my family tree on both sides, but there was nothing even slightly Mediterranean in our bloodline. We'd managed to maintain a surprisingly pure Celtic lineage, much to my disappointment.

There were two guys in the class: one was Greek and the other was Lebanese, and in their fitted black pants they managed to look like extras in a Ricky Martin video. But I couldn't be mistaken for a Spanish chick during a blackout on a moonless night. My skin is so pale it practically glows in the dark, and the Aussie sun is really good at bringing out my freckles. If I could just get all those little dots to join together I'd have a very flamenco tan, but I didn't really think that would work. And investing in a fake tan would only make my skin the same color as my hair. The redheaded trait is a stealth gene and it chooses its prey with care. I was the only one in my family to get it. The rest of them are spunky brunettes who'd blend into the crowd in any European café. I'd be the one embraced by the group of drunk tourists who wanted me to join them in a verse of "When Irish Eyes Are Smiling."

The intermediate students talked about Spain and flamenco, and I learned a lot from those weekly conversations. I learned that flamenco comes from the Spanish gypsies, *los gitanos*. Nobody knows where the Spanish gypsies originated from, but it is believed that they came from India, and traveled through the Middle East, across the north of Africa and into Spain, bringing flamenco with them.

I also discovered that flamenco isn't just one kind of dance: within it there are hundreds, if not thousands, of different styles, each with its own *compás*, or rhythm, and with its own music, history, and tradition. I was beginning to see that to learn it all would take me lifetimes. We started out with one of the simpler styles, *soleá por bulerías*. (By the way, how cool is that name? *Soleá por bulerías*. It made me wish that someone would ask what I was doing on Tuesday, so I could say, "Oh, I have flamenco. We're doing a *soleá por bulerías*. It's very demanding.") My classmates talked about flamenco singers, dancers, and guitarists, and I learned to look suitably impressed when names like Vicente Amigo and Rafael Amargo came up in conversation, but I didn't really know who they were.

I wanted to learn more, so I staked out the world music section of my closest CD store and pounced on anything new that came in from Spain. I bought a couple of albums by the guitarist Paco de Lucía, which I played on a loop, and some flamenco pop from the group Ketama, but I was hungry for more music.

Tuesday soon became my favorite day of the week. On Monday night I'd pack my long skirt and dance shoes in my bag ready for class, and all the next day I'd eagerly watch the clock. One particularly slow Tuesday, Sascha and I shut down the register at twenty to six. There was no one around, so we locked up the back room and stashed our coats under the register so we could make a dash for the lifts as soon as the bell rang.

Then we got a customer. I heard the *Jaws* theme playing in my head as she walked across the floor in our direction. "Trent Nathan, Trent Nathan, Trent Nathan..." Sascha said softly, willing her to a different section. But it was no good. She was heading straight for us.

Shopgirl Rule #1: Smile!

Rule #2: Ask an open-ended question. Shopgirls are forbidden from asking any questions that can be answered with a simple yes or no. We must instead trap the customer into expressing their needs.

So with a smile that felt heavy on my lips I asked, "What can we help you with this evening?"

The customer wanted to look at suits, and although we told her we really didn't have time to show her the full range, she insisted. She asked for gray suits, black suits, brown suits, pinstriped suits. She tried them all on, then dumped them, one after the other, in a heap on the fitting room floor. It didn't matter how many times that happened, I could never get over the lack of respect some people have for exquisitely tailored clothing.

When the six p.m. bell rang, we had a mountain of clothes to put back on hangers and tidy away. We didn't get out of there until twenty past six, and even though I ran all the way to the station, and then from the station to the dance studio, by the time I arrived I was late, and Diana didn't like it when we were late. I always tried to be the perfect student, but today there was nothing for it. I hurried in, whispering apologies, and joined in the last part of the footwork drill.

I pounded my feet into the floor, letting out the anger I felt toward that customer. She had made me late for class just because she wanted to play dress-up. I stamped my feet harder. Diana was still clapping her hands and stamping her feet, shouting at us to go faster and harder. Of course it would never have occurred to the customer that I actually had a life and that my entire reason for being was not just to convince her she wasn't fat while finding her a bigger size. *Stupid, stupid, stupid!* I thought as I stamped my feet.

I thought of the time-wasters, the rude women who demanded to be treated like princesses when we were rushed off our feet and in desperate need of a drink of water. The people who tried to rip the security tags out of cashmere sweaters or who came in with raging BO and tried on a dozen different items, then left them strewn on the floor of the fitting room for us to pick up and send off to be dry-cleaned.

And as I drove my feet into the floor, I realized that I wasn't really angry at the customers. They had a right to come into the store, even at ten minutes before closing time. But what was *I* doing there? What had I been doing there for the last two years?

Diana stamped her feet and clapped faster. I held my own gaze in the mirror and realized that I was angry with myself. I was angry with the life I was living. I was angry that things hadn't turned out the way I'd imagined. Actually, anger wasn't the right word for it: I was furious.

Diana switched to hammer step, and I let myself drop into the floor with all my weight and stamp my feet. And though my thighs were burning and my feet were numb, I kept up the rhythm. Other students faltered and stopped, one by one, but I kept on, and soon there were only two of us left. All eyes were on us to see who would collapse first. Determined that it wasn't going to be me, I pummeled the floor with a force I didn't know I had; then, as I brought my foot down one more time, my shoe went *crack*! I stumbled forward and almost fell on the girl in front of me.

I lifted up my foot. The heel of my shoe had snapped. I couldn't believe it. I'd danced so hard I'd actually broken my shoe. I didn't even know that was possible.

At the end of the footwork routine, Diana beckoned me out to reception with her. One of her advanced girls, she explained, had just bought a pair of flamenco shoes from Spain, but when they arrived she found she'd ordered the wrong size. Diana took a shoe box out from under the desk. She lifted the lid; sitting inside the box was a pair of brown suede flamenco shoes, just like the ones I'd seen the advanced girls wearing. Diana took one out and handed it to me. It was heavier than I expected. The sole was made from a strip of wood that was hammered with dozens of tiny nails for extra strength and sound.

"They'll last you years," Diana said as I buckled them up.

I skipped back to the sprung floor of the studio to try them out. They sounded wonderful. The stamp was so much heavier and stronger than my old shoes had produced, and they were much more comfortable. "I could dance in them for days!" I said to Diana.

She raised an impeccably penciled eyebrow and said, "Why don't you?"

THE SHOE MAN

Or
Sit down and tell me who you are

Once I had my first pair of real flamenco shoes, I found it almost impossible to take them off. I was like a little girl who is so in love with her new party shoes that she insists on wearing them to bed.

At every opportunity I slipped them on and practiced clicking my heels and tapping my toes, and before long I had worn two holes in their precious soles. I showed them to Diana and she told me to go and see the Shoe Man. "He's the only person in Sydney who understands flamenco shoes," she said, handing me his card.

I remember the day I made my first visit to the Shoe Man, because it was the same day the new collection of Jimmy Choos arrived on Level Five. The news traveled like a wave across the floor, and by nine thirty-five everyone knew. At each counter the girls were taking turns to go up and get a look at the new shoes.

As soon as I arrived at work, Sascha handed me the feather duster. "Just look busy, darling. Back in a tick." And before I could open my mouth to ask what was going on, she'd disappeared up the escalator.

When Sascha returned it was to grab the calculator and figure out how many hours' overtime she would need to work to take home a pair of black stiletto heels with an ankle strap and an oversize buckle.

The result was: yes, she could have the shoes, but no life for the next six months. She sent me up to take a look at them and to tell her whether I thought they were worth maxing out her only remaining credit card. So I unclipped my name tag and took the escalators up to Level Five.

I walked past the school shoes, the Clarks, the orthopedic shoes, the work shoes, and traveled around the floor to where the toes were shinier and pointier and the heels higher and higher, until I reached the wall where the Jimmy Choos were displayed, like butterflies from a far-off rain forest.

And they were beautiful. Oh yes, they were perfection on five-inch heels. Sascha was right. Every single pair was worth giving up your Sundays for. I reached out and picked one up. It was shiny and impossibly high.

I gazed at this off-the-runway confection that any woman would give her firstborn for, and as I ran my fingers over the pencil-thin heel, I couldn't help thinking, "What good are these to me? I could break them with one stamp of my foot." I put the shoe back on its pedestal and squeezed out of the crowd. I didn't need Jimmy Choo. I had a date with the Shoe Man.

❊

I had imagined the Shoe Man's shop would be like Santa's workshop, with boxes of flamenco shoes piled high to the ceiling and dozens of little helpers sipping on sherry as they hammered tiny nails into thick wooden soles. So when I reached the address on the card, I thought I must have made a mistake. It was nothing more than a shop front with FIX YOUR SHOES WHILE YOU WAIT in peeling paint. Surely this couldn't be it. I hesitantly pushed open the door and stepped inside.

The walls were covered with posters for old stage shows, and a wooden shelf behind the counter held rows of resoled tap shoes, ballet slippers, sparkly ballroom shoes, and patent-leather lace-up jazz shoes. A young man in blue jeans and a leather jacket stood waiting, drumming his fingers on the counter. Then the door to the back room swung open and out stepped a man carrying half a dozen shoe boxes. This must be the Shoe Man.

If the shop had disappointed me, the Shoe Man didn't. With tanned olive skin, dark eyes, and black hair flecked with gray he looked like a flamenco artist off the cover of one of the albums I collected from the Spain section of the CD store.

He looked up at me as the young male dancer took pair after pair of identical tap shoes out of the boxes. "You here for ballet shoes?"

"No," I told him. "I dance flamenco."

"You?" He looked me up and down. "You are dancing flamenco?" That thought seemed to blow his mind. I felt a little disappointed that even though I couldn't *plié* to save my life it was easier for him to believe that I was a ballerina than a flamenco dancer.

When the young dancer had examined each pair of shoes, he packed them back into their boxes and counted out a wad of notes. "Come," the Shoe Man said to me as he deposited the money in the register. "Let's talk." He pulled open the door to his workroom and invited me to follow him. The workroom was a big open space with white walls and exposed wooden beams. "Sit, sit." He waved me toward a long wooden bench. "Sit down and tell me who you are." I sat down, and the Shoe Man went to the kitchenette and made us each a cup of instant coffee.

"Tell me, why did you want to dance flamenco?" he called.

"Because I love it."

He nodded and handed me a cup of scalding Nescafé. "And you are performing?"

I couldn't help but laugh at that. The idea of me in a big ruffled dress on a stage was just too funny.

"Why are you laughing?" he asked.

"I don't perform," I explained. "I couldn't."

"Why not?" he asked sharply.

"I'm nowhere near good enough."

"What you talking yourself down for? You think you can build a house in one day? No! You have to start with the foundation." He took a flamenco shoe off the workbench. "You see this?" He ran a calloused finger over the tiny nails that were hammered into the heel. "This is the foundation. But it is not enough on its own. The great dancer needs the foundation for the feet, and the foundation for the heart. Have you been to Spain?"

"No."

He must have heard the longing in my voice because his tone softened and he said, "But you would like to, eh?"

Like to go to Spain? It was my dream to go to Spain. My secret dream that was too precious to even articulate.

"Let me give you one piece of advice, then I fix your shoes. Deal?"

I nodded. "Deal."

"Dreaming is good, but living is better. Maybe it is time to start living your dream, eh? What do you say?"

THE SEARCH

Or
It's so you!

It was nothing more than an innocent online search. But an online search is never really innocent. What we type into Google reveals our deepest desires, and mine was to dance flamenco in Spain.

The conversation I'd had with the Shoe Man would return to me as I stood in line for bag check or on the unforgiving marble floors of Level Two. It was time for me to start living my dream. He'd been right, and I knew it. So I typed "dance flamenco in Spain" and clicked Search.

The first result that came up was for a dance school in Seville. They had new courses starting every week and even organized accommodation for international students. *I could take a month off work and just dance*, I thought. One whole month with no swipe card, bag check, or cold coffee in a paper cup for lunch. No ID codes, First-Class Service Rules, shelves to dust, or mirrors to Windex… It sounded too good to be true.

There was only one thing keeping me from tossing my dance shoes into a bag and jumping on the next flight to Seville, and that was money. I calculated that it would take me four months to save up what I needed for my airfare, classes, and living expenses, and every week I watched my bank account like a child watching a cake rise in the oven, until finally, in the last week of February, I had enough to buy my flight.

On payday I slipped out on my coffee break and hurried up the street to the travel agency on the corner. I sat down opposite a red-blazered travel agent and asked for her best price on a round-trip flight to Seville. As her fingers went clackety-clack on the keyboard, I wondered, *Am I crazy for doing this?*

Probably.

But wasn't it about time I did something crazy?

My mother was always at me to "do something" with my life, and she didn't mean a management course or an LLB in international taxation. My father would have liked to see me become an Oscar-winning film producer, or a high-flying venture capitalist, or really any job that involves running the free world from an island shaped like a skull. He was ambitious for me, and I was the oldest child, after all. But I always got the feeling that my mother would have preferred to see me tearing up the floors of an underground tango bar. She didn't care if I had a job or how much money I made; she just wanted me to live my life and "get on with it, for goodness' sake!"

But now that I was about to put it into action, the idea of walking into a flamenco class in Spain terrified me. I didn't even speak Spanish. Would I cope in a class full of gorgeous, dusky-skinned Sevillians? Or would I be humiliated in Spanish and laughed out of the country?

By the time the travel agent had found me a good fare, my head was so full of doubts and fears that I didn't know what to do. I asked her to hold the ticket for me for twenty-four hours while I made up my mind.

Was I really ready to go to Spain? I mean, who was I to think that I could just turn up in the birthplace of flamenco? But if I didn't go, then what? I had to make a crazy break somehow, because the thought of spending another year folding cashmere sweaters with tissue paper was enough to make me lock myself in the ladies' room on Level Three and never come out.

When I got back to the floor, Vivienne from Covers rushed over to speak to Sascha. "Michelle just called. They've arrived!" Michelle was Vivienne's friend at Hermès, and "they" were the new handbags that had just been flown in (by private jet, presumably) from Paris. I was intrigued by Vivienne and Sascha's breathless excitement. What could be so wonderful about these bags that they made these seemingly rational women go crazy? So I asked Sascha if I could go with her and Vivienne to Hermès, and as there were no customers around, and after Deborah said she'd watch our section, she agreed.

"Darlings!" Michelle greeted us as we walked in the door. Her pale blond hair was styled into an elegant bob, and she wore pearl drop earrings and an impeccably cut suit.

The plush carpet and low lights of the shop were already working their magic on me. I felt like I had entered Aladdin's cave. I gazed around at the smooth leather briefcases and organizers in signature Hermès orange. Long cashmere shawls were draped on stands, and silk scarves decorated with Indian elephants were framed on the walls.

Michelle disappeared into the back and returned moments later carrying a bag on a velvet cushion. She walked slowly, bearing aloft the Holy Grail of designer handbags. It was a black Kelly.

As my eyes fell on it, I realized that it was not just a bag—oh no. It was the stuff dreams are made of. It was small—just big enough to fit keys, sunglasses, and a lip gloss—and the very picture of elegance. I could imagine Grace Kelly carrying it by its perfect handle when she went out on the town in Monaco. I wanted it desperately, and I'd never felt that way about a bag before.

I knew enough about the physics of fashion to understand that a bag like that dangling from my arm would transmute my cheap black suit into Armani. I could wear fake pearls and they would look like Tahitians. This bag was my ticket to a new and glamorous existence.

Michelle could sense my desire. She smiled at me with her glossy mouth and said, "Take it." I reached a hand forward hesitantly and slipped it onto my arm, where it hung as if it belonged there.

"Daaarling...you should do it," Sascha said, angling herself behind me in the mirror.

Vivienne nodded and ran one lacquered red fingertip over the platinum appendages. "It's so *you*," she cooed. "You *have* to have it."

"Why don't you?"

Yes, why don't I? I could go to Spain next year, I told myself. It would give me another year to study flamenco here, and I would probably get more out of my trip if I waited. And then I could take my new bag with me. Hmmm...maybe instead of the Kelly I should get a Birkin so I could fit my dance shoes inside? All I had to do was say yes and it would be mine. It would only cost me my four months' savings plus the next two months' salary.

Sascha pulled out her phone and calculated the daily wear price. "Twenty-four cents a day, darling. It's a steal."

It was as if a cloud had descended over my brain. I could faintly hear my common sense telling me to put the bag back and step away. *Put the bag back...* With a superhuman effort I took the bag off my arm and sat it on its velvet cushion. Michelle barely raised an eyebrow. She had a list of women who would do anything for a Kelly, and if I didn't understand how lucky I was to be offered one, then I clearly didn't deserve it. She led Sascha and Vivienne over to a glass cabinet to show them the latest designs in scarves, pulling out scarf after scarf as though performing a magic trick. Butterflies and carnival masks and spring roses fluttered in the air as she held them up. *Maybe I should just get a scarf...?*

No, Nellie!

I knew I had to get out of that shop. A girl could lose her mind in there. I calculated that I had fifteen minutes before I had to be back on the floor, so I slipped out the door and ran down to the travel agency as fast as my slingbacks would take me. I collapsed breathless into the chair, handed over my card for the travel agent to swipe, and asked for an aisle seat and vegan meals.

For less than half of what the Kelly would have cost me, I booked six weeks in Seville. Six whole weeks away from the marble floors and the air conditioning and the panpipe music. For six whole weeks I wouldn't have to lock myself in a toilet stall to get a moment of peace in the middle of the day. Now it was time to live my dream, and dream my life, and live life like it was a dream.

Olé.

THE MACARENA

Or
I declare I love you

"P assport?" The dark-eyed immigration official put out his hand and raised an eyebrow as I rummaged in my bag.

I'd just stepped off the plane at Seville Airport after a thirty-hour flight from Sydney. My breath was furry, my eyes were bleary, and my face was as rumpled as my clothes. And here I was, face-to-face with the epitome of tall, dark, and handsome.

At the same time, my bag seemed to have transformed itself into an interdimensional vortex. Instead of my passport, I kept pulling out random objects I hadn't seen in years: old notebooks, those sunglasses I thought I'd lost, a Pez dispenser...

"Er..." I muttered, looking up at the immigration guys. There was not one but four, all standing languidly around the passport checkpoint, each more gorgeous than the last. I'd known Spain had a reputation for being up the steep end of the graph when it came to looks, but I hadn't expected to be confronted with the evidence before I'd even picked up my suitcase.

They nodded ever so slightly as the other passengers from my flight walked past and held up their passports. I couldn't help comparing this to the rigorous exit procedure at Sydney Airport, where after having my passport scrutinized by a stern man in a glass box who had made me cross my heart and hope to die that I wasn't an al-Qaeda operative/endangered-wildlife smuggler, I was asked a series of calculated questions about where I was going and for how long. But the Spaniards didn't even ask to see the photo page.

One of the guys leaned forward. He had bright green eyes, a two-day beard, and a uniform that fitted in a way that left me in no doubt of the bulging biceps beneath. He asked in the sexiest accent, "You have something for declare?"

"Um…no," I said.

"No?" he repeated, a wounded look crossing his beautiful face. "You no declare no thing?"

I mentally scanned the contents of my bag and tried to remember whether I'd thrown out that apple core. "Uh, no. Nothing."

"Are you sure?"

People kept coming past, showing their passports, and being waved through, but I still couldn't find mine.

"I have something to declare," the immigration guy said, leaning in closer. "I declare I love you." The rest of the guys started laughing. *Great*, I thought as I turned red.

"What for you come to Spain?" one of the other guys asked. That question instantly put me on guard. So that was their game. They were trying to trap me into admitting that I had come there to work without a visa or sell drugs or steal Spanish babies for shady international adoption agencies.

"Just a holiday," I said, a little too quickly. I tried to make up for my nervous reply by adding, "And to see some flamenco."

"Flamenco?" The guys exchanged glances. "What do you know about flamenco?"

"Um…" I floundered, feeling the pressure of eight smoldering eyes on me.

"See this boy?" he said, pointing to one of the other officials, who smiled suavely, flashing a set of Colgate teeth. "He is a very nice dancer. You want to see?" He started clapping and singing a flamenco tune, and his colleague stepped forward. He lifted his arms, clicked his fingers, and began to dance.

I stared, dumbfounded, as the guy who was supposed to be checking my passport for suspicious stamps or recent trips to Colombia wiggled his shoulders and stamped his feet on the carpet of the terminal floor.

"*Olé!*" cried the other guys.

"Enjoy your vacation," one of them added.

My fingers finally grasped my passport at the bottom of my bag. I pulled it out triumphantly, but they paid no attention. They were already waving through the next line of arrivals.

A sign on the wall in front of me said WELCOME TO SPAIN. That's right, Spain. It felt too good to be true, that after working and saving and planning and packing and repacking I had finally made it to the land of flamenco.

My parents had taken me to the airport in Sydney. Dad checked me in and used his frequent-flier card to get me lounge passes. He seemed as excited about my trip as if he were going himself, and I was relieved that he'd recovered from his initial anxiety about his eldest child throwing her life away.

I hadn't known how my parents would react when I told them of my plan to spend six weeks dancing flamenco in Seville. I finally broached it with Mum while she was making dinner one night, and she said the same thing she always said when I came to her with a plan: "Good idea, darling."

"But," I'd pressed, "you don't think I'm being irresponsible?"

"Nellie." She put down the potato peeler. "Being irresponsible is what being an adult is all about."

Then I went upstairs to my father's office where he was working on a script. "You're going to Spain to dance flamenco," he repeated back to me. Illuminated by the glare of the computer screen, his face was etched with concern.

"Yes."

There was a pause before he asked, "And where do you think this will lead you?"

The question didn't seem fair to me. It seemed that every other day my parents had young people coming to them itching to work in the film industry. My father would look at those kids, fresh out of school, and tell them to go off and live a life and come back to him when they had some real stories to tell. And now, when I was proposing to do just that, he just sighed and said, "It's your life, Nellie."

But when we said good-bye at the airport gate, that was all forgotten. Dad made sure my camera was set to the right aperture, then told me to check my email when I got in because he'd sent me an article from the *New York Times* with a list of the best tapas restaurants in Seville. And Mum told me not to worry, because everything was going to be wonderful.

I couldn't help getting teary as I said good-bye. But as I walked through the entrance into the "passengers only" section of the airport, I felt my excitement build. My journey had begun, and each step I took was taking me closer to my new adventure.

✳

As part of my booking, the dance school had organized my accommodation. I was renting a room in the apartment of a woman called Inés, who worked at the school office.

"Welcome to *Sevilla*," she said, opening her door wide and helping me in with my bags. Inés was in her late twenties and had brown hair to her shoulders with a long fringe and a big smile. She spoke good English and was used to showing foreigners around her home.

She had two bedrooms that she rented out to flamenco students. Mine was a narrow room with a single bed, a wardrobe, a bedside table, and a window that looked out over the courtyard. I left my suitcase and followed her as she showed me the rest of the apartment. There was a big living room with a little balcony and a small kitchen with an old gas stove and a wooden table.

"This is a really great part of the city," she said. "It is called La Macarena. Only two minutes walking from here is the long street called the Alameda de Hércules, which is full of bars and cafés and restaurants. It's a great place to go out for drinks or for dinner. You're not vegetarian, are you?"

"No," I said.

Inés looked relieved. "Good. Some of the girls who come here are vegetarian, and you know in Spain vegetarian does not exist."

"Actually," I said, "I'm vegan."

Inés looked at me blankly. "What is vegan?"

I explained proudly that vegans are like vegetarians, except they don't eat any products that come from animals.

"So what do you eat?" she asked.

"Lots of things. Brown rice, whole grains, lentils…" I went through the vegan's shopping list as Inés's eyebrows climbed higher and higher up her forehead.

"Wow," she said. "You are really going to starve."

Inés didn't realize that's what vegans do. When there's no bean curd to be had, we starve proudly, looking scornfully at those who say, "Let them eat cake." And anyway, what did I care about food? I was in Spain to dance, and that was all that mattered to me.

Inés looked at her watch. "I have to go to the office now. Do you want to come with me and see the school?"

"Absolutely," I said, forgetting my jet lag and the exhaustion I was feeling after the thirty-hour flight.

"*Vámonos*," she said. Let's go.

I think I first fell in love with Spain on that walk to the dance school through the narrow, winding alleyways of the old town. It was the middle of March, and spring was in the air, and flamenco music seemed to come from everywhere. It spilled down from open windows. A car drove past with flamenco blaring on the radio. A man chatting to a friend on the corner sang a few lines of a song, then went back to talking. Notes from a guitar floated toward us on the breeze. The five-minute walk from Inés's place to the dance school was like a flamenco odyssey.

I'd expected the academy to be a big stone building full of dancers waving fans about and swarthy guitarists skulking in every corner. But it wasn't imposing at all; it was just one of a row of white-painted, low-rise apartment blocks. Somehow that seemed even *more* exotic to me. I was intrigued by the thought that behind this unassuming facade there was a world of flamenco madness.

Inés pressed a buzzer next to a picture of a fan, and the gate clicked open. Off a little tiled courtyard were two dance studios. I followed Inés to the first door.

"This is the class you will start on Monday," she said as she waved to the tired-looking teacher who was trying to walk her students through some simple steps.

To my surprise, the students looked like tourists, not flamenco dancers. Some were wearing new red-and-black flamenco skirts, while others just wore tracksuit pants. Many of them seemed to be having a hard time coordinating their arms and feet. One gave up altogether and put her hands on her hips and counted softly to herself as she stepped forward and back. Looking around the room again, I saw that not one of the students was even wearing flamenco shoes.

"Maribél is an incredible dancer," Inés whispered. I could tell by the way the teacher moved that she was a good dancer, but there was nothing she could do with the class in front of her. It looked like none of them had had a flamenco lesson in their life. I could only imagine how Diana would have reacted if one of these girls had tried to walk into my flamenco class back home.

Inés told me to stay and watch for as long as I liked. I nodded and said nothing. What could I have said? As I watched the class from the doorway, all I could think was, *This is it? This is what I've come to Spain for?* It was beyond depressing. I wanted to walk in there and straighten bent elbows, bend straight knees, and pull back shoulders. But even the teacher seemed to have given up on that.

What about my dream of dancing flamenco in Spain? I'd envisaged something fast-paced and exciting. I *wanted* it to be too hard. I wanted to collapse at the end of the day, giddy with the new rhythms. I wanted to struggle and learn and get better. That's what I was here for. Yes, I'd been nervous; I'd been scared. But I *wanted* to be nervous; I *wanted* to be scared. Dancing flamenco in Spain should be scary! This class of tourists was just not what I signed up for.

As I lingered in the courtyard, I heard the sound of stomping feet and a man shouting. It was coming from the second studio. The door was closed, but from the sound of the feet, I could tell it was an advanced class.

I went over and listened at the door just as a man started to sing over the stamping feet. Now I had to see what was going on in there. I pushed lightly at the door, and it opened a fraction. I peeked through the crack in the doorway and looked in. The dancers spun around, colored skirts flying. In the corner I could see the guitarist; sitting next to him was an old flamenco singer who sang a heartrending song. The students leaned backward and curled their arms up above their heads.

As the music shifted to a faster tempo, I pushed the door open a fraction more. The dancers swayed their hips to the sound of the guitar, then the singer jumped up out of his seat and belted out the verse. The dancers jumped heavily onto the floorboards and threw themselves into fast footwork.

"*No!*" a man shouted.

The teacher strode into my sight line. I edged forward again and watched him demonstrate the steps, his black flamenco boots pounding the floor at lightning speed. I'd never seen anyone move that fast. He finished off the steps by spinning around one, two, three times and landing on two feet.

Whoa.

He clapped his hands and the students took the section again.

"No!" He stopped them and again tilted his body and spun around impossibly quickly, landing perfectly on both feet. The girls tried again; some finished on time, but others were still late.

I was getting dizzy just watching them. I hated turns. I would have been so much happier if they didn't exist in flamenco. I didn't like getting dizzy and I didn't like falling over, and spinning around on one foot practically guaranteed both.

The teacher grabbed a stick from the side of the room and shouted, "*Otra vez!*" Again! He beat the stick into the floor and counted, "*Uno, dos, tres!*"

The girls shifted slightly onto the balls of their feet, getting ready to pounce. The singer began the verse again, and the girls threw themselves into an explosion of footwork.

"*Fuera!*" Out! the teacher yelled.

If they were out of time, it was only by a fraction of a second, but that was enough to get a passionate lecture from the teacher. The guitarist started the music over and the teacher jumped forward and danced, slamming the floor with his heels. He moved so fast that his feet were a blur.

"*Otra vez*," he said. The guitarist resumed playing, and the girls wiped the sweat from their brows and prepared to take the section from the beginning. I pushed the door open a little farther and watched how the students moved into position with their arms raised perfectly above their heads, then slowly brought their arms down, twirling their wrists.

I heard the tread of the teacher's shoes on the floor, and then he pushed the door shut. I snapped my head back as the door slammed in my face.

And that about summed it up. *I wouldn't last five minutes in there*, I told myself. *I must be mad for even thinking about it. There's no way I can do that class!* But even as I tried to tell myself that, I knew it was no good. I had to find a way into that studio. The door that had just been slammed in my face was like a portal to a fabulous flamenco universe, and after one glimpse of it, there was no way I could go into the tourist class.

I found Inés sitting at her desk in a little office space on the second floor. "Did you see the class?" she asked.

"I did," I said. "But it looked very…basic."

Inés frowned. "Maribél is teaching the beginners' level. You made a reservation for beginners, no?" She riffled through the papers on her desk in search of my booking.

I explained that I had made that booking thinking the level in Spain would be higher than what I was used to in Sydney. "But there is another class," I said.

"Enrique's class?" Inés's frown deepened. "Enrique's class is advanced level."

I didn't want to beg, but I would do what I had to do. "Please, Inés, let me try. I've come so far just to dance flamenco. Please don't put me in the easy class. Let me try it. Just one class. Just let me do Monday, and if he says I'm not good enough, I'll go back down to the other class. Please."

Inés's frown softened. She took a pen and crossed "beginners" off my form and wrote "advanced" over the top. "I'll have to get Enrique's permission. And if you can't keep up with the group, you cannot stay in the class. But you can try on Monday."

"Thank you!" I said. I wanted to hug her, but the wide, paper-strewn desk was between us. So instead I skipped happily down the stairs and out of the school. It wasn't until I was halfway down the street that I realized what I'd done. In my effort to convince Inés that I could handle the advanced flamenco class, I'd forgotten that I couldn't. They were doing triple turns in there, and I couldn't even do one turn without falling over.

Maybe in Spain it would be different, I told myself. This was the other side of the world, after all. Maybe gravity would be more on my side here. Turning into the narrow side street that led back to Inés's apartment, I looked both ways to make sure no one was coming, then leaned onto the ball of my right foot and spun around. I stumbled at the end, but that was because there was some gravel under my shoe. I tried again, going for a double turn this time. At the end of it I almost fell over. Third time's a charm. I took a deep breath and turned again.

"*Olé!*"

I looked up and saw a man leaning down from an open window. I quickly straightened up and hurried away down the street. Once I'd turned the corner, I started to laugh. Okay, it was embarrassing, but I'd just had my first ever *olé*.

THE DANCER

Or
Would you like pig's ear with that?

Perhaps this trip had been a big mistake. I clearly wasn't the intrepid traveler I had imagined myself to be. Maybe the most crushing part of what we call "growing up" is seeing the gap between the people we *think* we are and the people we *actually* are. In my case it wasn't just a gap, it was a yawning chasm.

When I'd pictured myself in Seville, I'd imagined drinking red wine and dancing flamenco in little bars until dawn. But now, as I walked along the narrow streets of the center of Seville and passed those little bars, I was too scared to even go in.

Even though there was a cold wind that made me pull my jacket tightly around myself, the bars were so full that people were spilling out onto the street. Beautiful, dark-eyed Spanish people, all laughing and shouting and every now and again breaking into a flamenco song. *Just do it*, I told myself as I came to another bar. *Just walk in and order a glass of wine.* But I was too shy, so I walked on.

I'd been in Seville for a whole weekend by now and hadn't even managed to get myself a meal. When I'd tried to go out for dinner on Saturday night, I'd been told at each restaurant that the kitchen was closed until nine. Until nine? I wanted to protest; at nine I'd be passed out with jet lag! But I didn't have the Spanish to say more than "*gracias*," so I went back to the apartment, hungry and dejected.

Of course, I'd woken up starving on Sunday morning. And the cold water that dribbled from the showerhead didn't make me feel any better. Inés had warned me that Seville had a very temperamental water supply and that it was often cut off altogether. "Then we drink wine," she'd said with a grin.

After a quick shower, I wrapped myself in a thin towel and imagined the breakfast I would have at the first café I came across. It would be just like the ones I'd seen in my guidebook: hot coffee, thick slabs of toast slathered in rich green olive oil…a vegan's dream.

But it seemed that nothing in Seville was going to be that easy. First of all, it took me an hour to find a café that was open. I was up early, but even so—is nine thirty in the morning really too early for coffee? In Sydney you can always get a coffee at seven a.m. And a vegan bruffin, in the right part of town.

I finally found an open café, but as I walked in I was engulfed in a cloud of cigarette smoke. There were no tables, just bar stools on which perched a group of old men drinking red wine. But there were also two women having coffee, so I ordered myself a *café solo*, which is just as sad as it sounds—a lonesome coffee with no milk. I didn't know how to ask for soy milk in Spanish, and from the autographed pictures of bullfighters that covered the walls and the mounted bull's head above the register, I gathered that this place wasn't particularly vegan-friendly.

I tried to ask for some food, but with my nonexistent Spanish, that wasn't so easy. The waiter just stared at me as I mimed putting food into my mouth and rubbing my tummy. One of the ladies next to me pointed at a doughnut that she was eating with a knife and fork; I smiled at her politely and asked if there was anything else to choose from.

Eventually, the waiter scooped some chips out of a bag and put them on a plate for me. They looked like Japanese rice chips but had a strange taste that I couldn't quite place, almost like deep-fried sweat. What was I eating?

"*Corteza*," the waiter told me.

"*Qué?*" I asked.

One of the doughnut ladies smiled kindly and said in heavily accented English, "*Corteza* is skin from a pig."

Skin…from a pig. I was eating skin from a pig.

There was an odd smell in the air, and as I looked around, I noticed a tray of skinned rabbits by the coffee machine. Was that where the stink was coming from? As my eyes strayed farther, I saw a bucket full of live snails, looking like one writhing mass.

The waiter opened up a container and pulled out a heap of yellow things I couldn't identify. He chopped them up with a huge knife and arranged them on a platter, which he put on the counter for me.

"What is that?" I asked the lady next to me.

"This is very good," she said. "It is ear of a pig."

It was all too much. The smoke, the taste of pig sweat, the coffee I tried to wash it down with, which was somehow both burnt and watery at the same time. The skinned rabbits, the clicking of the shells as the snails slithered over each other, the glassy stares of the mounted bulls' heads on the wall, the women delicately cutting up their doughnuts with knives and forks. It was like I'd stumbled into some kind of surrealist horror film.

Walking through the city streets that evening, I shuddered at the memory and pulled my jacket tighter around myself as a cold wind whistled up the narrow alleyway. I wished that I was tucked up in bed, as unflamenco as that might sound. But instead I was on my way to see my first ever flamenco show, in a *tablao* in the old part of Seville.

Tablao is the Spanish name for a flamenco theater. These generally have a little stage for one or sometimes two dancers and a couple of musicians. *Tablaos* are often found in bars or restaurants, but the one I was going to was called Casa de la Memoria, and it was in an old Moorish palace.

Inés had insisted I go that night to see the dancer who was performing, Carmen Mesa. She'd told me it would be an experience I'd never forget, and though I was groggy with jet lag and still starving, I couldn't pass up a recommendation like that.

I took my seat in the interior patio of the palace, where the *tablao* was set up. The floor was paved with delicately painted tiles in shades of blue and green, and the walls were hung with vines and ferns. When the lights went down, I looked up and saw the stars twinkling in the sky overhead.

A flamenco guitar began to play in the darkness, and I felt that same thrill I'd experienced the first time I heard the flamenco guitar in the dance studio in Sydney. The notes seemed to form a net that tightened around me and pulled me into the moment.

Then a light appeared in the darkness. Holding a lantern, the dancer walked slowly out across the tiled floor toward the stage. She placed the lamp at the foot of the stage, illuminating the singer and the guitarist who sat behind her. The dancer lifted one foot ever so slowly, and with her chest puffed out like a bullfighter, she stepped onto the stage.

She raised her arms up above her head, then with a clap of her hands, jumped onto the balls of her feet and began to dance. She turned, one, two, three, four, five times. I watched her spin, wondering how it was possible that she could move so fast without toppling off the tiny stage. She let out a hoarse cry and landed on both feet, arms still raised above her head. The singer lifted up her head and shouted, "*Olé!*"

I sat in the audience with my body craned forward, my mouth hanging open and my eyes like saucers. The dancer was so sharp, so precise, so present, yet it was as if she was in another world. She'd been taken over by the energy that electrifies an artist and makes her capable of creating something that has never existed before and will never exist again. Yes, she was dancing on a stage, but she wasn't dancing for the crowd. She was dancing for herself.

And you know how in life you have those moments, those little revelations or epiphanies or whatever you want to call them, when life just suddenly makes sense? Right then, as I gazed at the dancer, all I wanted was to be like her. I wanted to experience what she was experiencing. I wanted to feel what she felt. Everything just clicked into place inside my head and I realized that this was what I'd been searching for. This was what I'd traveled to Spain to find. And yet it was something that was so far from the world I'd come from, and so different from what my future was supposed to contain.

After years of feeling lost, I suddenly knew what it was that I wanted out of life. At the time, it was too soon for me to put it into words, I was just overtaken by excitement. And it wasn't even about flamenco anymore. I just knew that I wanted to live the way that dancer danced on the stage. I wanted to attack my life with that passion, to live with her joy and her devotion to her art. I wanted to take risks like the quintuple turn, knowing that I could all too easily spin out of control. I wanted to feel my feet on the very edge of the stage and sway like I was about to topple over, then wink at the audience and let them laugh in relief. I wanted to live without being afraid of life, of passion, or of falling off the stage.

And I realized I had been right to hold on to the idea that there was a life out there for me waiting to be lived. I'd been right saying no to a plan B, because if I'd pursued a plan B, I would have missed this moment, right here among the small crowd of a tiny *tablao*.

THE *BIEN*

Or
Toma que toma!

I relived the show in my dreams that night. Tossing and turning, I saw again the way the dancer's feet had attacked that tiny stage. I wanted to be her. Yet when I'd looked closely at her beige-colored shoes, I'd noticed that they were wrecked from dancing. How was it that such an extraordinary artist had to dance in ruined shoes? It was a strange concept for me: I came from a world where people could afford to buy an extra pair of shoes whenever they felt like a bit of a lift. We even have a term for it. It's called retail therapy, and we're told it's healthy.

The more I dwelled on this, the more remarkable the dancer seemed to me. That is the dedication of the artist: training her entire life to put on a show regardless of whether she was paid for it. I couldn't have had a sharper contrast to the world of Level Two.

I opened my eyes and saw the first hint of morning light out the window. As I lay there, I could still hear the rhythms of the guitar and the dancer's feet in my head. I promised myself that I would throw myself into my classes and dance my feet to the bone. I would train night and day if that was what it took, but I would learn to dance like the dancer in the *tablao*.

But the confidence and certainty I felt as I lay in bed burst like a bubble when I stepped into the changing room of the dance school later that morning. A group of girls spoke in Spanish as they sprayed on deodorant and pinned up their hair, and two Japanese girls in long black skirts stared into space as they practiced rapid footwork on the tiled floor.

There seemed to be an invisible divide between the gorgeous Spanish girls in their shrugs, leotards, and worn-down flamenco shoes and the giggling tourists who were getting ready to go into the beginners' class. Two American girls were talking much too loudly in English; the sound of their voices made me wince, because I knew I should be in their class. I called them tourists, but how was I any different?

Some people thrive under pressure, but not me. My brain checks out, my stomach seizes up, and my body shakes like jelly in a thunderstorm. I've always been that way. And not just for big things; exams, flights, phone calls that I don't want to make, all that kind of stuff makes me nervous. Raise the stakes a little and I'm a mess.

As I left the changing room, I saw the teacher, Enrique, walking up the corridor toward the studio. When I'd peeked into the studio Friday, I hadn't seen much more than glimpses of his racing feet and fluid silhouette, but as he was walking toward me, I realized he was the very embodiment of all the romantic dreams I'd ever had.

Maybe this was why I'd come to Seville. Maybe it was written in the stars that we would meet. He was going to be my dance teacher, and after hours of sweating over complex footwork, we would fall in love. It would be a whirlwind love affair that would later be made into a Hollywood movie starring Antonio Banderas and Kirsten Dunst. And we would take our adorable flamenco-dancing kids to the premiere...

"*Eres la chica nueva?*"

He had stopped outside the studio and was talking to me. I swallowed and tried to see if my vocal cords still worked. "Uh?"

"*Vas a tomar la clase?*"

"Eh?"

"*No hablas español?*"

"No…?"

He gave up and walked past me into the studio, and I felt myself deflate in the face of my own idiocy. I really had to learn some Spanish. I scurried to the back of the room where I hoped I would be as inconspicuous as possible.

"*Chicas, vámonos!*" Girls, let's go. He clapped his hands and all the girls started to dance.

That's it? I screamed silently from the back of the room. No instructions, nothing? How on earth was I supposed to know what to do? But I seemed to be the only one who had absolutely no idea of what was going on. Everyone else knew the routine by heart. This was my worst nightmare come true. Deciding I had to just do something, even if it was wrong, I tried to mimic the girls in front of me. Toe, heel, tap, shuffle, ball, heel—ahhh! what the hell?! And now to the left, toe, heel, shuffle, point, ball, heel—aha! That was it! I cracked the code!

Enrique raised his voice above the noise of stamping feet and said, "*Con faldas!*" With skirts! The dancers picked up the corners of their skirts and held them out, swishing them to the right and to the left as they moved. I stopped momentarily at this beautiful sight. All the girls moved with an ultrafeminine glamour, holding a perfect curve in their backs and twirling the ruffled skirts around to right and left. But just as I lifted my skirt and held it out, trying to imitate the movement, again they changed the routine on me.

What a disaster. I wished I could sink into the floorboards—anything rather than standing like an idiot while these beautiful Spanish girls danced rings around me.

The guitarist walked in and sat down to tune up. When the girls came to the end of the dance, Enrique added on a new step, a lightning-fast combination of stamping feet, tapping toes, and I didn't even know what else.

The class started to practice the new step, repeating it over and over, and Enrique walked between the rows, listening carefully. Someone was out of time, and he knew it. Of course it was me. He walked between the dancers, every now and again stopping the class and telling one girl to do it on her own. Then he would nod his head and move on.

I started to panic. I had absolutely no idea how to do the step, and I knew that if he asked me to repeat it I would just burst into tears. I got more and more nervous as he came closer and closer to my corner, and the more nervous I got the more my feet clattered on the floor.

Once he made his way to my back corner, he knew he'd found his culprit. He silenced the class and pointed at me. Everyone turned around to stare. I took a deep breath and did my version of the step.

He shook his head and demonstrated the step again. I stared at his feet, but he was moving so fast that I couldn't see what he was doing. Feeling everyone's eyes on me, I grabbed at my skirt and did something, but I was so far off that the sound of my own feet made me wince.

"*Escucha*," he said. I looked at him blankly. He pointed to his ear. Ah…he was telling me to listen. He repeated the step again, and this time instead of watching his feet I tried to hear the rhythm.

I took a deep breath and replayed the sound in my head, then, without giving myself time to think, let my feet copy the rhythm pattern back. Enrique nodded and said, "*Bien*."

Bien. That, if I wasn't mistaken, meant good. He said "good"! I gave a sigh of relief. I'd passed the first test. I was so happy I missed the next step that Enrique added on to the end of the sequence, and once again I was the only girl in the room who had no idea what she was doing.

I guessed I might as well get used to that.

❊

As I got changed after class, I repeated to myself over and over again, "I did it." I was the worst person in the class, and I knew I didn't deserve to be there, but it was the flamenco class of my dreams, and if I had to practice for hours every day just to keep up, I would.

Just as I was about to leave, a woman walked into the changing room. She was in her midtwenties, with jet-black hair, pale skin, and large, almond-shaped eyes. One thing I'd learned on Level Two was how to size up a customer in an instant, and I immediately noticed that her skirt was new and expensive, and the Louis Vuitton tote she was using as a dance bag was no fake. She put a foot up on the bench to unbuckle her shoe, which was the deepest, velvetiest purple. Before I realized I was staring, she had caught my eye in the mirror.

"I love your shoes," I said.

She gave me a wink. "Me too," she said. "I bought them here, in Plaza del Salvador. But you know I need to get another pair, in beige. I saw a dancer at the Casa de la Memoria with that color shoe."

I knew straightaway she was talking about the dancer I had seen the night before at the *tablao*. The image of those beige shoes all scuffed and streaked with black, tapping away on the tiny wooden stage, was fixed in my mind.

"You saw her also?" She pressed her hand to her heart. "I just love her clothes. The suit she wore in the beginning, the shirt with the ruffles and the bolero-style jacket? We have a shop in Zurich that sells this kind of thing. And the dress, the orange one? That is my favorite color. Orange, not like Hermès orange, but brighter, you know?"

I asked her if she was Swiss, but she shook her head and said, with a bat of her fanlike eyelashes, "No, I'm Persian."

Persia…I did a quick mental cross-reference and came up with: Middle Eastern country, possibly mythological, famous for carpets.

She saw my hesitation and helped me out. "Today it is called Iran."

Ah, right. *That* Persia.

We left the school together, and as we walked, she told me her name was Zahra; like me, she'd come to Seville to take dance classes for a few weeks. She asked if I'd join her for a coffee, and I hesitated. After my traumatic experience with the pig skin, I had decided to avoid Spanish cafés. But Zahra had already taken me by the arm and was leading me toward her favorite place.

We stopped at a cute little café that had a few tables out underneath the orange trees. The blossoms were just starting to open, and their fragrance wafted down to us. "I love this smell," she said. "I want to find a perfume that smells like this. In Spain it is called *azahar*, you know? It is an Arabic word."

"Do you speak Arabic?"

"Yes, I studied it at the university, and I use it a lot in my work."

"What do you do?" I asked.

"I manage Middle Eastern investment for a bank in Zurich. And you?"

After hearing that she managed the wealth of some of the most oil-rich nations of the world, I was embarrassed to tell her that I was a shopgirl.

"Oh, that must be so much fun!" she said. "I worked in a shop as well after I finished in the university. I just loved it. Of course, now I work in the bank, which is a very good job for me, but it is so stressful."

As we lingered over our coffees, a delivery truck pulled up outside the café. Two men climbed out and started unloading beer kegs from the truck. One man stood up on the tray and hurled the kegs down to the pavement below, and the other man grabbed them as they rolled across the street. One keg broke open as it hit the ground and beer spurted out of it like a fountain, but the men barely glanced at it, just kept on with their work.

"Can you imagine if this happened in Switzerland?" Zahra asked, looking down at the lake of beer that was forming in the street. "Zurich is like the Swiss watches, you know? Everything has to be perfect. But here the people live with…with *toma que toma*! I love this expression. It is what they say in the flamenco shows."

"What does it mean?" I asked.

Zahra shrugged. "I don't know. *Toma…toma* means 'take,' no?"

"Take it, take it?" I suggested.

"Yes! This is what the singers always say to the dancers in the flamenco shows. Take it, take it!" She started to repeat it each time the delivery guy threw down a keg of beer. "*Toma…que toma… que toma…*"

She called the waiter over with a wave of her impeccably manicured hand and ordered a second coffee. Then she lowered her Armani sunglasses and gave me a wink. "This is Spain, *chica*. *Toma que toma!*"

THE G WORD

Or
Turn, turn, turn

I slipped my feet into my flamenco shoes. They had molded to my feet and felt like an extension of my body. Every time I put them on it was like coming home.

Inés had told me I could come and use one of the studios in the evenings when all the classes were over. It was my only way of keeping up with Enrique's class. Every day I stumbled through the new choreography, memorizing all I could. Then in the evenings, when no one was around, I slipped into the studio, buckled up my dance shoes, and went through the steps by myself. This was my favorite hour of the day. It was just me and the mirror and the fading light that filled the studio with a dusky glow. I kept the fluorescent lights off and danced in the twilight, watching the long shadows I cast on the wooden floor.

As I went over the steps, I thought about my new teacher. Was he not the man I'd been dreaming of all my life? A flamenco-dancing Don Juan with eyes like a pirate and a soft, caressing voice... I was in danger of sounding like a frustrated Harlequin heroine, but it was true: he was the kind of man I'd always dreamed of but never really believed existed.

Comparing him to the guys I knew back in Sydney made me laugh out loud. I didn't have much of a social circle back home, which was understandable given that I spent 60 percent of my time in women's fashion, at least 30 percent asleep, and another 10 percent lying in bed trying to convince myself to get up. The only way I was going to meet someone was if he bumped into me while I was trying to do my lipstick on the bus, or came up to Level Two in search of a birthday present for his mother. The guys I did know were mostly my friends' university-going boyfriends and their friends. They generally talked about things they were studying or social issues or other things that even in my most imaginative mode I could hardly describe as romantic. But even though I had no reason to believe that my fantasies would ever be fulfilled, I'd dreamed of the perfect man. He'd be tall with dark hair and darker eyes that would meet mine across a crowded room, and I would know immediately he was the one I'd been waiting for. And he would sweep me into his arms without a thought as to whether I might interpret his actions as presumptuous or sexist. He wouldn't ask me what kind of music I was into or what type of beer I liked, or whether I'd read any good Dostoyevsky lately, because he wouldn't care. We'd just look into each other's eyes and know that we had found what we were looking for...

I was so swept up in my romantic daydream that as I leaned in for the triple turn my foot got tangled up in my skirt and I stumbled forward, almost falling over. In frustration I cried out, "Arrrrgh!"

"*Tranquila.*"

I jumped and turned around. Standing in the doorway was Enrique. How long had he been there? I was grateful that the lights were off; there was no way he could have known what I'd been thinking about, yet I felt sure that my thoughts were written across my face.

He walked in and stood next to me in front of the mirror. Then, lifting up with impeccable balance, he spun around, once, twice, three, four times. "*Ves*? See? *Fácile*," he said. *Fácile* means "easy." I thought I should explain that, because I don't consider a quadruple turn your standard definition of "easy."

"*Inténtalo*," he continued. This word I didn't know, and I wished that I could cling to my ignorance, but I could tell from his face that he was saying, "Now *you* try it."

I knew going into the turn that it wouldn't end well, and I didn't even get the full way around before I stumbled.

After watching my attempt, Enrique lifted up onto the ball of his foot and gestured to me to do the same. I tried to copy his posture. He came around behind me and corrected my arms and directed my eyes straight ahead, a little above my sight line. I swayed there in the music-box-doll position, afraid to breathe in case I toppled over. Then he placed one hand on my waist and another on my shoulder and spun me around.

I fell over almost immediately, but Enrique told me to get back up on my tiptoes and try again. When I was balanced with my arms in two perfect curves, he pulled back my shoulders, lifted my chin, and steadied me again before spinning me around. I tried to keep the position, but the force of his push only got me halfway around before I fell—right on top of him. He caught me, and as I looked up at him and realized that I was in his arms, I almost forgot my embarrassment.

It couldn't have been more than a few seconds that I rested against him, but it felt like an eternity. His hands were on my waist to steady me, but I had no desire to regain my balance. His dark eyes searched my face, and again I was thankful that the light was too low for him to see me blush. He ran one finger along the line of my jaw and said, "*Guapa*."

And in a flash the moment was over. I straightened up and he stepped back, and again I was up on my toes ready to be pushed into another turn.

※

"Inés, what does *guapa* mean?" It was the next morning and I was in the kitchen putting on oats for porridge and Inés was firing up the coffeepot.

She laughed at this question. "Are the Spanish men calling you *guapa*?"

"What does it mean?" I repeated, worried now that it was something unflattering.

"*Guapa* is beautiful."

"Oh," I said, stirring my oats. I hadn't expected that. I'd just assumed that it meant "klutz" or something like that.

As I walked to the dance school, I replayed the scene in my head, now with the English subtitle. It was suddenly so romantic. Dancing alone with him, the golden light of the sunset slanting in through the windows… The sweet smell of orange blossoms filled the air, and the sun warmed my skin and made the cobblestones gleam. The sound of a flamenco guitar wafted down from an apartment, making me think it would be a good day to fall in love.

THE SEDUCTION

Or

Meat is vegetarian

Inés had been right when she said I was going to starve. After three weeks I was still searching for vegan food. All the restaurants in Seville seemed to serve the same thing: tapas. Meat tapas, fish tapas, pork tapas, and deep-fried tapas. There were no salad bars, no kebab shops, no Hari Krishnas doling out free *dal*. I combed the streets for a sushi train but just kept passing the same old Spanish restaurants with pigs' legs in the windows and bulls' heads on the walls. *What's with these people?* I asked myself as I wandered through the streets looking for a non-Spanish restaurant. I'd never known a people who were so in love with their own cuisine that they had absolutely no other restaurants. Tapas, tapas, tapas…didn't they ever just want a pappadam?

The local supermarket had only white rice, white flour, and white sugar, which I was sure would be the death of me. All the books I'd read on healthy eating had succeeded in making me absolutely terrified of pretty much everything. I knew that white flour leaches nutrients from your bones, cooked spinach robs you of calcium, milk is toxic, sugar is a drug, caffeine gives you wrinkles, potatoes cause tumors… Really, I felt I was never safe. One of my friends back in

Sydney was a medical student and absolutely militant about the dangers of sunlight. "Do you know how long you can stay in the sun before it causes permanent damage to your skin?" she used to ask me whenever she saw me out without a hat. "One second. That's how long it takes to ruin your skin."

But here I was in Seville sitting in the dappled sunlight with Zahra every morning drinking coffee. You can't drink Spanish coffee without adding a bit of sugar to mask the burnt taste, so I'd gradually been seduced from sipping straight black coffee with my back to the sun, to drinking *café con leche* (coffee with milk), to now indulging in *café con leche* with half a sachet of brown sugar mixed in and the soft Sevillian sun on my face.

And to tell the truth, I was enjoying the seduction. I'd been secretly thrilled the day I went to the bakery and discovered they only had white bread. What choice did I have? I had to buy a baguette. As I broke open the crust and breathed in the smell of fresh bread, I remembered with a grimace the bitter sprouted-grain loaf that I used to buy from the co-op back home. Spreading on a little bit of Inés's butter, I whispered to myself, "Only in Spain." Still, at night I would lie awake worrying about my descent into decadence. I could feel the free radicals crawling over my face and eating away at my flesh. I wondered, *Will I survive Seville?*

In my search for healthy food, I ventured out to the main department store in the middle of the city. Even the center of Seville maintained the air of a village in the south of Spain. The streets were all painted white and lined with orange trees, and the little boutiques had painted fans in the windows and mannequins decked out in extravagant flamenco costumes. Following the international code of department stores, there on the lower ground floor was a food hall, and they had a section with preprepared meals.

Unfortunately, all the labels were written in Spanish, and as far as

I could tell, there were barely any vegan options. It was mostly pork and chicken and crumbed seafood. But they had stewed green beans and some kind of casserole that looked vegetarian, so I got a serving of each and hurried home to eat the first real meal I'd had in days.

The casserole was good, but I couldn't tell what was in it. I was halfway through when Inés came into the kitchen, looked at my lunch, and said, "I thought you said you were vegan? You're eating *riñónes*."

I froze. I didn't know what a *riñón* was, but it didn't sound like a vegetable.

Inés didn't know the word for it in English, so she got the dictionary from the lounge room. "*Kid-neys*. It is very typical."

Kidneys. I was eating kidneys. I didn't care how typical it was. Inés couldn't stop laughing at the expression on my face, but I didn't share the joke. When I told her with a throb in my voice of my struggle to find healthy food, she asked, "Why don't you go to the market?"

"There's a market?"

It turned out there was a bustling market close by, in a big white-washed building behind an old stone church. I'd walked right past it without having any idea it was there; the problem was that I couldn't get used to shops shutting at one and reopening at five, and kept going out shopping when everything was closed.

I went out early the next day to explore this new market. I wove my way through the crowds of shoppers and past cheese shops and butchers with strings of red chorizo sausages hanging from the awnings and pigs' legs with hoofs still attached. (Who's buying *that*?) I wandered between the rows of stalls all selling Technicolor fruit and veggies and stopped at a stand that had flamenco playing from an old radio. As I waited to be helped, I tapped my feet against the concrete floor.

"*Olé, Olé*!"

I turned around and saw a man in a green apron carrying a crate of mandarins. "*De dónde eres?*" he asked. Where are you from?

"Australia," I said.

"Au-tralia…" the fruit seller repeated, wonderingly. "And did you swim all the way here?" The other fruit sellers laughed, delighted with the joke.

He asked what I wanted, and I pointed at the pears and said, "*Tres,*" then a couple of oranges and a bunch of grapes.

He packed them in gray paper and weighed them on the scales. "*Ya tá?*"

I didn't know what that meant, so I just nodded and repeated back to him, "*Ya tá.*"

On my way out I passed a little stand that sold different kinds of bread: heavy ryes and loaves studded with pumpkin seeds and caraway, and in a little fridge I saw they even had tofu loaf and sprouted-grain bread. My heart sank right down to my sneakers. I could say good-bye to my morning baguettes. Now that I'd found organic spelt bread, I couldn't keep pretending white bread was my only option.

I picked up my pace and walked quickly past the healthy bread stall. Let's just pretend we never saw that…

❉

There it was, shining in the morning sun: a great wall of shoes. Flamenco shoes of every imaginable color were on display, every shoe that had ever appeared in the midnight fantasies of obsessed flamenco dancers. They were all perfect, all begging to be taken down and broken in with ankle-twisting footwork.

But I only had eyes for one pair. I'd noticed them as soon as I stepped in the door: a perfect pair of red shoes. As I picked one up, my inner shopgirl gave me the sales pitch: "Every woman needs a pair of red shoes. They brighten up any outfit." But I didn't need convincing. These shoes were mine.

Zahra picked up a beige shoe. "This is my shoe, *chica*. You know people think it's good to match the color of the shoe to the color of the dress, but the shoe should match the color of your skin. It makes the leg look longer."

Long legs or no long legs, I was in love with my red shoes. And when I tried them on, even Zahra knew there was only one thing to say: "You *have* to have them!"

We each left the store with a new pair of shoes, swinging our bags back and forth like excited children. As we darted in and out of shops, looking at oversize earrings and gazing at hand-painted fans and heavy embroidered shawls, I realized something wonderful: I was having fun. Since I had started working on Level Two, I couldn't go into stores without noticing shelves in need of dusting, smears on the glass cabinets, and price tags hanging out of garments. I'd find myself overcome by the need to straighten hangers and organize pieces according to size. But with Zahra, shopping had gone back to being a game.

We walked through the streets, gazing at window displays of extravagant flamenco dresses. "When do they wear those dresses?" I asked as we stared at a particularly outrageous red-and-white polka-dot dress with matching accessories.

"It is for the feria." Zahra explained that the Feria de Abril is a big festival that happens every year after Easter, and everyone gets dressed up and dances *sevillanas*, the traditional dance of Seville. "See, *chica*!" She pointed at a poster with a painting of a woman in a flamenco costume looking seductively over a fan. I'd seen these posters all over town but hadn't understood what they were for.

I noted the date on the poster—it was for the day before I was to leave Seville. When I told Zahra, she stopped and looked at me.

"Really? Me too!" It was a wonderful coincidence. We'd both booked our return flights for the day after the first night of the feria.

All week Zahra had been telling me she wanted to go to a tapas bar she'd heard of called El Rinconcillo. "It is so *toma que toma*. It is a flamenco tapas bar. We have to go!" When we'd finished shopping, we decided to go there for lunch. "It's the oldest tapas bar in Seville," she said, leading the way through the streets of the Macarena, following her own internal GPS.

I wasn't so excited about the idea; I figured there would be nothing even vaguely vegan on the menu, and I hated being the girl who nibbles on bread and gazes longingly at food she can't eat. And I knew that Zahra would try to tempt me into eating something delicious. She'd noticed how thin I was, and how much weight I'd lost since we first arrived. It was only natural that I'd lose weight: I was dancing three hours a day and struggling to find enough food. But Zahra didn't approve.

"Look, *chica*! This is it." It certainly looked like the oldest tapas bar in Seville. The front of the building was covered with colorful painted tiles, and garlands of onions and garlic hung from the dark wooden beams above the bar.

We elbowed our way through the crowd to a spot at the bar. From there we could see the waistcoated waiters bringing sizzling dishes from the kitchen. There were servings of fish in tomato sauce, deep-fried squid, and various kinds of meat.

"What do you think?" said Zahra. "We take one meat, one fish— ooh! What is that?"

I told her to order whatever she wanted but that I couldn't eat any of it. She dismissed me with a wave of her hand and called the waiter over to give him our order. The waiter marked a line of mysterious numbers down in chalk on the wooden bar in front of us. It took us a moment to figure out what it was; then we realized that he was chalking up our tab as we went. Such a simple but effective system, which I suppose relies on the honesty of the customer not to lean over and smudge off a couple of numbers with a sleeve.

Our first two tapas were almost hurled across the bar. The plates spun around and settled in front of us. They were *bacalao*—salted codfish—and *carrillada*, beef cheek.

Zahra took a piece of the codfish. "You have to taste this!"

"I can't," I said.

"Why not?" she asked, surprised. "Fish is vegetarian."

Fish is vegetarian, indeed! I thought angrily as I broke off a piece of bread and munched on it. I hadn't eaten anything that morning, and the smell of so much food was almost enough to make me fall off my stool.

"*Chica.*" Zahra pushed the plate toward me with a twinkle in her eye. "Only in Spain."

I regretted having shared with her the secret of my baguette; now she was using my own words against me. But then again, I thought, breathing in the smell of the fish, how often does one have the chance to eat tapas in Seville? And, as Zahra would say, such *toma que toma* tapas...

I sighed and picked up a fork. "Only in Spain," I said as I sliced the fish with the edge of my fork and raised it to my mouth. Then I experienced heaven. "Oh my God!" I moaned through a mouthful of what had to be the best fish I'd ever eaten.

But Zahra had already moved on to the second dish: beef cheek, cooked so slowly that it falls apart on your fork. Her eyes rolled back in her head. "It's divine. You must try it!"

"I can't. That's meat!" I protested.

"This is vegetarian meat," she said through a mouthful. I was weak and I knew it. The smell of the meat was too much for me to resist, so I decided that there was no use fighting it. Only in Spain.

And if I'd thought the fish was good, it had nothing on the beef. It was so tender I could have sliced it with a spoon. Before I'd finished my first mouthful, another plate came spinning across the bar toward us. *Albóndigas*, meatballs in rich gravy.

"Don't worry," said Zahra. "This is vegetarian meat also." It was so delicious that we mopped the plate clean with bread.

When we'd finished eating, I stared down at the empty plates that were lined up in front of us. I couldn't believe what I'd just done. I was a disgrace to the vegan community. When I got home, I'd have to hand in my co-op card and my green bags and go into the brown rice rehab program.

"You know, this is really incredible," Zahra said, looking around her. "The bars here are always full of people. Do these people have jobs? Who is in the office?"

I had no idea. Zahra was right: at nine o'clock the cafés were full of people having their morning coffee, and they were packed again at eleven as everyone came out for their second coffee of the day. From twelve the streets were filled with people out drinking aperitifs, one o'clock was time for tapas, three was time for lunch, then everything closed down for siesta until five.

"I tell you, *chica*," Zahra said, looking around at the Sevillians who were getting louder with each glass of wine. "These people know how to live."

THE COMPÁS

Or

¿

'¡|€¢∞2å¨Ç*^–}[ª

"Come on…where are you?"

I'd been sitting at the computer for fifteen minutes, pressing every key in every possible combination, trying to find the @ symbol.

"Come on," I begged the keyboard. "Just show me where it is!"

All I wanted to do was check my email, but the Spanish keyboard was making it impossible.

"Come on, you stupid thing…"

The computer was in a little library on the third floor of the dance school. It was a place where students could come to watch videos or check out CDs, brush up on flamenco theory or check their email. Well, supposedly.

¢∞¬#5[]ń…}ç¿

Hang on. Most of those symbols I'd seen before, but ¿ was new to me. An upside-down question mark? I was pretty sure I didn't have that on my computer back home. What did it mean? Why would anyone use an upside-down question mark? I pondered this for a moment before going back to my search for the @.

'·2$)($¨^*¿¡

What? They have upside-down exclamation marks too? But why did the Spanish feel the need to invert their punctuation? Do the upside-down symbols have a different meaning? Do they mean the opposite? What's the opposite of a question?

Finally I hit on the @ and was able to get into my email account. Of course, when I started typing, I had the same problem trying to find the right keys.

In the end my email looked like this:

Hi everyoñe¡

Please excuse the rañdom punctuation…I¡m still tryiñg to figure out how to use a Spañish keyboard. Check this out: ¿'¿?¿!ç¡!

Pretty cool„ huh¿

As I walked back to the apartment, I could hear a man singing flamenco. It was *la hora de la siesta*, siesta time, which was from about three to five o'clock. I was always amazed by how this bustling city became a ghost town for two whole hours during the middle of the day. Inés had told me that it was considered rude to call someone during *la hora de la siesta*, because you would be disturbing their afternoon nap.

But the singer's voice broke the afternoon silence, and as I came to the old stone church on the corner, I saw it was a street sweeper. He was standing beneath the orange trees, leaning on his broom with his eyes half-closed as he sang.

The wind blew the orange blossoms he'd swept up away down the street, but he didn't notice. The blossoms, or *azahar* as Zahra had called them, were fast becoming my favorite thing about Seville. It was the first time I'd been in a city that had its own fragrance. I wished I could buy a bottle of it so that wherever I went I could breathe in Seville, but there was no way any perfume could capture the smell of these streets. It was a mix of the sweet smell of the orange blossoms, the fried fish from the corner tapas bar, and the whiff of cigarette smoke from the man who'd just walked past. I knew that this smell would always remind me of these days in Seville, walking up and down these little streets on my way to and from dance class with my head full of rhythms.

"Da da dum…da do di da, da da, da-da…" I repeated softly to myself. The only way I could memorize the footwork patterns from class was to practice them over and over again. And even then I normally managed to get them confused between classes. They were such complex patterns that I found it almost impossible to keep them in my head.

I always stayed in the studio after class was finished, repeating the new steps again and again, trying to make them stick in my head. But I hated practicing when there were people around, because I knew I was making mistakes, even if I didn't know what they were.

Today, Enrique had poked his head in while I was practicing and had seen me repeating the new choreography out of time. He had stopped me and told me to clap the *compás*, and I was forced to admit my shameful secret—I didn't know how.

He stared at me in disbelief. How could I have made my way into his class without knowing *compás*? Of course I knew *of* it: I knew that every different flamenco style had its own rhythm pattern and that was what all the clapping in flamenco was about—someone's got to keep the time. I just never wanted it to be me, because it's really, really hard.

Enrique started clapping the beat, slowly. I watched his hands. He clapped some beats louder than others, and left some out altogether. This kind of clapping is called *palmas*.

"*Soleá*," he said.

I knew that *soleá* was the name of the type of dance that we were doing and that there were twelve beats to the bar, but that was about all I knew.

He started clapping again, this time numbering the beats out loud, emphasizing certain beats. "*Uno, dos, TRES…siete, ocho, nueve, DIEZ. Uno, dos, TRES…siete, ocho, nueve, DIEZ.*"

Okay, so: one, two, three, then seven, eight, nine, and ten. But what happens to the four, five, six, eleven, and twelve? They're silent? And the three and the ten are accented? I followed along with him, but I still kept getting mixed up.

Enrique took my hands in his and clapped them together. "*Uno, dos, tres…siete, ocho, nueve, diez. Uno, dos, tres…*"

But I gazed up at him, lost in those flamenco eyes, and everything he said simply went in one ear and out the other.

Afterward, I followed him out into the hall. He took a pen and wrote on a scrap of paper, *Sólo Compás*. He explained to me very slowly in Spanish that this was the name of a CD that I had to buy and wrote down the address of a shop where I could get it. He told me to listen to it all the time—at home, when I was having my coffee, when I was walking down the street. "*Todo el tiempo*," he emphasized. All the time.

❋

The shop that Enrique sent me to, Compás Sur, was a little CD store in the center of Seville dedicated to flamenco. My eyes wandered over the racks: the CDs were alphabetized by the artist's name. Some of the more famous names I recognized, but the vast majority were unknown to me. I smiled, remembering the way I used to pore over the dozen flamenco albums in the dusty back corner of the CD store I went to in Sydney. Now I'd found the shop of my dreams.

The sales assistant came out from behind the counter and asked if I needed help. "*Sólo Compás?*" I asked, and he indicated with a wave of his hand a large section of the store. That's right, section. I'd thought that *Sólo Compás* was a disc, but it was in fact the name of a brand that produced CDs that were, as they say, *sólo compás*, or "only rhythm."

I looked around at all the different styles to choose from. Some of them I'd heard of, like *bulería*, *soleá*, *alegrías*, *tangos*, and *sevillanas*. But there was a whole heap more I'd never encountered before, with names like *tarantos*, *siguiriyas*, *tientos*, *fandango*, *granaína*, *farruca*, *malagueña*, *toná*, *caña*, and *zambra*, to name just a few. As my eyes scanned the titles, all I could think was, "How on earth am I ever going to learn all this?"

When I got back to the apartment, I chose one of the half dozen *Sólo Compás* CDs I'd bought and put it in the stereo in the lounge room. The first sound was a man saying "Ay!" Then a guitar started to strum with the chords muted, followed by a percussion instrument and someone clapping.

I turned up the volume so I could hear it while I made lunch. One, two, three, open the fridge. I drummed my nails on the door to seven, eight, nine, and ten. One, two, three, take out the rice, seven, eight, and a bag of green beans. Carry it to the bench, two, three, close the fridge with a kick, seven, eight, turn on the gas, *click click click*, light the flame. Put the pot on the stove. Rinse the beans and shake off the water, two, three. Take a knife, *chop chop chop*. Throw the beans in the pot. Put on the lid, turn down the flame.

Lunch in *compás. Olé, olé.*

❊

I listened to my *Sólo Compás* CDs at every possible moment of the day and night, just like Enrique had told me to. I listened to the different rhythms on my headphones as I walked to and from class, in the market while I did my shopping, even in the café. The simplicity of the recordings let the sounds around me filter through, and rather than taking me away from my surroundings, the music gave form to the noise of daily life.

In the café the whir of the coffee machine blended into the rhythm pattern on my headphones. The sounds of spoons clicking against cups and cups clattering against saucers merged in with the beat. One, two, three…I stirred my *café con leche*. And seven, eight, nine, and ten.

I also played the CDs when I practiced alone in the studio, and having to stay in *compás* changed the way that I danced. I started to see the reasons behind Enrique's choreography. Every twirl of the wrist and flick of the hips had its place in the *compás*, and each must be on their beat for maximum impact and drama.

At the end of the week, Enrique's guitarist was joined by a singer, and they both accompanied Enrique as he choreographed a new section for the dance. Then his eyes caught mine, and he beckoned me to come to the front of the class.

Me? What did he want me for? I walked nervously to the front of the room. Enrique told me to clap *compás* as he demonstrated the new footwork, and I got that flushed, nervous, dry-mouthed feeling that is usually felt by people who are about to throw themselves down a water slide that didn't look so scary from the bottom. *It's easy*, I told myself. *You know how to clap, don't you? Just put your hands together and…*

All eyes were on me as I began to clap. The guitarist picked up the rhythm and started to play. Enrique stepped forward, his arms raised, his eyes on the floor in front of him; he seemed to be waiting for inspiration. Then it hit him and he attacked the floor with rapid footwork. I had to keep all my focus on the beat so I didn't lose the *compás.* Enrique spun around, clicking the heel of his boot against the floor on the offbeats as he turned, then he landed and continued to dance as the singer started his verse.

By the end of the section, I could no longer tell if I was in time, but Enrique nodded and said, "*Muy bien.*" I did it! I did *palmas* for *soleá*, and I didn't mess it up. I didn't clap on the wrong beat, or go too slow or too fast or pass out from the pressure. I did it!

It was an important moment for me, because it showed me that I was able to keep the rhythm for a singer, guitarist, and dancer. For the girl who a week before had only a vague idea of what *compás* meant, it was a big step forward, and I had Seville to thank for it, because in Seville *compás* is everywhere and I never lacked opportunities to practice.

Sevillians grow up with flamenco and know *compás* intuitively. The street sweeper who sang outside the church didn't have to count to know where he was in *compás.* When I passed him I listened carefully, trying to pick up what style he was singing. And I noticed that when the sun was shining brightly he sang *alegrías*, which I guessed was because *alegrías* means happiness.

The next day as I was walking to the café to meet Zahra, I saw the street sweeper again. He was singing a slow song and I stopped to listen to him. What style was that? It sounded like a *sevillanas*, but it was much too slow. Maybe it was a *fandango*?

"*Hola,*" he said, seeing me standing there.

"*Fandango?*" I asked, and he nodded. "*Gracias!*" I said, and continued on my way. And as I walked on I heard his voice ring out again.

He doesn't know it, I thought to myself, *but he's made my day.*

THE *SEVILLANAS*

Or

Pasa…Gira…Pasa!

S pain was seducing me, and I was such a willing seductee. Every day she stripped off another piece of my armor, and she did it in a way that was so delightful that the staunch vegan who had been proudly starving herself was now drinking red wine at midday and ordering tapas without even checking the ingredients.

Only in Spain.

Only in Spain could it feel so normal to be so indulgent. Just a glance over your shoulder was enough to tell you that everyone else was doing it. And it wasn't just the wine or the tapas or the sugar in my coffee. Every day I was being seduced by the dark eyes that watched me from the front of the classroom.

That's right, I was falling for Enrique. Falling like an apple off a tree. Plummeting through the air without a thought to the bump I'd get when I hit the ground. I knew I couldn't call it love. How could it possibly be love? I didn't even know him outside of the classroom. I didn't know what he was like at home, though I had a pretty clear mental picture of his über-glamorous dancer lifestyle.

I could imagine him weaving through the traffic on his sleek black motorcycle, ducking under bowers of orange blossoms to arrive at his elegantly Mediterranean loft with its terra-cotta-tiled terrace littered with random sculptures, and succulents growing out of empty wine bottles. And he'd let himself in to his bohemian dancer's apartment—all polished floorboards with mismatched chairs—and he'd light a cigarette and lean on the windowsill, looking out over the rooftops of Seville, and think to himself, *I wonder what she's doing now?*

Yes, that was my dream. And through his eyes I saw a world covered in polka dots. Because a life with him would be one of wild, flamenco madness, like the day we did a *sevillanas* in class. We'd finished early, and seeing there were still ten minutes on the clock, Enrique decided to take us through a *sevillanas*. One small problem: I'd never danced a *sevillanas* and had no idea what the steps were.

As soon as the guitarist strummed the opening chords, the girls divided up into pairs. There was an odd number of students in the class, and I was the one left without a partner. Enrique came quickly to the back of the room and stood opposite me. I copied the girls around me and lifted my arms above my head.

No doubt Enrique couldn't have imagined that a girl could get into an advanced flamenco class without having learned *sevillanas*. In Seville the kids are dancing *sevillanas* before they can walk. Everyone dances *sevillanas*, whether at the Feria de Abril, or in a corner bar with a glass of wine after work. But as soon as we started to dance he realized. Around us the girls were stepping forward and back, their skirts swishing and their arms circling elegantly around their heads, but I just stood there helplessly.

Then the girls started spinning around each other, their arms twirling. "*Pasa!*" Enrique said, instructing me to step forward and swap places with him. "*Pasa!*" he repeated, and we switched places again. "*Gira!*" he said, and we both spun around.

The music sped up and I skipped forward, spinning around,

and then skipped back, spinning as I went, then forward again, and back. I was getting dizzier and dizzier, and on the next step forward I crashed into Enrique. He steadied me, then pushed me into position. Was it just me, or was the music getting faster? Enrique clapped the rhythm, and looking at him, I wished that we were in one of those smoky little *sevillanas* bars, pressed close together by the crowd...

As we lifted up our arms to begin the final set, Enrique gave me a look that said, "I hope you're ready." He told me to look into his eyes, and then we went straight into the turns.

"*Pasa*." We spun around each other, then our eyes met and he repeated, "*Pasa*," and we spun around again. "*Gira...pasa...gira... pasa...*" Turn, pass, turn, pass... We circled around each other, our eyes meeting each time we passed, and the faster we went, the more unsteady I was on my feet. Enrique put his hands on my shoulders to steady me, then spun me around again: "*Gira!*" Again I landed, and we locked eyes and circled each other again.

When the guitarist strummed the final chords, my head was spinning, but I threw my arm up in the air and we all cried out, "*Olé!*"

That evening Zahra and I met for a glass of wine in our favorite little bar, just around the corner from the dance school. Zahra was quite possibly the only person alive who was more obsessed with flamenco than I was. She was the only one of my friends I didn't have to explain my passion to. It didn't matter that all our conversations were about flamenco, and I didn't feel like a weirdo when I went on and on about things like *compás* and how much I hated turns. For us the weirdos were the people who didn't like flamenco.

The only difference between us was that she was more into the flamenco outfits, the colors, the different looks and accessories. And maybe that was because it all looked so good on her, with her sleek black hair and almond-shaped eyes, and the hourglass figure that made her look like one of the dancers on the posters in the tourist shops she was always dragging me into.

So of course when I told her about my first *sevillanas* experience, she said, "*Chica*, that is so cool! We have to go find one of those bars where the people dance. Then you can teach me. Or, better, we find some *ojos* to teach us!" *Ojos* means "eyes," but Zahra used it to describe Spanish eyes, which are like dark lagoons of mystery and seduction framed with luscious fronds of flirtation. It had become our code word for handsome Spanish men.

Our only problem was that we didn't know where these *sevillanas* bars were. So when the waiter came over with the bottle of *rioja* to fill up our glasses, we asked him if he knew of a place.

"*Claro!*" Of course! He pulled out a pen and wrote down a name on a serviette. With a wink of one dark eye, he told us he'd be there that night.

Zahra waited until he was a few steps away before saying, "*Muchos ojos!*"

We found Bar Andaluz underneath a stone bridge in the old part of town. It was the kind of place you would never find unless someone told you about it, yet even on a Thursday night the bar was so packed that we had to squeeze through a throng of perfumed and cologned bodies just to get in the door.

"*Chica,*" said Zahra, as we pushed through the crowd, ducking under glasses and lit cigarettes, "look at all these *ojos!*" We were surrounded by gorgeous Spanish men, all clapping to the rumbas played by the flamenco group on the stage. Then the band played the introduction to *sevillanas*, and everyone divided up into pairs and got ready to dance.

Looking at the people dancing, I could barely recognize this as the same dance we'd done in class. Some of the couples circled their arms around their heads the way my classmates had, but others kept their arms low or just twirled their free arm and held a drink in the other. The steps were adapted for a crowded dance floor, and looking around, we could see that there weren't two people who danced it the same way. It seemed everyone had their own personal *sevillanas* style.

I felt a hand on my arm, and a man spun me around to face him. He was tanned and smooth-cheeked, and looked suave as only a Spanish man can in a crisply ironed pink button-down shirt. I looked around for Zahra and saw her standing opposite her own partner, lifting her arms above her head and twirling her wrists like a born-and-bred *sevillana*.

"*Olé*!" my partner said as the dance began, then, "*Pasa…Gira… Pasa!*" as he gestured to help me with the movements. At the end everyone in the bar threw up one arm and shouted, "*Olé!*"

Zahra and I danced for hours, and with each set we got better. Each new partner taught us a different variation or a little flourish to add to the steps, and we didn't stop laughing all night.

As I twirled from partner to partner, I realized that I just love Spanish men. I love the way they wear pink and spray-starch their shirts, and that "going out with the boys" means dancing flamenco until the bars reopen for breakfast. I love the way they flirt, still believing that a song will win a fair lady, and I love the way they make a girl feel like she's the star of her very own Broadway musical.

"Watch this!" Zahra said, her dark eyes sparkling. She cried out, "*Toma que toma!*" The crowd cried back, "*Que toma, toma! Que toma que toma, que toma!*" as they danced. I still didn't know what *toma que toma* meant, if it meant anything at all. But it was just so much fun to say, and the Sevillians couldn't seem to resist it.

"You try it," Zahra insisted, so I called out, "*Toma que toma!*" and

THE DANCING JESUS

Or
You dip the fried stuff in the chocolate stuff

I don't know what time the drumming started. I woke up in the early hours of the morning and heard it through my window, then went back to sleep and the drum merged with my dreams. It was a slow and steady beat: *dum…dum…dum…*

When I woke up again later in the morning, I could still hear the distant drumbeat coming in my open window. At first I didn't pay much attention to it; by now I'd gotten used to the unusual sounds from the streets. There was the man who would walk past my window playing panpipes; when the local people heard him coming, they all went down to the street with their knives for him to sharpen. Then there was the *butanero*, who came past calling out, "*Butano!*" He sold the big orange gas canisters that powered the houses of Seville.

The sounds of the knife man and the *butanero* had become part of the soundscape of Seville that I loved. Music seemed to be in the air, and even the cry of the *butanero* reminded me of the voice of a flamenco singer. So now I didn't think twice about the drums; I knew it would be another Spanish ritual that I had yet to discover.

I was meeting Zahra for coffee that morning, and as I left the apartment, I heard the sound of wailing music. It sounded like a marching band tune being played backward. I turned a corner to find that the road was blocked by hundreds of people. They all stood watching as a procession made its way down the street, a crowd of hooded men carrying a statue of Jesus. Leading the procession were two men in white robes swinging incense burners, followed by another two robed men beating big drums, and a brass band playing the slow, mournful music.

This was Semana Santa, Holy Week, the Spanish Easter celebrations that go on for seven days and finish with Easter Sunday. The crowd surged toward the statue of Jesus, crying out prayers and reaching out to touch it. Then the drumming stopped and the procession halted in the middle of the road. The crowd fell silent; everyone seemed to be holding their breath. When the Jesus statue started to move, slowly, from side to side, the crowd erupted into rapturous cheers: "*Olé, Olé! Jesús, olé, Olé!*" What was going on? I couldn't understand it. Why were they shaking the statue, and why did this make the crowd go wild?

I asked an old man next to me and he said, "*Jesús está bailando!*"

"Jesus is dancing?" I repeated it back to him, thinking I'd heard him wrong, but he confirmed with a radiant smile, "*Sí, sí! Jesús está bailando!*" I looked up at the Jesus statue. He wasn't looking so good. His face was contorted in agony and streaked with blood from the crown of thorns on his head. His body was wasted and his bones were protruding...and they were making him dance? I guess in Seville there's no excuse not to *toma que toma*.

This was certainly going to be more colorful than Easter back home, which consisted of Sunday lunch with the family (me picking the goat's cheese out of the goat's cheese salad and eating some of the roast veggies that hadn't touched the lamb) and coming up with ingenious reasons why I should break my diet to eat chocolate.

The Spanish certainly seemed to take Easter seriously. The street was completely blocked, and every attempt I made to move through the crowd was met with angry shouts and hisses from the people around me. How on earth was I going to get to the café?

At the rate the procession was going I figured it would take me at least an hour to cross the road, so I turned around to see if I could find a way through the backstreets. But as I walked back toward the apartment, I heard the sound of another brass band playing a funeral march.

Coming up the street toward me was a different procession. These men carried a giant doll in a lavish purple gown with a massive crown on her head and one pert tear glistening on her cheek. I guessed she was the Virgin of something or other. Were they going to make her dance, too? She was certainly dressed for it.

Just then I got a text message from Zahra telling me she was trapped in a café on a corner near her apartment. The message ended: *They are eating something wonderful. Come here!*

The siren song of a mysterious and culturally specific delicacy! After only three weeks in Seville, I was beyond trying to resist. I knew that whatever it was they were eating in that café would not be made of tofu, but I didn't care. I was already planning my route to the corner café like a guerrilla tactician.

It took me half an hour to cover what was on a normal day a two-minute walk, and the incense wafting through the streets was starting to make me cough, but I got there. Zahra was standing in the doorway of a café that was packed with Sevillians eating coils of yellow pastry. The smell of deep-fried dough was even stronger than the incense.

Pushing our way through a crowd of women draped in black lace, we somehow got to the bar. Behind the counter, a man in a white uniform was cranking a machine that turned out a thin coil of yellow paste into a vat of bubbling oil. Whatever this new delicacy was, it had to be wonderful: anything that involves that amount of bubbling oil must be good. The dough was fried until it was crispy then placed on paper to dry for all of about five seconds before it was chopped up and served to the customers, who tore off pieces and dunked them into cups of coffee or thick hot chocolate.

From the signs up around the bar that said CHURROS €1.50, I guessed that these were churros. I wondered briefly what the macrobiotic take would be on deep-fried yellow stuff and liquid chocolate. The yellow stuff looked very yang, and the chocolate was clearly very yin, so I supposed that about evened it out.

We ordered a plate of churros and two cups of hot chocolate, which appeared before us at lightning speed. I tore off a piece of that yellow dough; just touching it covered my fingers in grease. Then I dipped it into my cup of chocolate as the other people were doing and bit into it.

Outside on the street, thousands of people were having a religious experience, but sitting at the bar of the café, I had one of my own. That mouthful of crispy featherlight dough covered in grease and dipped in thick hot chocolate was so divine I had to close my eyes for a minute. Zahra was trying to talk to me, but I held up my hand to say, *I can't eat this and listen to you at the same time*. She understood.

❋

The drumbeat went on day and night for the entire week. I could hear it when I lay in bed at night, and it was the first sound I heard when I woke up in the morning. It beat while I brushed my hair and cleaned my teeth and while I was getting dressed to go to class.

Out on the street I used the sound to navigate the quickest way around. When it got louder, I knew there was a procession somewhere nearby, so I'd take a side street to avoid getting caught again among a thousand pious Spaniards. This didn't always work; sometimes there was no avoiding the processions, and by the end of the week my jacket was streaked with wax from ducking under the giant tapers that the hooded men carried, and my clothes and hair stank of incense. Although the processions were streets away, we could even hear the drums in the studio, and the smoky incense wafted in through the windows. Sometimes I thought that the drumming had stopped, but it was just that I had gotten so used to the sound that I stopped hearing it.

On Saturday night Zahra and I went out without a plan. We wandered through the little archways and down the cobblestoned streets, going from bar to bar around the bullring in the center of town. We heard singing and followed the sound until we found ourselves in a tiny bar where a man was singing *copla*, traditional Spanish songs.

After a glass of wine we went back out onto the streets and wandered again until we heard a guitar. We followed the melody to a tiny bar where a guitarist was beating out a *bulería* and a girl in ripped jeans twirled around him with castanets between her fingers.

After that we wandered down to the river that runs through Seville, Río Guadalquivir. We crossed an old stone bridge and walked slowly through the streets, stopping to gaze into the brightly lit shop windows at spectacular flamenco dresses. Next year, we promised, we'd both come back and buy one.

We kept walking until we heard more live music and saw a crowd of people outside an old bar. They were standing by the door, all pushing, trying to get in. We joined them, pushing our way in just far enough to catch a glimpse of what was going on inside.

A woman in a black dress with heavily painted eyes and a bright red mouth stood in front of the crowd. She balled up her fists and belted out a love song. But she was not singing for any man. She was singing for her beloved Seville. When you fall in love in Seville, she sang, you fall in love *with* Seville.

A man came through the bar handing out cards with pictures of one of the Jesus statues on them. Underneath was written *El Jesús del Gran Poder*, the Jesus of the Great Power. I didn't understand; how was the Jesus of the Great Power different from the Jesus of the Sacred Heart or the Jesus of the Wasted Flesh or the Jesus of the Pained Facial Expressions? How many Jesuses were there? And what about the Virgins? Everywhere I looked in Seville there seemed to be a Virgin, but they all had different names. There was the Virgin of Pains, the Virgin of Miracles, the Virgin of Eternal Sorrows. Surely there was only one Jesus and one Mary, but the Virgin painted on the tiles above the entrance to Inés's building was different from the picture of the Virgin in the frame that hung above the radio at my favorite fruit stall in the market, and the Virgin that was paraded down Calle Feria was different from the other Virgins carried down different streets.

And everyone seemed to be particularly attached to their own version. The man with the card explained to me passionately that *El Jesús del Gran Poder* was very important and I should keep him with me always. Looking at the card, I didn't feel much of a connection to the statue's wooden features, though I did like his floor-length purple velvet cloak with gold brocade. The Sevillians certainly like their gods to be well dressed.

Just then, the lights went out in the bar. The only light came from the candles around a small framed picture of a Virgin that hung on the wall. The musicians began to play and the singer gazed up reverently at the illuminated figure and sang to her.

Zahra and I extracted ourselves from the crowd and went back onto the street. We turned a corner into a little lane and stopped, both struck by the scene before us. The moon was hanging so low in the sky that I felt if I reached up on my tiptoes I could touch it, and the stars looked like the twinkling fairy lights on the ceiling of Santa's Cave on Level Six of the department store back home.

I knew that my stay in Seville would soon come to an end. I could feel time speeding up: every day seemed to go faster and faster, like it was moving to the rhythm of *bulerías*. The day would come when I would have to pack up my suitcase and get on a plane back home.

But how could I possibly go back to that world I had run away from? How could I go back to eating lunch at twelve and dinner at six? I'd learned to take my coffee with a dollop of brown sugar in the warm midmorning sun; how could I go back to coffee in paper cups on the run? And how could I go back to breathing in air conditioning after the incense of Semana Santa, or squirting perfume on my wrists when I'd gotten used to crushing orange blossoms and rubbing them on my neck?

How could I live without flamenco? Here flamenco was part of daily life, not just restricted to an hour and a half once a week. And there weren't any *sevillanas* bars in Sydney where I could pick up new moves and dance until dawn.

In any case, I knew I had to dance. My body had gotten used to the daily training, and I was living on endorphins and *compás*. When I caught sight of myself in the mirror in the studio, I found it hard to believe that the girl dancing confidently in red shoes was the same one who had tried to hide at the back of the class just weeks before.

I didn't know what I was going to do when the time came to say good-bye. The very thought filled me with dread. In Spain I was living on cloud nine, and I didn't want to go back down to earth.

We walked back across the old stone bridge over the river. "This is a magic night," Zahra said. "Anything we wish for tonight will have to come true." And so I closed my eyes and made a wish. I wished that I could live in Spain forever.

THE KISS

Or

Sí, claro, toma que toma!

Zahra smoothed her hands over the bodice of her new flamenco outfit. It was her favorite color, not Hermès orange, but brighter, and the skirt was white with big orange polka dots and three layers of ruffles.

This was her final fitting; in three days' time both she and I would be sitting on airplanes that would propel us back to our homes. It was an odd coincidence that we were both flying home on the same day, and that it was the day after the opening of the Feria de Abril.

Zahra was lucky to have her dress finished in time as this was the busiest time of the year for dressmakers: everyone wanted a new outfit for the feria. The shop was packed and there was barely room for me to stand. Shopgirls were helping women into long ruffled dresses, taking note of last-minute alterations, and bringing out shawl after shawl to drape over the dresses.

Zahra was pushed away from the mirror by a woman in a bright red dress who wanted to see her own reflection. A stressed shopgirl followed her carrying a selection of combs; with an apologetic glance at Zahra, she held the different combs up above her customer's head for her to pick one.

It looked like Saturday afternoon on Level Two. In a week I'd be back at work. I didn't want to think about it. The saddest thing about leaving was that I had only recently begun to feel at home in Seville. Adapting to a new culture, especially one so different from my own, wasn't easy, and it wasn't until the end of my stay that I actually started to feel like I was in sync with the people around me. Everyday life was starting to feel like less of a struggle, and I'd accepted that searching for a smoke-free café and a supermarket open on a Sunday in Seville was as pointless as it would be to expect flamenco-singing police officers or a glass of red wine for a dollar fifty in Sydney. It just wasn't gonna happen. And as soon as I let go of my ideas of how the world should be, I was able to enjoy all the Spanishisms I had come to love. I had learned that midday is a perfectly respectable time to have coffee in the sun, just as midnight is a perfectly good time for dinner. I'd even temporarily suspended my veganism. "Only in Spain," I said to myself each time I indulged, knowing that when I got home I'd go back to brown rice and tofu.

I knew I had to return to Seville, and I dreamed of coming back to live. I imagined myself doing my weekly grocery shopping at the market, instead of Woolworths Metro. I pictured myself sitting in the café every morning, listening to the strum of a distant guitar, before swinging my dance bag over my shoulder and going off to class. But how was I going to do it? I racked my brains for a solution, but I couldn't find one. I didn't speak enough Spanish to get a good job, and the minimum wage in Spain was too low to permit me to live and dance. If I wanted to come back to Seville, I was going to need a plan.

※

That evening I went back to the school to practice. When I walked in, I could hear music coming from the studio. The door was closed, so I stood outside and listened, remembering how I had stood in that same doorway not so long ago watching the advanced class.

I could hear a singer, a guitarist, and a percussionist, as well as the sound of a dancer's shoes on the floor. The dancer was in the middle of a fast and complex footwork pattern. The music dropped out, and just the percussionist kept going. The dancer was racing the beat, going faster and faster.

I closed my eyes and tried to imagine the dancer drilling his feet into the floor, not daring to break his concentration even to wipe the sweat from his brow. Then there was a triumphant *stamp, stamp, stamp!* and a pause where I could imagine the double or triple or quadruple turn, then the dancer cried out, "*Ay!*" and landed on the floor.

It was Enrique. I could tell from the sound of his voice. I wished I could look into the studio; I would have loved to see him dance. I thought about pressing on the door to see if it would spring open as I'd done once before, but I didn't dare, so I went off to get changed.

But just as I was coming out of the changing room the door of the studio opened and there was Enrique, his eyes sparkling. "*Australiana!*" he said, seeing me. "*Qué haces aquí?*" What are you doing here? I told him I'd come to practice, and he said, "*Ven.*" Come.

As I followed Enrique into the studio, he told me that the dance he'd been rehearsing with the musicians was the same one that we were doing in class, and that he was adding a crazy footwork section to the end of it. He clapped and told the musicians to get ready to go again from the beginning. I looked around, confused. What? He wanted *me* to dance?

"*Venga,*" he said, telling me to get ready to start. The guitarist strummed the introduction, and I felt my arms lift up above my head as they had done countless times before. My wrists twirled and twisted, my fingers reaching out and curling back in, and then at a strum of the guitar, I grabbed the end of my long skirt and— *ratatatatatatatatatata!*—drilled my feet into the floor in the first section of the dance.

"*Olé!*" the singer said, but I was already moving on. The dance went so fast that I had to always be two steps ahead of myself. The singer began the verse, and I twisted and twirled to the music. Dancing with live flamenco musicians was something I'd only ever experienced from the back of the classroom, hiding behind a group of better dancers, hoping that no one would notice me. But this was a totally different experience. I could feel the guitarist's eyes on my feet as he followed me, while I kept my ear cocked to the percussion to stay in time.

All those evenings alone in the studio paid off in those few minutes. When it came time to jump up and slam the floor with my shoes, I didn't hesitate, and I knew just when to pause and linger over a roll of the shoulder and a flick of the hip.

"*Que toma que toma!*" the singer cried.

As I came to the end of the dance, Enrique came up and danced beside me. We went into those complicated steps that had so intimidated me when I had first seen Enrique performing them, and this time I nailed them. And when we went into the triple turn, I heard Enrique say, "*Vamos, niña!*" and I leaned in and threw myself around, one, two, three times!

"*Olé!*"

That one was me. I laughed with joy at the thrill of my first ever triple turn, landing perfectly on two feet at the same moment as Enrique. Our eyes met in the mirror as we clapped our hands, slapped our thighs, and skipped forward, one, two, three, threw one arm up in the air as if to tell the world to go to hell, and turned on our heels. I lifted up my skirt and swished it from side to side as we danced around in a circle.

"*Olé, Australiana!*" the singer said with a wink.

That was as much of the dance as I knew, so I took a step back and watched as Enrique went into his footwork solo. He stood in the middle of the room, his gaze fixed ahead of him, then slowly lifted his foot and went into the first rapid section.

"*Olé!*" the singer said as Enrique once again paused, clapping and listening to the *compás*. Then he threw himself into another complicated section, and then paused. After a couple of bars he started again, this time building up and building up until his feet were racing over the floor so quickly they were just a blur.

He stared straight ahead, his lips barely moving as he counted to himself. His boots hit the floor harder and harder and then he spun around once, twice, three, four, *five* times, landing with his arms outstretched and his head thrown back. "*Olé!*"

Enrique stood like this a moment as the singer jumped out of his chair and sang a verse. Then he opened his eyes and started to dance again. I joined him in the middle of the floor, swishing my skirt and twirling my wrists as we moved around the studio, waving good-bye to our imaginary audience and pretending to go offstage as the singer sang his last words and the guitarist strummed the final chords of the song.

The next day was my last class with Enrique. It was the Friday before I flew out, and it was the day before the Feria de Abril. I threw myself into the dance, reminding myself that it would be the last time.

But in spite of my determination to make my last class the best, I was out of *compás*. Perhaps it was because part of me was already on that plane over the Pacific. Though I tried to throw myself into the steps, I couldn't recapture the joy I'd felt dancing alone with Enrique and the band.

When the class was over, I stayed behind and went through the dance again, trying to glue it into my memory so that I could take it home as a souvenir from Spain. As I was dancing, Enrique appeared in the doorway and asked me if today was my last class. I nodded, sadly, and told him it was.

"*Cuando vuelves?*"

I hesitated before answering this question. When was I coming back?

Enrique saw my hesitation and pressed me to come back soon. "*Has aprendido mucho en poco tiempo.*"

He was right. I had learned a lot in my short time in Seville. I remembered how he'd tried to speak to me before my first class and I'd just stared back at him like a stunned possum. Now I could understand him.

"*Sí,*" I said.

The only problem was I couldn't speak Spanish, as he pointed out with a smile. "*No sabes decir más que sí?*" You don't know how to say anything but "yes"?

"*Claro,*" I said, pulling out another of the words that Zahra and I had picked up on our nights out dancing.

"*Claro?*" he repeated.

"*Sí,*" I said.

"*Sí? Sí qué?*"

I laughed at the nonsensical exchange and said, "*Toma que toma.*"

He laughed, hooked one arm around my waist, and swung me into a dip so low that my head was only inches from the floor. "*Toma que toma,*" he said, and he kissed me.

And if a kiss was ever Hollywood, this was it. It was a kiss to build a dream on, suspended in the arms of a flamenco dancer with one red shoe pointing up toward the ceiling.

Perhaps before that moment I'd had a chance at going home and leading a normal life, but the moment he took me in his arms my fate was sealed.

"*Vuelve*," he said. Come back.

Yes… Why don't I?

THE FERIA

Or
Only in Seville

On our last night in Seville, Zahra and I went out for a farewell dinner in El Rinconcillo, the tapas bar where I had first been seduced by Spanish food.

It was the night of the opening of the Feria de Abril and there was a festive atmosphere in the bar. The Sevillians were all dressed up to dance. The women were in frills and ruffles and polka dots, and the men looked like bullfighters in high-waisted trousers and waistcoats. Even the children were dressed up in mini flamenco costumes. And all around the bar people were singing *sevillanas* and clapping *compás* with glasses of sherry balanced between their fingers.

This time Zahra and I didn't hesitate before ordering our favorite dishes, and I tried not to look sad as I ate my vegetarian fish and meat. "Only in Spain," I said, trying to sound lighthearted but not getting close. The knowledge that my time in Spain had come to an end hung over me, and I couldn't even enjoy our final dinner together. I felt like weeping into the bread basket.

Over the six weeks that I'd been in Seville, I'd taken all the rules that had held my life in place in Sydney and replaced them with "only in Spain." Only in Spain did I get to dance flamenco every day.

Only in Spain did I drink milk and eat white bread and chocolate and fried squid. Only in Spain was sleeping for two hours in the middle of the day not only acceptable but encouraged. And only in Spain could I dance *sevillanas* until dawn.

I'd gotten so used to living this way that I didn't know how I was going to go back to the life I'd left behind. The swipe card and black suit and the 422 bus and First-Class Service Rules. The quiet streets, smoke-free bars, wine at ten dollars a glass, and I could forget about live music.

And then there was that kiss.

That damn wonderful kiss. I kept reliving it over and over in my head, the way that he had held me and gazed into my eyes. What frustrated me was knowing that it could have been that way from the beginning if I hadn't been so shy! But how could I have known that the impossible was possible? How could I have guessed that the man I was dreaming of was also dreaming of me? Now there was no time left. I was counting down the hours like Cinderella watching the clock, knowing that soon her carriage would turn back into a pumpkin.

We finished the last of our wine, and I told Zahra that she could go to the feria without me. I just didn't have it in me to go out and celebrate. All I wanted was to go to bed and cry.

The waiter came to collect our plates and asked if we were on our way to the feria. Zahra told him that she was but that I was going home to bed. He stared at me for a moment, dumbstruck.

He carried our plates away and came back moments later with a bottle of liqueur and two shot glasses. He poured out two shots and waited expectantly. I took one and swallowed it down. Then he pushed the second shot toward me too. I lifted the shot glass and drank it.

"*Ahora quieres bailar?*" he asked. Now do you feel like dancing?

"No." I shook my head.

The waiter filled up the shot glasses again. I took one and gulped it down. "*Ahora?*" he asked. Again I shook my head. He pushed the fourth shot in front of me, and I obediently tipped it back.

I closed my eyes and felt the world spin. It was my last night in Seville and I wanted an early night: What was I, crazy? Had this time in Spain taught me nothing? The night is for dancing, not for sleeping!

"Okay," I said, a little dizzy. "This is my last night in Seville and I'm going to the feria."

"*Olé, mi niña!*" the waiter cried, pouring me another shot for luck. Then he tapped his watch and told us it was already eleven thirty. The feria would open at midnight with the *alumbrado*, the lighting of the lights. If we didn't move fast, we were going to miss it.

Our plan had been to jump in a cab, not realizing that every taxi in a fifteen-mile radius of the center had been prebooked for the occasion. So instead we ran. We ran as fast as two girls in heels could run. We ran through the old streets of the Macarena, chasing each other around corners and in between orange trees. We raced down streets lined with flamenco boutiques. Zahra faltered in front of one window with a mannequin in a couture flamenco gown with cascading ruffles. "*Vamos, chica!*" I said, and she tore her eyes away and kept on running.

We ran down Zahra's favorite street, a little alleyway that always smelled of *azahar* and fried fish, and out across the plaza, past the cathedral, dodging women in flamenco costumes pushing baby carriages, and through crowds of men dressed up like bullfighters and drunk on sherry.

We raced past the bullring and down to the river where hordes of people were making their way to the showgrounds, carrying open bottles of whiskey and wine, beat-up guitars, and boxes they used as drums. We ran and ran and ran until finally we reached the entrance to the showgrounds.

There was a crowd of thousands of people waiting for the lights to come on and the gates to open. We stopped, panting for breath, just in time to hear the tolling of the bell. It was midnight.

"We made it, *chica*," Zahra whispered.

On the twelfth stroke of the bell a giant fan unfurled in lights in the sky, followed by another, then another. The crowd erupted into cheers as the three gold-and-red fans twinkled in the dark night sky.

The gates were thrown open and the crowd surged into the showgrounds. But Zahra and I just stood there staring up at the beautiful sight of the three fans created out of light in the sky. The fan is the perfect symbol for Seville. It's just like the city itself—fun, flirtatious, outrageous.

I couldn't help but wonder again at the strange timing of my trip, how I had booked my flight back home for the next day. It seemed almost as though the lights had been turned on for me: I was meant to be here, I was meant to see this.

Doesn't everything happen for a reason? I need to believe that it does. I don't do random; I see too much magnificent synchronicity in life to believe that it's all just chance. I was on a journey that had started when I opened that copy of *Harper's Bazaar*, and I knew that my adventure was only beginning. My return home was just a pit stop, I told myself. There were still thousands of flamenco nights ahead of me.

Standing there, I made a promise to myself. "I'm coming back," I said silently. "I'm coming back, I'm coming back, I'm coming back…"

THE NEW SEASON

Or
Where's your culo*?*

My parents picked me up at Sydney Airport, and as I gazed out of the car window at the deserted streets, I was shocked by how quiet the city was. Okay, I knew I wasn't in Spain anymore, but I was in the biggest city in Australia and it wasn't even six o'clock, yet every café, bar, and restaurant that we passed was shut. Where were all the people?

I had a few days off before I started work again, so Mum suggested I hang out at the beach while I got over my jet lag. My parents had a little beach shack on the Northern Beaches that they used for weekends and holidays, so I went up there and spent a couple of days gazing at the sea.

In the mornings I'd take a book down to the beach and try to read, but I always found myself staring off into space. All I wanted was to be back in my little room among the streets of the Macarena. I missed the smell of the orange blossoms; I missed the drum of Semana Santa; I missed those nights dancing *sevillanas* with Zahra.

I played the CDs I had brought back from Seville on a constant loop, even leaving the music on when I went to sleep. I would wake up in the middle of the night thinking I could hear again the sounds of the streets of Seville, people passing by my window, singing and laughing, and a guitar playing off in the distance. What can I say? I was hopelessly, head over heels in love with Seville, and there was nothing I could do about it.

❉

One morning I went down to a café opposite the beach for a take-away coffee to prop up my lazy eyelids. As I stood in line, I became nostalgic all over again, remembering the day I asked Inés if there was a café near the dance school that sold takeaway coffee.

"Coffee to take away?" she had echoed.

"Yes, you know, for when you're in a hurry and don't have time to sit down and have a coffee, so you drink it while you're walking."

"Drink coffee while you're walking?" Inés had repeated back to me. "How can you drink coffee while you are walking? That is like smoking a cigarette while you are running. In Seville, when you want a coffee, sit down and take a coffee. The world will wait for you."

I sighed as I took my takeaway cappuccino, remembering that soon I'd be back on Level Two, where the world most certainly would not wait the five minutes it might take me to have a coffee in peace. Again I wished that I was back drinking Spanish coffee in the warm morning sun.

It was as I wandered out of the café that I heard the sound of stamping feet. I stopped and looked around. Surely not?

The sound was coming from an old Boy Scouts hall opposite the beach. I walked across the lawn, thinking that surely I must be going mad. There was no way that what I was hearing could possibly be flamenco. But as I peeked in the doorway, I knew that I had found my new teacher.

She was magnificent, a *toma que toma* Spanish goddess in forest-green flamenco shoes. As soon as I saw her tearing up the sandy floor of that little wooden building in true Andalucian flamenco style, I knew that some greater power was orchestrating my life, because it was just too weird that I would find myself in the presence of this flamenco diva just as I was wishing myself back in Spain.

I waited by the door until the class was over, then ventured into the old hall and asked the teacher about joining her class. She introduced herself as Marina. She was Australian, from a Spanish family, and had spent years studying flamenco in Spain. And she looked like a flamenco dancer. She had a beautiful Mediterranean complexion tanned even darker by the Australian sun and thick black hair that fell down to her waist. She asked me where I'd learned to dance; when I told her about my six weeks in Seville, she cried, "*Ay! Sevilla!*" and told me about her own time dancing there when she was younger. We reminisced together about the *tablaos* and bars and nights on the Alameda.

I told her that I wanted to go back to Seville to live. I felt strange saying those words out loud for the first time. Of course it was what I wanted, but I hadn't actually gotten as far as saying it. But if my eyes were too bright and my voice too wistful, Marina didn't notice. She just waved away the idea and told me that if I wanted to "go pro," I had to go to Madrid.

Go pro? I looked at her wonderingly.

"*Claro!*" she said, then raised a finger in warning. "You gotta work hard. You gotta work harder than everyone else. But if it's what you want to do, the only place to go is Madrid, to the Amor de Dios." The Amor de Dios was a famous flamenco academy, where Marina herself had studied.

"Everybody teaches there." Marina listed famous flamenco dancers whom I was ashamed to admit I'd never heard of: La Tati, La China, Antonio Reyes, Cristóbal Reyes, La Truco…

"But…me? A professional flamenco dancer?"

"Why not you? Most of the best dancers these days are foreigners. You're starting late, but that's okay with flamenco. This isn't ballet; a flamenco dancer's got a long life span. But you've gotta want it."

I didn't even need to think. I just said, "I do."

"Then you've gotta go to Madrid."

She went on telling me stories about the famous teachers at the Amor de Dios. About Cristóbal Reyes, who wore sunglasses and chewed gum all through class then spat out the gum into the corner of the room whenever he stepped forward to demonstrate a step. She told me about La Tati, who grew up as a penniless gypsy girl in a small village and who hung out every day outside the neighborhood flamenco school, copying the sounds from the class with her bare feet on the street outside.

She reminisced about Paco Ortega's class, which was full of castanet-playing ballerinas. "That'll be you!" she said, and I laughed, feeling thrilled by the very idea. She mapped out for me my entire training schedule and filled my mind with so many dreams, I felt as though my head was spinning.

I thought about it on my way back to the city. Go to Madrid and become a flamenco dancer…it just sounded too crazy, too much like someone else's life. A hobby is one thing, but a profession? I guess I just didn't believe it was possible; I'd never imagined becoming a dancer.

But how could I have imagined it? My high school career adviser never suggested that I consider flamenco dancing. There's no bachelor of arts/flamenco dance at Sydney Uni, and there was no *Mastering the Art of Flamenco Dance* for me to stumble upon on my parents' bookshelf.

It was a dream, but did I really want to turn it into a reality? Did I really want to leave Sydney? Okay, maybe it didn't have all-night *sevillanas* bars or flamenco guitarists around every corner, but it was the city I had grown up in.

I thought about all the things I loved about my city. The beaches, the cafés, the shopping, and just wandering down by the harbor. But as I thought about these things, I had to ask the question: When was the last time I enjoyed Sydney? I was normally so exhausted after work that the only thing I had the energy to do was soak my feet in hot water and watch a DVD. Even the vegan restaurants I used to haunt had lost their appeal. I'd gotten used to tapas for lunch and tapas for dinner. Mock chicken made out of tofu just didn't do it for me anymore.

The reality was that Sydney had become the seven a.m. alarm, the morning commute, and days standing behind the counter, writing up the sales book and trying not to think about the varicose vein forming in my legs.

I thought about leaving my family. Though I knew I would miss them, I wasn't leaving forever. I'd come back every year for Christmas. And anyway, hadn't my parents raised me to be a traveler? Ever since I was young they encouraged me to treat the whole world as my stage and not limit myself to one country or one way of life.

More than worrying about what I was leaving behind, what I worried about was what was ahead of me. Madrid. I didn't know anything about it, apart from what Marina had told me, but I figured it was a big city full of lots of people speaking Spanish. How was I going to survive? *Was* I going to survive? Would I end up sleeping rough in my red shoes? Would I run out of money and have to sell matches or bunches of violets to keep body and soul together until I got consumption and finished my days coughing up blood in some charmingly bohemian garret?

Yes, I was afraid. On one hand I had the dream of moving to Spain and dancing flamenco, and on the other hand I had the paralyzing and debilitating fear of doing just that. A dream is such a beautiful thing, but when you try to turn it into a reality, it can go horribly wrong. *Maybe I should just stick with the dream...*

I've never been good with fear. I'm afraid of everything: of spiders, of pollution, of hurting people's feelings, of making a mistake on my tax return, of heights, of cancer, but most of all I was afraid of seeing my life go by without living it. That was the fear that trumped all the others. I didn't know if I believed in God or in a life after this one. All I knew was that I had been given a life to live, and that was a great gift, but also a great responsibility.

And time passes so quickly. The years seemed to be speeding up, and I knew that I could face my fear of aging and of death if, on the day that I looked in the mirror and saw the first lines around my eyes, I could smile and remember all the times I'd laughed and cried and drank wine in the sun. I knew that if my face had stories to tell, I wouldn't mind getting older.

And if I lived my life, and I mean really lived it—if I ran away with the gypsies and danced flamenco in a red dress under the full moon of a summer night in Madrid—then I could face any challenges life threw at me, and even death itself, because I would know that I had really lived this one precious life that I had been given. But it isn't easy being a girl who is afraid of everything. I had to create a kind of hierarchy for my fears. And in the end, the fear of letting go of this chance to live my dream was greater than my fear of what lay ahead of me.

So I made a decision about fear: I couldn't afford to let it control me or stop me from doing what I wanted to do with my life. I took a deep breath and felt the fear in my body. It was that cold, panicky feeling I knew so well. It flashed images of disaster across the screen of my mind, and I let it, for about ten seconds. Then I said to myself very clearly: *Yes, I'm afraid. And that's okay, because I'm going to do it anyway.*

"Chica!"

It was my first class with Marina, and I was already getting yelled at in Spanglish.

"Where's your *culo?*" she asked, tilting her head as if trying to see where I'd hidden my butt under my skirt. "What, did you leave it on the bus?" The rest of the class and even the guitarist were stifling their laughter.

Okay, yes, I'd lost a lot of weight. But if I was going to be a dancer, wasn't that a good thing? I was proud to be the thinnest student in the class. Aren't dancers normally just muscle and ambition? Not flamenco dancers, Marina told me with a waggle of her finger. A flamenco dancer needs to have at least the fat content of a King Island Camembert. "'Cause when you're onstage you need to make every movement look bigger," she explained. "If you don't have hips and you don't have a *culo*, you have to work twice as hard, and you're already going to have enough work to do! Go down to the market and buy yourself a *culo* and stick it on there!" She mimed attaching a big bottom to the void where mine should be.

At the end of the class, I told Marina that I had made up my mind—I would go to Madrid. "Good girl!" she said. We got take-away coffees from the café and sat on a bench overlooking the beach to talk through the plan for my new life.

"A lot of the girls getting into the companies these days are foreigners," she said. But to get a job in a company, it wasn't enough just to be able to dance flamenco. Company dancers need classical Spanish, which is like ballet combined with traditional Spanish folk dancing. And I was all for folk dancing, but not in pointe shoes.

I didn't want to have to learn ballet. Much as I would have loved to be able to move with the perfect control of a classically trained dancer, the idea of going into an adult ballet class terrified me. Though I could fudge my way through a flamenco turn—sometimes

I'd even fluke a double or triple turn—there was no way I could pirouette in ballet slippers like a doll out of a music box. But Marina told me that if I wanted to take my dancing to the next level, there was nothing for it.

To survive over there, Marina told me, I could teach English. Madrid, she said, was full of academies that organized teachers for in-office classes in big companies; the work would give me enough to live on if I was prepared to live simply. I was lucky because I had dual nationality—a British passport as well as my Australian one—that allowed me to work legally in Spain.

I wanted to leave straightaway. But of course that wasn't possible. Marina pulled a pen and a little notepad out of her dance bag and calculated a budget for me.

"Okay, so to survive and dance for three months, you're going to need three thousand euro, which is about five thousand dollars, plus your flight. So let's say seven thousand dollars."

Seven thousand dollars? There was no way I could get seven thousand dollars. It would take me a year to save up that money. "What if I get a job in my first month?" I asked.

Marina redid her calculations and came up with the slightly more attainable amount of five thousand dollars.

Okay, I said to myself. *It's May now, and if I do nothing but work until Christmas, I should be able to make it. And if not, I'll just go with what I have.* I'd make it happen, because I was sure about one thing—on December 31, I would be in Madrid ready to start my new year Spanish.

THE DAYS OF
CHRISTMAS

Or
Four fetching sweaters, three stone slacks, two trench coats, and a pinstriped Max Mara suit...

"*Mi tía tiene un gato negro*. My aunt has a black cat. *Mi tía tiene un gato negro*," I repeated as I stepped off the bus onto the busy city street. "*Mi hermana tiene una camisa blanca*. My sister has a white shirt." The serious man's voice came to me through my iPod earphones. "*Mi hermana tiene una camisa blanca*," I repeated, just as seriously, as I walked to work.

I had promised myself that I would learn as much Spanish as I could before moving to Madrid, and *Learn Spanish in Your Car* was part of that promise. Of course I didn't have a car, so I renamed the program "Learn Spanish on the Bus."

But time was going by so fast, and my vocabulary was still limited to family members, animals, numbers, colors, and days of the week. I was still having trouble with sentence structure and verb conjugation, and tenses just did my head in.

I walked up the street toward the department store, then stopped and stared. It couldn't be. Not yet. The new season spring fashion in the window had been replaced by...gingerbread houses. A line of wooden toy soldiers stared out through the glass, and around them a model train set ran through an inch of fake snow.

Surely it wasn't Christmas already? How was that possible? It seemed only weeks ago that I'd made the decision to move to Madrid on New Year's Eve.

At the bag check counter, I saw a sign pinned to the wall announcing that auditions for Santa's Cave would be taking place in the lunchroom at noon. *This can't be happening*, I thought. *I'm not ready for this. It's too soon. And I haven't even learned any Spanish yet!* "My sister has a white shirt" and "my aunt has a black cat" weren't going to help me get an apartment and open a bank account in Madrid.

When I stepped out onto Level Two, there were men in overalls on top of ladders fixing garlands of tinsel to the roof. *Stop it!* I wanted to yell at them. *It's not Christmas yet. It's too early!*

Not that I could talk. I was notorious for getting Christmas fever in November. I just always loved Christmas, so I'd plan a decoration concept for the house, choosing the color palette, writing shopping lists, looking at MarthaStewart.com for cute gift ideas. I'd plan my Christmas baking, and on December 1, I'd already be rolling out gingerbread to Bing Crosby Christmas albums.

But this year was different. This year Christmas meant packing up and going off to face an uncertain future on the other side of the world. And though I wanted that more than anything, I still had the panicky feeling that the clocks were being wound forward on me.

"I suppose I should say Merry Christmas," I said to Sascha as I went into the stockroom to clip on my name tag.

"I hate Christmas," Sascha said.

"You can't hate Christmas," I said. "Christmas is reindeers and pudding and baby Jesus, and it's the only time of year you get to hear Dean Martin on commercial radio."

Sascha raised one eyebrow. "Maybe you should audition for Santa's Cave. You'd make a good elf."

A new roster was pinned up on the wall with our hours up until

Christmas. I ran my eyes over it: I was going to be working six-day weeks for the next month. "We're on Christmas hours already? You've got to be kidding me." While I was happy for the extra money, I was going to have to negotiate to get Saturdays off so I could have some classes with Marina before leaving.

I'd been taking private classes with her in the Scouts hall opposite the beach, trying to get up to speed with what I'd need to know for the Amor de Dios. She'd taught me to dance *sevillanas* like they do in the theaters, not in the bars. How to dance with a fan, opening and closing it with a flick of the wrist, and of course the most important thing: castanets. She'd ordered a set for me from Spain, and I still remember my excitement the day they arrived.

She presented them to me in a box wrapped in maroon paper with thin gold stripes. I carefully lifted the sticky tape, like I was unwrapping a Christmas present, and opened the box. Inside was a little pouch that held my castanets. They were made of dark polished wood, and as I slipped them out of the pouch, they clattered together, making the most wonderful sound.

Marina showed me how to put my fingers into the woven cotton loops and then pull them tight so they fitted perfectly in the palms of my hands. She put hers on and demonstrated tapping her fingers so that they clicked together. *Tac-a-tac-tac, tac-a-tac-tac.*

"Come on, let's give 'em a go," she said. I got up off the bench, and Marina and I stood facing each other, our arms held out in front of us. She drummed her fingers on her castanets, and I tried to copy the rhythm. It was much harder than it looked, especially getting a sound with my little finger. Then we opened our arms wide and I tried again: *tac-a-tac-tac.*

Marina lifted her arms above her head and I did the same, trying to use the castanets at the same time. It was impossible. I could barely make a sound at all. Marina started circling her arms, clicking her castanets together. I tried to follow, but after a couple of minutes my arms were aching so much that I had to drop them.

In the three months since, I'd improved a lot, but dancing with castanets was still a challenge, and with Christmas approaching, there wasn't going to be enough time for me to practice.

※

In retail, no one gets Christmas Eve off. In the department store, every section had all their staff out in force. The managers became like generals, assigning everyone specific tasks they were not allowed to deviate from, unless it was to bust a shoplifter.

Of all the jobs, mine was the worst, no question about it. I'd have much preferred to be on the fitting rooms, hanger detail, or gift wrap, which was reserved for our Christmas temp, Victoria, who had a flair for neatly pleating tissue paper. Instead, I got the job of repricing all the stock in the three hours left before midnight, writing the reduced prices for each individual garment on little red stickers.

"Aren't there machines to do this?" I asked as I went through the seven-page list. But I was talking to myself. Sascha was on the register, ringing up last-minute sales to stressed-out Christmas shoppers laden down with bags of pudding and chocolates, tinsel and lights.

I started out with suits, which were going down by thirty percent. I wrote $1,350 on twenty-two stickers. The red dots were swimming in front of my eyes. I'd been working since eight o'clock that morning and I was almost delirious. Around the floor I could see other girls doing the same task. Some sections had proper printed stickers that had been sent out from their head offices, while others even had fancy pricing guns. I was leaning on the glass display cabinet, squinting over the price list and writing up every sticker, my writing becoming increasingly illegible. But it was all going to be so worth it, I reminded myself. When I walked the corridors of the Amor de Dios, I'd be glad I suffered through one final Boxing Day sale.

The same Christmas mix had been playing over the speakers on a continual loop, and it was driving me crazy. I knew the playlist by heart: "Jingle Bell Rock" merged seamlessly into John Lennon's "Happy Xmas," adapted for synthesized panpipes. I could almost hear poor John rolling over in his grave. That then segued into "The Twelve Days of Christmas."

"On the first day of Christmas, my true love gave to me," I sang to myself, "a pinstriped Max Mara suit."

This is insane, I thought again, looking around the floor. The same two-thousand-dollar beaded Dinnigan dress that would be unwrapped on Christmas morning was already hanging on the sales rack at fifty percent off. The Trent Nathan trench coat you bought for your mother was now forty percent off. And that red-and-green Moschino twinset that you just *had* to have for Christmas Day was already two hundred dollars cheaper.

I knew that those same pieces would be returned on Boxing Day. "They just didn't fit right," the regretful customers would say. And they would linger and wait until we went on our much-needed coffee breaks, then pick up the same items from the sales racks and buy them again at the reduced price.

"Can you blame them?" I asked no one in particular as I peeled the red stickers off the roll and tagged every T-shirt in the pile at thirty percent off. "On the fifth day of Christmas my true love gave to me, five white tees, four fetching sweaters, three stone slacks, two trench coats, and a pinstriped Max Mara suit."

At the bottom of a pile of sweaters, I found a wad of scrunched-up green silk. I pulled it out; it was a floor-length Akira dress from the Australian Designers department. Come on, now. Is that the spirit of Christmas? What kind of person would come into a department store on Christmas Eve just to try to hide the last size eight Akira dress so that no one else could get it before the Boxing Day sales? They should be at home with their families or helping out at a soup kitchen or something, not trying to stash designer dresses under piles of knits.

The beautiful dress was crushed almost beyond recognition. I slipped it onto a hanger and carried it over to Liz, who I knew would be frantically combing the racks looking for it, dreading the thought of having to fill in a lost merchandise report.

"On the sixth day of Christmas, my true love gave to me, a bias-cut silk Akira dress, five white tees…" I sang as I skipped across the floor. Everywhere I looked the sales girls were trying to simultaneously swipe credit cards, reticket garments, and answer the persistently ringing phones without losing their cool. "Four fetching sweaters, three stone slacks, two trench coats, and a pinstriped Max Mara suit."

I was right: Liz was pulling her hair out trying to find the eighteen-hundred-dollar dress. And though she was relieved to have it back, the wrinkled silk would need an hour under a cool iron before it was fit to go back on the display rack, and on a night like Christmas Eve that was not an option.

"Darling…" I turned and saw Deborah standing coolly behind me in her impeccable gray suit. "I need someone to mind my section for an hour while I do my shopping. Sascha said she can spare you." Thank God. Christmas had come early for me. I stuffed the roll of red stickers in my pocket and followed Deborah back to the Armani concession, a white marble oasis in the midst of the surrounding chaos.

"We haven't been that busy this evening, so you shouldn't have any trouble," she said and dropped the stockroom keys into my hand. "*Ciao, ciao.*" She slung her Ferragamo bag over one shoulder and sauntered off into the madness.

I watched as customers darted past with their heavy shopping bags. Deborah was right: it was quiet in her corner. The night ticked slowly by, and I entertained myself by running my hands over the beautiful clothes.

One jacket in particular caught my attention. It was a warm cream-colored creation with mother-of-pearl buttons in a two, just my size. I took it off the rack and held it up to myself in the mirror. It was pure perfection. I wondered what it would look like on. *Maybe I should try it. Why not? It was Christmas, after all, and everyone on the floor was too busy to pay any attention to what I was doing.* So I unbuttoned my black blazer and slipped on the cream jacket. Wow. So this was what it felt like to wear beautiful clothes.

"Look at you!" It was Nathan from Moschino. He was wearing his green and red Christmas cravat with a sparkling red tiepin and carrying glasses and an open bottle of champagne. "Just thought I'd bring you a little Christmas cheer!" He set the glasses down on the register. "One of my good customers left it for us. Don't let anybody see!" He stood with his back to the selling floor and poured out two glasses of bubbly. "Chin chin!" he said, as we clinked glasses. "I love the jacket! You should tell Deborah to put it away for you."

Yeah, right. Even at half price it was still enough money for me to live and dance for a month in Madrid. "Bottoms up!" he said, downing the rest of his champers before scurrying off to spread more cheer.

My next visitor was Amanda from Escada. She was carrying a gold box full of chocolate truffles. "It's quiet in here. Take one, quick!" she said, handing me the box.

"How's it on your end?"

"It's a madhouse!" She shook her head. "That jacket is divine. Don't let Deborah catch you in it!" she warned as she crossed over to offer truffles to the girls at Collette.

This is more like it, I thought as I bit into the chocolate and took a sip of champagne. Merry Christmas. Then I looked up and saw Deborah walking across the floor toward me. I froze. She had asked me to watch her concession, and I was wearing a two-thousand-dollar jacket, drinking champagne, and eating chocolate.

Deborah saw me and stopped dead in her tracks. Her eyes blazed. It was too late for me to suck the melted chocolate off my fingers. She took two steps toward me, her red lips pressed together.

"It's so *you*!"

It took me a moment to realize I wasn't in trouble. Deborah hadn't even noticed the chocolate or the bubbly. She was looking at the cut of the jacket. "You have to try it with the skirt," she said, taking the cream skirt off its wooden hanger and shooing me into the fitting room. "Didn't Nathan leave a glass of champagne for me?"

As I tried on the gorgeous cream skirt, I sang to myself, "On the seventh day of Christmas, my true love gave to me…a cream Armani jacket, a silk Akira dress, five white tees, four fetching sweaters, three stone slacks, two trench coats, and a pinstriped Max Mara suit."

Definitely the worst thing about trying on clothes in Armani is having to take them off again. I sighed as I clipped the skirt back on its hanger, and reminded myself that I'd have no use for a cream suit in the Amor de Dios.

The doors of the department store closed at midnight, but we didn't make it out of there until twelve thirty. The place was a mess. Frantic, near-hysterical customers had tossed merchandise off shelves and onto the floor, and every single item had to be returned neatly to its place before we were allowed to go home. Bright red sale signs had to be attached to mannequins and the glamorously named "dump bins." When we finally dragged ourselves to the elevators, we were exhausted. It was officially Christmas Day.

"Merry Christmas," I said to Sascha as we waited for the lift. Sascha gave me a look that told me exactly where I could put my "Merry Christmas," and we boarded the elevator with a group of tired shopgirls and rode down to the ground floor.

I'd started work at eight, and I'd be getting home at one thirty on Christmas morning. *But it's all worth it*, I said to myself as I walked down the dark street to the bus stop and waited for the twelve forty-five bus to arrive.

"On the twelfth day of Christmas," I sang quietly, standing alone at the bus stop, "my true love gave to me, a brand-new life in Spain."

THE AMOR DE DIOS

Or
I'm in Madrid; how cool is that?

The dancers lifted up onto their toes and spun around, clicking their heels one, two, three times and landing lightly. Then, lifting their arms like birds about to take flight, they twirled their wrists and stamped their feet into the floor.

Olé.

It was my first day at the Amor de Dios, and I stood at the back of the classroom gawping at the other dancers. They all moved together like the corps de ballet of the Spanish National Dance Company. Perhaps that's what they were.

It was my first class and I could barely join in, but I didn't care. I was just so thrilled to be standing there on the famous sprung floors. I'd arrived in Madrid, as I'd promised myself I would, on New Year's Eve, with my red shoes, castanets, and just enough money in my purse for the train fare to the city and a *bocadillo*, a sandwich.

I was so excited as I dragged my suitcase up out of the underground station and into my first Madrid day. I was so happy to have finally made it to Spain that I didn't even mind getting lost in my search for my hostel. And when I finally found the street, I was too delighted to care that it was lined with prostitutes. I just admired their fabulous animal print coats and wondered where they got their awesome vinyl platforms. As I hoisted my suitcase up the stairs to reception, the smile on my face was a mile wide, and even the sight of the swastika tattooed on the receptionist's forehead didn't put a dent in it.

"*Buenos días!*" I said in my most "I'm in Spain; how cool is that?" voice.

"*Buenos días,*" he said, smiling back at me with curious eyes that said, *I wonder what she's on and where I can get some?*

"*Estamos en España!*" I said. We're in Spain!

"*Sí,*" he responded with one of those indulgent grins generally reserved for babies and drunks. He handed me a key and told me that my room was down the stairs.

Down the stairs? Weren't hotel rooms generally upstairs? But this wasn't a hotel; it was a hostel I'd found in the "At Your Own Risk" section of my *Spain on a Shoestring* guide.

As I rattled the key in the lock, I told myself that at the price I was paying, it would be normal for the room to lack some comforts. "Oh," I said, looking around the room that was to be my home away from home. Comforts like…lights, perhaps? Or windows? Clean sheets, or even…sheets? There was at least a basin, and some mysterious cables that hung from the ceiling. It took me a little while to realize that my room wasn't actually a room at all; it was an old elevator shaft with a plaster ceiling added. But I didn't care. I unzipped my suitcase and took out my red shoes and castanets and placed them carefully on a shelf that seemed to be held up by Blu-Tack, turning it into a flamenco altar. I'd made it to Spain, and my days of being a shopgirl were no more.

I'd arrived on December 31 for symbolic value: new year, new country, new life. What I didn't realize was that I'd have to wait a week before starting classes. I had expected the Amor de Dios would be closed on New Year's Day, but nobody told me about el Día de los Reyes Magos.

El Día de los Reyes Magos, or Reyes as I came to know it, is held on January 6. It is the day of the three kings, the ones in the song that came following the star, and it's like Spanish Christmas. These days the Spanish also celebrate "American Christmas" on December 25, so what happens is that December 25 to January 6 effectively becomes one long holiday, because there's no point going back to work for a couple of days in between those days and New Year's Day. And as this year Reyes fell on a Sunday, the holidays lasted till the seventh.

While I could appreciate this nifty arrangement, I'd come more than ten thousand miles to dance flamenco, and for the first week I was in Madrid the dance school was closed because everyone was off eating *roscones*, giant doughnuts filled with cream. And it wasn't that I expected everyone to stop having Christmas so I could dance. Except…well, that's exactly what I expected. I mean, come on, *January*? That's New Year's resolution time, time to buy that yearly gym membership or Bikram yoga pass. Quit smoking, read more books, learn to speak Mandarin or dance flamenco.

I don't think the Spanish go in for New Year's resolutions, but I soon discovered that they have at least one strange New Year's Eve tradition. The hostel where I was staying was right next to Puerta del Sol, the square that is the official center of Spain. This was where the people came to watch the clock strike midnight and celebrate the New Year. So on my first night in Madrid, I put on a leotard, then a sweater, then two more sweaters and my coat to go out and join the festivities.

I had a thick scarf that Dad had bought me for my trip, and as I wrapped it around my neck, I remembered my last New Year's Eve in Sydney, walking down to Bondi Beach at a quarter to twelve in a summer dress and a pair of thongs. I carefully tucked the ends of the scarf into the neck of my coat to keep the icy air out, and remembered the way I had run into the surf with my girlfriends as we heard the fireworks go off. But this year I had traded my Sydney summer for a European winter, and even the cold added to the sense of adventure. *Maybe it'll snow*, I thought as I ventured out to the street and down to the Puerta del Sol, where thousands of Spaniards were gathered in front of a gray stone clock tower, waiting for midnight.

On every corner there were people selling little packets of grapes. My guidebook had explained that it was a Spanish tradition to eat twelve grapes at midnight on New Year's Eve, one on each tolling of the bell. Around me I could see people in woolen caps and heavy coats, holding their grapes in one gloved hand and a drink in the other, watching the clock and waiting. I bought a packet of grapes and wove my way through the crowd to get closer to the clock.

We all held our breath, waiting for the stroke of midnight. I inched the first grape closer to my lips. I was determined to do this right. It was the first important Spanish tradition I was taking part in and felt like a momentous responsibility. I had to prove that I could be Spanish too.

At the first stroke of midnight, everyone started cramming grapes into their mouths. I chewed and swallowed mine as quickly as I could. At the final tolling of the bell, the crowd erupted into cheers. I was swept up in the wave of joy that passed over them all, pulled into the arms of people I had never even laid eyes on before. Old women hugged me and kissed my cheeks, saying "*Feliz año*!" Happy New Year! All around I could hear corks popping, and someone pushed a plastic cup of Spanish champagne into my hands.

But then I had a whole week with nothing to do. So I grudgingly did the touristy stuff. Madrid has some of the most incredible art in the world, but it was all I could do to keep myself from tapping the heels of my boots on the marble floors in front of *Guernica*. I hadn't come to Madrid to look at paintings; I'd come to dance.

The day the Amor de Dios reopened, I was up and dressed at seven in the morning. Just as I was packing my red shoes in my bag, I got a call on my mobile.

"*Guapa*!" It was Marina, calling from Sydney. "Are you dressed already?"

"Yes," I confessed.

"I knew it!" she said, laughing. "What did you have for breakfast?"

"Er…a kiwifruit," I said, not mentioning that I'd had to rip it apart with my fingers because I didn't have a knife.

"I knew you wouldn't be taking care of yourself! Go to the café underneath the Amor de Dios and order yourself *pan con tomate y un café con leche*."

Pan con tomate is my favorite Spanish breakfast, toasted bread with tomato, drizzled with olive oil and sprinkled with salt. In my time in Sydney I had gone back to being vegan, but that didn't mean I couldn't be a little indulgent. "Well, *guapa*, I'm just calling to wish you luck and tell you how proud I am of you."

I couldn't help the tears that welled up in my eyes. It was so kind of Marina to call me up on my first morning of class, and it made me realize how lucky I was to have such wonderful people in my life. I suddenly felt homesick, and I was afraid of what was ahead of me. But I'd made my decision about fear. I wasn't going to let it stop me doing what I wanted to do with my life.

In my excitement about my first day at the famous school, I forgot to take the address with me. It was about a ten-minute walk to Antón Martin, the suburb where the dance school was, but it wasn't until I got there that I realized I didn't even know what street I was supposed to be looking for.

I wandered around in circles, listening for the sound of stamping feet. The Amor de Dios is *the* flamenco and classical Spanish dance academy, and one of the most important dance schools of the world, so I'd assumed it couldn't be that hard to find, but there didn't seem to be anything in Antón Martin except for a huge building that housed a produce market. The streets around it were lined with fruit and veggie shops, cheese shops, and butchers. I couldn't see any signs of the world-renowned center for *toma que toma*.

A fishmonger stopped me as I came past his store for the fifth time and asked me what I was looking for. "El Amor de Dios," I said.

"Ahhh!" he cried. "*Vienes a bailar flamenco!*" He twirled his rubber-gloved hands above his head, then pointed to the big market building and told me to go to the top floor; that was where I'd find the dance school.

At first I didn't believe him. I thought it might have been a joke, especially as all the other fish guys had come out from behind the mountain of crushed ice and were nodding and grinning. But they insisted, and I was tired of circling, so I ventured inside the market.

What kind of a dance school is in a building like this? I thought as I passed butchers and fruit stands and olive stalls. But as I climbed the stairs the shouts of the market were increasingly drowned out by the rumble of stamping feet, and the smell of fresh fish was overpowered by cigarette smoke. A man with swarthy skin and long black hair stood smoking in the stairwell next to his guitar case. He stared at me with dour eyes as I climbed the final flight of stairs and stopped in front of a brass plaque that read EL AMOR DE DIOS, CENTRO DE ARTE FLAMENCO Y DANZA ESPAÑOLA.

I stepped through the doorway and into the dance school of my dreams. It was just like Marina had said it would be. The walls were hung with black-and-white photos of the school's famous teachers, and the reception area was full of Spanish dancers: girls in long skirts with dark hair pulled up on top of their heads, and boys in flamenco boots with long hair hanging down to their shoulders. They chatted in Spanish as they practiced footwork, tapping their feet at lightning speed.

The notice board was covered with signs for classes. Inmaculada Ortega was teaching *bata de cola*. Cristóbal Reyes was doing a workshop on *farruca*. Antonio Reyes had technique at two p.m., followed by choreography at three. I gazed up at the notices, thinking, *I can do any of these classes. Any class I want.* I wanted to do all of them. I wanted to learn *bulerías de Jerez, alegrías, soleá, tientos, tangos,* and *tanguillos.* But I had to start with one, so I picked a choreography class.

There was a white-haired old lady at the reception desk, and I tried to ask her in my broken Spanish how to sign up for the class. She waved me away and told me to go straight to the studio and pay the teacher directly.

I walked down the corridor to the changing room, gazing at the framed pictures of the Amor de Dios's teachers, and every time I passed a studio where a class was going on, I stopped to have a peek inside. One studio had a few girls in ruffled skirts with yards of train. The girls were spread out around the room so that they had space to kick and twirl their long, long skirts. They wobbled and strained as they tried to lift up their skirts, which must have weighed at least ten pounds each, with one leg. In another studio half a dozen girls in pointe shoes twirled around, clicking castanets above their heads.

I found the changing room at the end of the corridor. It was full of girls changing in and out of ruffled skirts and brightly colored shoes. Girls in tights and leotards sauntered out of what I assumed to be a ballet class. One girl was stretched across a bench in the splits, lazily adjusting her leg warmers. Everyone was slim and sinuous and Spanish, and I wished desperately that I could blend in a little more.

My excitement was fast turning into terror as I prepared to go into my first class. Wishing I could be just a little less visible, I wet my hands and tried to smooth back my red hair, but I was still too pale, too thin, and just too damn foreign not to feel like everyone was staring at me.

I watched the other girls in the mirror as I changed into my dance clothes. Clearly dancers, as opposed to dance students, they walked with straight backs and turned-out feet, the way only real dancers do. And as the girl next to me buckled up her shoes, I noticed that her calves rippled with muscle.

Dancers had always seemed to me to be impossibly cool creatures who lived off wheatgrass shots and endorphins and lived in lofts with floorboards and no furniture because it would only get in the way of their continuous practice. I hoped one day that would be me, but until then I was somehow going to have to get through a dance class with these pirouetting princesses.

The fear grew inside me as I made my way down the corridor to the studio. The previous class was still going, so I joined the girls waiting in the doorway, peering past them to see what was happening inside. The studio was absolutely packed. There were at least thirty dancers going through a beautiful classical-inspired flamenco dance, all fluid arms and tricky turns.

At ten o'clock, the teacher clapped her hands and the students filed out of the studio and joined the swarm of dancers in the corridor. I went straight for the back corner of the room, and watched as the class filled up until there were four lines of dancers.

The teacher was the last in. He welcomed everyone back from their holidays, then clapped his hands for the class to begin. I took a step back and watched the dancers go into the choreography they'd been rehearsing over the Christmas break. Watching the exquisite poetry of their movements made me forget my fear. Standing there at the back of the room made me feel like I'd stumbled onstage during a performance of *Carmen*.

One day that will be me, I thought as I watched the way the girls lifted up their long skirts with one leg as they spun around.

One day.

THE APARTMENT

Or

Don't let your feet touch the ground

My mother always told me when I was growing up that artists live on air. After a few weeks in Madrid, I started to understand what she'd meant. The desire to create something beautiful out of thin air is what drives you on, and even if you don't know how you'll make it to the end of the month, or even the end of the day, you can live on the dream that you're chasing and your feet won't touch the ground.

But my mother didn't know just how high above my present circumstances I was having to levitate. If there was one thing Mum always insisted on, it was beauty—she could make any place beautiful with a new tablecloth and a bunch of flowers in a jam jar. But even she would have been at a loss faced with my hostel room. My parents thought I was staying in a nice midrange hotel, the kind with a TV and individually wrapped mini soaps. They didn't know how far I was prepared to go to economize.

Mum never needs to know, I told myself as I spread out my supplies for lunch on my hostel bed. I had a carton of gazpacho, a tortilla, and half a baguette that I'd bought at the supermarket the day before. The cold air in the room was as good as a fridge, and the gazpacho was cool and fresh.

If I'd stopped and thought about what I was doing, I would have said that I was mad. Coming to a big city like Madrid to compete with thousands of Spanish dancers was beyond arrogant—it was insane. So I chose not to think about it. What was the point? It wasn't as if I had a choice. I was in love, pure and simple. I was in love with flamenco, and I knew that I wouldn't be able to live without it.

It never occurred to me to think about what I was giving up by embarking on this mad adventure. A voice of reason might have pointed out that these were the crucial years of my life to get an education and a good job and start putting money away; otherwise, I'd find that while I was off chasing down a hopeless dream, the ship of my life had sailed. But I chose not to listen to that voice of reason. I drowned it out with the flamenco music in my head. I leaned back and closed my eyes and saw again those dancers at the Amor de Dios twirling in front of my eyes.

❋

Marina had told me to check the notice board at the Amor de Dios for a room to rent. I looked over all the handwritten notices. Someone was selling their dance shoes, size seven, dark green, ninety euro. There was an ad for Japanese conversation classes, flamenco guitar tuition, babysitting, a seamstress experienced in making flamenco costumes… I looked up at all the different ways the students tried to make money. Someone was offering English lessons at five euro an hour. Five euro an hour? That was seven dollars. My morning coffee had cost me two euro fifty. How desperate were these people? And would that be me one day?

There was only one ad for a room. It was in Tirso de Molina, the suburb before Antón Martin and only about a ten-minute walk from the school. I wrote down the phone number and hoped for the best.

That afternoon I walked from my hostel, across the Plaza Mayor, the main square of Madrid, and down to Tirso de Molina. I followed my map along a narrow street lined with tall stone apartment buildings. It seemed to be a couple of degrees colder in this part of town, perhaps because the sunlight couldn't make it in between the crowded rooftops.

I found the apartment building and pushed open the heavy wooden door. It was even colder inside than it had been out. I heard my heels click on the stone floor. I pressed an illuminated button and a dim light came on.

A man was waiting for me at the top of the stairs. "*Hola, hija*," he slurred, putting his hand on my shoulder and giving me a kiss on each cheek. His skin was creased like someone had scrunched up paper and smoothed it out again. He had a hooked nose and sharp cheekbones, and his hair was thick and black and cut in a mullet. Leaning on a brass-capped walking stick, he waved me into the apartment.

His name was Miguel, he said, lifting his head like a chieftain, and he was a gypsy from one of the most important flamenco families in Spain. I was impressed. I'd never met a gypsy before, much less a flamenco gypsy. The idea of moving into a flamenco house was exciting, but my heart sank as I looked around. It was an old apartment that had been roughly divided up into different rooms with flimsy walls and shabby curtains. Miguel showed me what he called the best bedroom. It was separated from the corridor by a pair of glass doors with curtains for privacy. Inside there was a small single bed pushed up against the back wall underneath a high window that made the room look like a prison cell.

I thought about it, but there wasn't much to think about. It was a step up from where I was, and I needed to get into cheaper and more permanent accommodation. So even though it was dark and dingy, I told him I'd come around the next day with the first month's rent.

THE PRESENT
PERFECT

Or
Everyone is beautiful at the ballet

This is how cold Madrid is in January: I was sitting on my creaky bed in the Tirso de Molina apartment, under the blankets, dressed in tights under jeans and a sweater and a scarf, and I was *still* cold.

I was leafing through an English-language newspaper looking at job ads. Some of the ads for English teachers asked for a bachelor's degree or CELTA certification, some asked for a minimum of three or four years' experience, some wanted bilingual applicants. There were two ads that asked simply for native English speakers, so I called each and made interviews for the next day.

They say that you should dress for an interview as if you've already got the job. I'd been adamant that I wasn't going to bring my black suit with me, but as I rummaged through the contents of my suitcase looking for something appropriately teacherish, I regretted having taken that stand. The best that I could do was jeans, a sweater, and a scarf. I hoped it would be smart enough.

At the first office I went to, I was given a form to fill out. It asked for my name, address, education, marital status (are they allowed to ask that?), number of children, and availability. The last question left me stunned: *What is the lowest amount you will accept per hour? €…*

I should have put the pen down there and then and walked out. But I didn't. I filled in the application, though I must have answered something wrong because they never got back to me.

At least I had another interview. This one was for a reputable English academy with offices all over Spain. When I got there, a coordinator took me into a classroom and started explaining why I should work for them. It didn't take me long to realize that he was desperate. He needed a teacher to start immediately, and I guess I looked enough like someone who spoke English for him not to even bother with my CV. Instead he gave me a pile of textbooks, the address for my first class, and a map.

❋

The present perfect…past perfect and future perfect…is there a perfect present? It certainly wasn't this present. I was on a suburban train that was taking me to the outskirts of Madrid. It was so early in the morning that it was still what I considered to be nighttime, and I was packed in with the rest of the sleep-deprived commuters, reading the grammar lesson that I was supposed to be teaching that morning.

Now, I'd always assumed that I spoke English. But flipping through the pages of the grammar tome in my hands, I was starting to have my doubts. What is a gerund? What is a transitive verb? What am I going to do if my student asks me to identify the subject or the object in a sentence? What exactly did I learn at school? A lot of World War II, but no past continuous.

I started imagining different possibilities for future perfect.

Future perfect #1: I get a phone call right now telling me that the class is canceled, and I get off this train at the next stop and have a hot *café con leche* as the sun rises.

Future perfect #2: I click my heels together and magic myself away to Seville.

I closed my eyes and clicked the heels of my sneakers together. Nothing happened. So I went back to the textbook and read about embedded clauses.

Tom, who is only six, can speak three languages.

Well, hooray for Tom. Nellie, who is twenty-two, apparently can't even speak English.

By the time the train arrived at my stop, first light was breaking. The company was a fifteen-minute walk from the station alongside the highway. Globs of sleet hit my face as I walked through the slippery gutter. It was like having a Slurpee spat at me through a straw.

My student's name was Andrés. I found him in a glass-enclosed office on the sixth floor of the modern building. He was in his late forties and wore a stylish suit and Loewe tie. He had a shaved head, which suited him, and wore a pair of wire-rimmed glasses. He was typing an email as I walked in and held up his hand for me to wait until he clicked Send.

Then he took off his glasses and fixed me with his bright blue eyes. "You are American."

"No," I said.

"English."

Again I shook my head. Andrés furrowed his brow before asking, "Where are you from then?"

"Australia," I told him.

"Australia!" he cried, jumping out of his seat. "Look at this!" He beckoned me over to his computer. The image on his desktop was of a surfer suspended on a spectacularly nasty wave. "Do you surf?" he asked me hopefully.

Andrés spent the better part of our ninety-minute class talking about the years he'd spent traveling in search of the perfect wave. He explained to me the pros and cons of Maui and Indonesia, the coast of South Africa and the south of France, waving his hand impatiently every time I tried to correct his broken English. His eyes became wistful as he talked about the tube waves of the famous surfing beach Mundaka in his native Basque Country, in the north of Spain.

Andrés let out a sigh. "How did I finish here?" He looked around his plush office as though it were a cage, then leaned across his desk and said, "Do you know how these multinationals function?" I shook my head. "They must to grow all the years. Always getting bigger. Why?" he demanded.

"Uh…I don't know."

He leaned back in his chair and said, "Nobody knows." He lowered his voice to a whisper, as if afraid that the walls might hear him. "We have to feed the monster.

"And tell me," he continued, changing the subject. "What is an Australian girl doing in Madrid?"

I told him that I had come to Madrid to dance flamenco. His eyes widened, then he burst out laughing. "You? Dancing flamenco? Ba-ha-ha! Is even more funny than me dancing flamenco."

"Don't you like flamenco?" I asked him.

Andrés was suddenly serious. He shook his head. "No."

I was surprised. I'd assumed that all Spanish people loved flamenco. But Andrés set me straight on that point.

"One, I am not Spanish. I am Basque. Is different. And two, in my country we do not like flamenco. It is gypsy music. We have our dance. Have you see it? The dancers play a flute and kick their legs in the air. It is a very stupid dance. I recommend you see it. When you finish with flamenco, you can learn Basque dancing."

I walked back to the train station feeling relieved that I'd got through the class without having to actually teach anything. But at the same time I was a bit worried about that. What if Andrés were to turn around and complain that I was a lousy teacher? I couldn't afford to lose this job.

When I went back to the academy that afternoon to pick up more attendance sheets and textbooks, I confessed all to the coordinator. "Look," he said, "Andrés is the president of the company, so if he tells you he doesn't want to do the lesson and just wants to talk, then let him. From what I heard from his last teacher, he's not very interested in learning English."

"So then why is he taking classes?" I asked.

"We get a lot of students like that," the coordinator explained. "English classes are a perk. Companies offer them, often instead of giving their employees a raise. So the students go along. Every now and again you'll get someone who's motivated to learn, but most of the time they're not."

That sounded all right to me. As the coordinator loaded me up with textbooks for new classes, I hoped desperately that the rest of my students would be as uninterested in the lessons as Andrés.

❋

"Everyone is beautiful at the ballet..." I hummed the song from *A Chorus Line* as I slipped into my ballet shoes. I was trying to keep my *ánima* up—my spirits. I was about to go into my first ever ballet class and the idea scared me to death.

Actually, it wasn't quite my first class. I had taken ballet once before. I was six years old, and I remember my mother pulling me out of the car as I went limp in her arms, letting my feet drag across the pavement like a mini Gandhi in a pink tutu. Once we got inside I wailed and sobbed so hysterically that Mum was forced to give in and take me home.

Now, sixteen years later, I was going to give it another go.

But this time there was no one to drive me home. Then again, I wasn't wearing a pink tutu either—though I will confess that I was wearing leg warmers. How could you go to ballet class without leg warmers? Isn't the whole point of doing ballet to have an excuse to do *Flashdance* fashion?

I loved the dance class look. I watched the girls who came into class in ripped T-shirts and sweaters and observed how they had transformed an oversize tee into a shrug, or woolly socks into ankle warmers, trying to memorize just where they had made their incisions so I could copy the look on some unsuspecting piece of clothing.

Today there were two other girls in the changing room getting into their ballet gear and they looked suspiciously like ballerinas. Especially the girl in the pointe shoes. Why do I have to do this? I considered walking out, but I thought of Marina and the way that she'd waggled her finger at me and told me that I had to work hard, harder than everyone else, if I wanted to dance professionally. I just had to bite the bullet and learn ballet.

The class started out innocently enough. The students, six girls and two boys, were lined up along the barre (which is for some reason spelled the French way, even though it is really just a bar), and the teacher told us to get into first position. I didn't know what first position was, but I was able to copy the others. Basically, you stand with your feet pointed out like a duck and your arms lightly separated from your body. For second position you slide one foot to the side a little. Third and fourth are also variations on this pose, I discovered to my relief.

But then the teacher got serious and told us to do things that I knew were going to be painful, like putting one leg up on the barre. I think it was intended as a gentle stretch, but I could see stars in front of my eyes, like a Looney Tunes character that had been hit over the head with a mallet. Around me the other dancers were sliding into effortless splits with graceful arms bent over their turned-out legs, but it was all I could do to keep my heel from slipping off the barre while my face turned white from the pain.

But then it got worse. I hadn't realized how great an ally the barre was: as long as I clung to the barre I was safe. There were horrible things to come, things with strange names, like *jeté*. That's when you leap off the ground like a gazelle and hang suspended in midair for an obscene amount of time before touching down on the tips of your toes and skipping off.

The teacher cued up a tape of tinny piano music that lent itself perfectly to such ridiculous prancing, and told us all to go to the corner of the room. I watched the dancers in the line ahead of me take a few running steps and then leap into the air, toes pointed, legs outstretched, arms floating, and face turned to profile. Then they landed with a scowl that said, "That was rubbish! I do not deserve to call myself a dancer!" (in a Russian accent).

One after another they ran forward and leaped into the air. My knuckles whitened as I gripped the barre tighter. *I'm not doing it*, I thought. *It's not just that I can't—of course I can't—but that I won't. There's no way I'm going to even try that. I'll die of embarrassment. I won't. I won't. I won't.*

"*Vamos!*" the teacher yelled at me. Great. Now everyone was watching. "*Venga!*" There was nothing for it. I ran forward, stretching out my arms, and jumped. I jumped higher than I'd ever jumped before. Even so, I was in the air for approximately half a second before hitting the ground with a BOOM that made the mirror tremble.

F@#%¡¡*¡* I said to myself as I dropped my head and hurried back to the barre.

I hate ballet.

I was so angry and humiliated after my first class that I felt as though I had steam pouring out of my ears as I walked to the changing room. I muttered furiously to myself as I strode past the dance classes: "Why am I doing this? Why am I choosing to put myself through this obscene indignity? What kind of adult person would allow herself to be humiliated, and in Jiffies? I never want to even set foot in another dance class for as long as I live. Whatever made me think that I could be a professional dancer? It must have been temporary insanity. I hate this. I'm going home and I'm going to get on with my life and get a communications degree, and I'll get a job with a diverse range of responsibilities, including filing and making filter coffee, and I'll get an apartment and a houseplant and some debt and I'll be serious and sensible for a change, and I'll shop at David Lawrence…"

In the changing room I splashed some water on my face and told myself, "Just breathe. It's only your second day. Things are going to get better." I put the idea of going home and going to university back in the case at the bottom of my mind with the label "In case of emergency, break glass."

I hadn't come all this way to give up just because I couldn't pirouette. If ballet meant daily humiliation, then so be it. *I've worked the registers on Boxing Day*, I reminded myself. *And if I've survived that, I can survive anything.* So I hummed to myself as I put on my red shoes, "Everyone is beautiful at the ballet."

THE TOUGH TIMES

Or
Ojos, *take this chica and* toma que toma!

Madrid is famous for being the European city with the highest number of bars per capita, but I suspect it also has the highest number of churches. Perhaps the churches in places like Rome are more attention grabbing, but in Madrid there's a little church around every corner.

My favorite was the Baśilica de San Francisco el Grande, which was just a short walk from Tirso de Molina. I loved its bare stone walls and high stained-glass windows. I preferred the anonymity of the cathedral to the smaller neighborhood churches. In the cathedral I could just sit and feel like I was invisible. Tourists would come in and out, and every now and again people came in to pray.

Around the cathedral were wooden statues of saints with out-stretched arms or halos of stars over their heads, but I didn't know who they were. They seemed content to stare off into the distance and ignore me too, so that was fine. I would have liked to light a candle as I saw other people doing, but it didn't really seem right to say, "Ah, excuse me, you in the robes with the doves at your feet, would you mind praying for me?" I felt I should at least have some idea of who I was talking to.

As I sat there one day, a policeman came in off the street and knelt down in front of a Sacred Heart Jesus. I marveled at the way people could just kneel down like that in a public place and do something that seemed to me so private. I couldn't. I would be afraid I was doing it wrong and everyone was looking at me.

I felt comforted by the peace and quiet of the old building, but I didn't really understand religion. I'd always heard from teachers and the media and society in general that religion was for sheep who need a shepherd, not for intelligent people who think for themselves and get their news from the *New York Times* and the *Guardian*. So whenever I saw the priests setting up the altar for mass, I knew it was time for me to move on.

I had other favorite haunts around Madrid. One was the Reina Sofía art gallery. On Sundays, when it was free, I'd go and sit in front of a Picasso, then wander through the Surrealist section and maybe watch some of one of the Luis Buñuel films they ran on a constant loop, then leave by way of the Robert Capa room.

I also liked going to Buen Retiro Park in the center of Madrid. It was still too cold to sit on the grass, but I loved to walk around the lake. And when it got too cold to be out, I'd go back to the apartment and sit in my room with blankets around my shoulders, trying to be positive and avoid answering the question that wouldn't leave me alone: What am I doing here?

Yes, I had come to Madrid to dance flamenco, and I was dancing. But it was a struggle, and with my ballet classes I had to deal with daily humiliation. And while it was a slight improvement from the hostel, the apartment where I was living was nothing like the sunny attic I'd dreamed of. It was so cold and cramped and filthy that the only place I could stretch out my muscles after a day of dancing and tramping to and from English classes was under the covers of my creaky bed.

But it wasn't just about that. I had never imagined that it would be easy, and I knew that with time I would find a better job and a nicer place to live. It was Madrid. I had left my home and come to this foreign city in the hope that I would find a place where I belonged, but instead I was wandering the streets feeling as invisible as a ghost.

Every morning I woke up at what I considered the middle of the night to take the train to the outer suburbs to teach English to businesspeople before their workday began. Andrés had given my classes rave reviews, so the academy had given me more and more classes until I had to turn down work, or I wouldn't have time to dance. Though I needed the money, I had to remember what I had come to Madrid for.

My pay was so low that every decision became a choice. Piece of cake or rent a studio for an hour? Buy a magazine or take a dance class? Things like eating out or even a couple of extra sweaters for the cold weather were luxuries I couldn't afford.

After dance class I'd sit in the little café in the market beneath the Amor de Dios until it was time to go off and teach. I'd listen to the music on the radio and watch the way the vibrations from the stamping above made my coffee ripple.

One morning a familiar song came on. It was one that Zahra and I had danced to in Seville. I pulled out my phone and dialed her number in Switzerland.

She answered the phone with "*Toma que toma!*" I held up the phone so she could hear the music. "*Ay, chica,*" she said, "I miss you so much!" I told her that Spain just wasn't the same without her, and she said, "Don't worry. As soon as I can take a long weekend I will come to visit you. I will find you an *ojos*, and I will say, '*Ojos*, take this *chica* and *toma que toma* till I get back!'" I laughed as I hung up the phone. Though I knew it wasn't easy for her to take time off work, just the thought of her coming to visit made me smile.

There was a little flamenco dress shop opposite the Amor de Dios. I loved to go in and gaze at the dresses, running my hands over the material and every now and again taking one off the rack and holding it up in front of myself in the mirror.

Generally I hated going into shops when I had no intention of buying anything. I was always conscious that I could be keeping the shopgirl away from her coffee or her magazine or her daydreaming. But this shop was run by a lovely woman called Lola and her husband, and they always welcomed me in, even though they could tell I didn't have a lazy two hundred euro to spend on polka dots. But they liked to chat to me about flamenco and my classes and how I was finding life in Madrid. They knew how hard life was for foreign girls; they had them in their shop every day and had heard all the stories. And they'd seen the successes too. "Don't let it get to you," they always said. "Things will get easier."

I hoped they were right.

One of my new English classes was at the Ministry of Foreign Affairs. The academy asked me to take over the class because the students hadn't been happy with the last teacher. "They can be difficult, this group," the coordinator told me. "I'm sure you'll be fine, though; just make sure you go in prepared."

Prepared was the last thing I was. When I got to the classroom, a long, high-ceilinged room decorated with tapestries and oil paintings, there were two women sitting waiting for me. I asked them where everyone else was, and they told me they were the only students. "The others stopped coming," said a woman called Paloma in barely accented English. "They did not like the teacher." Paloma's eyes traveled from my scruffy sneakers and jeans up to the coffee stain on the neck of my sweater. She fixed me with a sharp look and asked, "What are we going to learn?"

"Today we're going to start by reading," I said, handing out copies of an article from the *Guardian* about a new airline operating in Afghanistan that the coordinator had given me to use. I thought back on the way my high school German teacher had made us read in class, listening intently and every so often making a firm but gentle correction. I did my best impression of her, and amazingly I must have pulled it off. At the end, my two students smiled and thanked me before going back to their offices.

After the class I was so proud of myself for simply getting through it that I went back to my favorite shop. Lola greeted me with a kiss on each cheek and asked me how things were going. "*Bien*," I told her. I'd just had a successful English class and maybe things were going to start looking up for me. The little triumphs I had were so few and far between that I was determined to celebrate them, because each one was bringing me a step closer to the life I wanted to be living.

There was a pair of earrings on display that I had been dreaming of ever since I first stepped into the shop. They were silver, chandelier style, and set with little blue stones. They were gypsy princess earrings, and Lola agreed: I *had* to have them.

❊

The next Monday morning there was a new sign up on the notice board at Amor de Dios saying that La Tati would be starting up her classes for the year. I was so excited to see her name up on the board. Not only was La Tati one of Spain's most legendary flamenco dancers, but she was also Marina's ex-teacher, so of course I had to take her class.

As I waited outside the studio, I saw an old woman ambling up the corridor. Her dyed red hair was pulled back into a bun, and she wore an old coat over a long skirt. A dozen dancers had already taken their places in the studio, and I took my usual spot in the back, nervous but excited to be learning from such a legendary dancer.

The first half of her class was footwork. La Tati threw complex steps at us, which we were expected to pick up and repeat back with machinelike precision. I tried to fudge my way through it, but I hadn't counted on La Tati's ear. After a particularly tricky step, she listened carefully, then stopped us. Someone was out. Who was it? *Oh God*, I thought as I tried to disappear into the corner.

La Tati walked across the room until she was standing in front of me. The class was silent as La Tati counted me in: "*Uno, dos, tres...*" There was nothing for it. I tried to do the step on my own, but I knew what I was doing was wrong.

Tati lifted up her long skirt and showed me the step, breaking it down into stages. Then she barked an order at me in Spanish.

What? I looked around blankly. The girl next to me translated her words: "She say do it three hundred times before tomorrow," giving a shrug that said, "Sucks to be you."

Three hundred times?

At the end of the class, everyone went forward to give La Tati the seven euro she charged for the class. As the girls were counting out their euro, Tati pointed at me and said, "*Para ti, viente.*" At first I thought that I must have misunderstood her: everyone else was paying seven, and she was demanding twenty from me? I tried to protest, but La Tati threw her arms up in the air and shouted at me in Spanish. I had no idea what she was saying, so I reluctantly handed over a twenty-euro bill, which was my entire daily dance budget.

I didn't have enough money to take another class that day, so instead I shelled out an extra five euro to rent a studio. Surely La Tati had been exaggerating. She couldn't really expect me to do that step three hundred times. But when I remembered the look on her face, I decided that she was probably serious.

So I repeated the step, counting *one, two, three...* By twenty-one, my legs were already aching, but I kept on going. *Thirty, thirty-one...*

The ache moved up to my hips. *Forty, forty-one.* When the pain became too much, I stopped and shook out my legs. Then I started again. *Fifty, fifty-one, fifty-two…* My toes were starting to hurt. *Sixty.* I stopped to catch my breath, then carried on. *Seventy.* I felt like my legs were about to fall off. *Eighty.* I can't do it.

By the time I reached one hundred, the pain in my feet and legs was so bad that I had just zoned out. I kept on, breathing and counting. *One hundred and ten, one hundred and eleven.* By one hundred and fifty I had stopped feeling the pain; I was just listening to the sound of my feet. I had slipped into an almost meditative state.

Two hundred. I started counting back down. *One ninety-nine, one ninety-eight…* I couldn't even remember what the step was anymore; my feet were moving on their own. *One seventy.* I held my own gaze in the mirror to keep my focus. *One forty-nine, one forty-eight…*and suddenly my body was flooded with joy. I stopped counting the steps. I didn't even want to stop dancing. I just kept on going and going and going until I felt suddenly faint. The floor was moving beneath me. I staggered to the side of the room and collapsed.

As I stretched my legs out in front of me, the pain came flooding back. It was like knives stabbing into my feet, legs, and hips. I lay there, slumped against the wall, wondering how I was ever going to stand up again. Somehow I got up and made my way to the changing room. I didn't even bother putting on my jeans, just pulled my jacket on over my T-shirt and skirt, then carefully took off my shoes and slipped my sore feet into sneakers.

The walk home had never seemed so long before. Each step was agony. I tried to walk on the smooth pavement, avoiding the rough cobblestones that pressed into all the sore spots on my feet. When I finally got back to the apartment and pulled off my shoes, I saw why I'd been in so much pain. My socks were stained with blood. What had I done to myself? I shuffled to the bathroom and peeled off my socks, then swung my legs over the side of the bath and ran water on my feet. The water came out icy cold and stung the burst blisters on my toes.

Miguel knocked on the door and asked if I was okay. He came in and looked down at my injured feet, then asked me what had happened. I told him it was from dancing. He beamed at me and took my face in his hands and kissed my cheeks. "*Qué bonito es el flamenco!*" he said. Isn't flamenco beautiful!

Yes, it was beautiful. I was throwing myself at life like the dancer had thrown herself into the quadruple turn on the tiny stage of the *tablao* in Seville. And I was proud of the blood on my feet. It was a symbol of the passion I felt for what I was doing, even though it was hard, and even when it hurt.

THE LATINAS

Or
Nellie, like the hairspray

Here's something I hate: getting out of bed. You could give me a million reasons to get out of bed and I still won't do it. And it's even worse when my alarm goes off at six a.m. and I know that it is minus three degrees in my room and there's an icy floor waiting for my toes. On mornings like that, the only way for me to hoist myself out of bed is to remind myself that if I don't move *now* I will miss the train that will get me to class on time, causing me to lose my job and my only source of income, thereby setting off a chain of events that will lead to me standing outside a homeless shelter waiting for a plastic cup of coffee from a harried-looking Missionary of Charity.

Heaven forbid.

Every morning I had to hold that image in my mind while I quickly stepped into my jeans and splashed water on my face, threw my makeup in my bag and scrabbled around looking for my keys, wasting another ten minutes, then ran helter-damn-skelter to the metro station and propelled myself down the stairs.

All the while I tried not to stop and ask myself the question, "Does this scene look familiar?" Wasn't this exactly what I came to Spain to avoid? If anything, hadn't my situation gotten worse? I was getting up earlier to commute farther to make less money by working harder than I did before. What had happened to running away with the gypsies?

It was Tuesday morning, and I was late for class with Andrés. It was dark and the only other people on the street were wandering drunkenly home after a night of partying. I raced down the station stairs and put my monthly pass through the metro turnstile. I ran forward, expecting the metal spoke to move, but instead I just got a big thump in the stomach and a red light flashed to say my ticket wasn't valid. I tried again at the next machine and again the red light came up.

I could hear the train pulling into the station. I thought about jumping the gate, but there was a ticket inspector in the booth, so I darted over to him and told him there was something wrong with my ticket. The inspector ran my ticket through a machine to check that it was okay, then calmly stepped out of the booth and walked me back to the turnstile.

I could hear the sound of the doors closing as the train prepared to leave the station. I was going to be late again. The inspector calmly opened the gate for me to pass through. He smiled at me and said in English, "Don't worry, be happy."

Don't worry, be happy? Didn't he understand I was going to be late for work? How could I not worry?

I'm not good at not worrying. It's easier for me to get out of bed than to stop worrying. In fact, worrying about the consequences of not getting out of bed is the only thing that gets me up in the first place.

Taking it easy, relaxing, being in the moment are things that I appreciate in theory but that don't seem to have any practical application in my life. I get the beauty of being in the now, but even that idea stresses me. Should I be in the now, now? Like, now? I think I'm missing it. Was that now? Oh, now? I can't do this, I give up. That's pretty much how it works for me. When I think about taking it easy and not worrying, it's always as a future project that I will get to after I've dealt with all the things I need to worry about first. And during those first few weeks in Madrid, it wasn't like I didn't have enough to worry about.

I knew that worrying wouldn't solve my problems, but I couldn't help it. I felt like I was always walking on the edge of catastrophe, like a tightrope walker without a safety net. Sometimes I felt invigorated by my new life, but more often than not it was just overwhelming.

That was why I found it so refreshing to be around people who were relaxed about life, like Mariela, who worked in the café where I went for breakfast every morning after my first English class. Mariela was a Venezuelan woman with two daughters who was doing a part-time hairdressing apprenticeship. She had black hair with purple streaks that was cut into an asymmetrical bob, and had a mischievous smile that was never far from her lips. I didn't know that she was Venezuelan at first, and when I asked her if she was Spanish, she gave me a long look, then threw her head back and hooted with laughter. "*Una negrita como yo?*" A little black girl like me? she'd said, laughing at my ignorance.

Mariela's boyfriend was an artist who made a living doing caricatures of tourists in the Plaza Mayor. He also came to the bar every morning for breakfast. One day he drew a caricature of me dancing flamenco on a serviette, which I folded up and slipped into my wallet where it sat among receipts, metro passes, and museum tickets. They were little pieces of the puzzle that one day would form a whole picture so that I could look back and understand the journey that I was taking. At least, I hoped it would make sense one day.

My class at the Ministry of Foreign Affairs was held twice a week, and at the second class I had two new students. Paloma had told them that the new teacher was an improvement from the last, so they decided to give me a chance. The next week I had five students, then seven, then ten. Every class I'd come in to find a new face gazing up at me expectantly, waiting for the fun to begin. And the more students I had, the more interesting the class became.

The trick to teaching English, I was learning, was finding out what your students are passionate about; my students at the ministry loved to argue and debate about Spain and Spanish politics. That was perfect for me, because I was always asking them questions about things that I didn't understand. Like the day I was running late for class and the road was blocked by a hundred men dressed up in top hats and frock coats carrying a giant papier-mâché sardine. I'd come to accept a lot of strange things in Spain, but when the men in tuxedos tried to fill my pockets with sweets, I really needed an explanation.

"It's the burial of the sardine!" the class told me. They explained that it was Ash Wednesday, the final day of the carnivals and the first day of Lent. The men in frock coats were doing a mock funeral parade, my students explained to me, to mourn the end of the festivities.

"And will they actually bury the sardine?" I asked.

"Of course," my students said. "They bury it in the park. Don't you celebrate Carnival in your country?"

I thought about that, but I couldn't recall ever seeing giant fish being carried through the streets of Sydney.

"What holidays do you celebrate?" my students asked.

"Well…" I pondered that for a moment. "I guess we have Australia Day."

"Do you wear your traditional costume?" they asked. I didn't know that we had a traditional costume. "But," they protested, "what is the costume you wear for your festival days?"

"Well," I said, thinking carefully about how Australians dress up to celebrate our "festival days," "I guess it would be jeans and a T-shirt."

"No!" they said. "Really?"

The new student who had joined that day, a white-haired, bespectacled man named Antonio, politely raised his hand and asked, "Who is the patron saint of your village?"

I had to think about that one. The patron saint of Sydney… Well, there was only one person it could be. "Kylie Minogue," I told them.

They gasped in scandalized delight. "And your Virgin?"

That one was easy. "Nicole Kidman," I told them.

※

One thing I needed to do was get out of the apartment in Tirso de Molina. If there was one simple way I could improve my quality of life, that was it. I couldn't keep shivering through the nights, brushing my teeth over the cruddy bathtub because the bathroom sink was broken, hanging my wet laundry up around my bed, and going to sleep with two pairs of pants on just to stay warm. Plus I needed an apartment with a kitchen I could actually use. Each time I walked into the kitchen, there would be something to make me walk straight back out again, whether it was a mountain of dishes in the sink, graylooking seafood that had been put out to defrost and then forgotten about, or a stew that made the whole apartment stink. On top of that, with the expense of my dance classes, there was no way I could continue to keep paying the rent. I was earning very little from my English classes and paying for my dance classes with my Australian savings, but they wouldn't last forever, and in the meantime I needed to find a cheaper home. The problem was that I didn't know where I'd find one.

A girl called Brigita had just rented the room opposite mine. A young Brazilian girl who'd also come to Madrid to study flamenco, she was paying for her classes by working nights serving drinks. She'd get home in the early hours of the morning smelling of smoke and exhausted after being run off her feet all night, then go off in the mornings to dance. Brigita had only been staying in the apartment for a few days when she came into the kitchen in tears. She told me that Miguel had asked her what kind of work she did. When she told him she worked in a bar, he asked her if she had drinks with the customers. "He thinks I am a prostitute just because I am from Brazil!"

"I'm trying to find a new place to live," I told her. "When I find something we'll move together." This idea calmed Brigita down. I promised I wouldn't leave without her and said that I was sure it wouldn't take me long to find us a new place. Of course I wasn't sure of that at all. I'd been stressed enough about finding a room for myself; now I had to find two rooms.

I lay in bed that night wondering how on earth I was going to do it. I needed an apartment that was warm and clean and safe, and cheap enough so that I didn't have to worry about impending doom every time I made an ATM withdrawal. I decided that I'd ask absolutely everyone I met if they knew of anyone who had rooms for rent. Someone had to know of something.

I started out by asking Mariela when I saw her in the café the next morning. To my surprise she leaned across the counter and told me that she rented out rooms in her own apartment. She said she currently had a double room available with a view of the street, and another room with two single beds. I couldn't believe it. That was exactly what I was looking for. I arranged to go and see it that day after class.

Mariela lived in a neighborhood called El Rastro. It was in the old part of the city, and the streets were lined with antiques stores and junk shops. Every Sunday there was a big flea market. It was the perfect place to go if you wanted to buy an old bullfighter's costume, a rusty typewriter, a lace mantilla, or elaborate hair combs to wear to the feria.

Mariela's apartment was above a Moroccan furniture store that had a selection of brightly colored tea tables and carved wooden stools set up on the pavement. I followed Mariela up the stairs to the second floor, and she opened the door to a dimly lit apartment. There was a narrow living area with a couch, a television, and a dining table. The kitchen was tiny with a small gas oven, and there was a little patio where they hung up their washing.

On the far side of the apartment was the double room. When Mariela opened the door, I immediately fell in love with it. It was large with a big bed pushed up against glass sliding doors that opened out onto a tiny balcony. From the window I could see down onto the street where all the shopkeepers had set up their wares to tempt passersby. Arranged on the pavement were oil paintings in gilt frames, old light fittings, and brass-capped walking sticks. The shopkeepers sat outside in the sun with their *cafés con leche* and cigarettes, calling out to each other across the street.

I came back later with Brigita, and she loved the place just as much as I did. The second bedroom with the two beds was ideal for her because her sister would be arriving soon from Brazil and there was plenty of room for both of them, and the price was perfect.

So Mariela had two rooms rented out, and Brigita and I had found a new place to live for a perfect price, in an apartment full of light and fun and beans and rice. It was a four-bedroom apartment, but with me and Brigita and her sister, there would be a total of eight women living there. Mariela lived in one room with her mother and two daughters, and then there was another Venezuelan woman called Andrea who lived in the room next to mine.

"*Cómo te llamas?*" Andrea passed me in the hall the day I moved in and asked me my name for the second time.

"Nellie," I said.

She repeated it, struggling with the pronunciation. "*Ne...ll...i...e...* Ah! Nellie, *como la laca?*"

It took me a moment to translate *laca* to "hairspray" in my head. But then I remembered seeing bottles of hairspray in the bathroom with the name "Nelly" in pink letters.

"Yes," I said. "I'm Nellie, like the hairspray."

THE FIESTA

Or

Let tomorrow look after tomorrow

I got much more than I'd expected when I moved in with the Latinas. I'd been looking for a new place to live, but what I got was a whole new family, a great big Latino family, and they welcomed me into their lives like I was one of their own.

Mariela's two daughters were called Andy and Mandy. Andy was fourteen and Mandy was ten, and they were both absolutely adorable. I was normally the first one home in the afternoon, and Mandy would always insist I mix her a glass of chocolate milk when she came home from school; then she would sit on my bed with her homework and try to convince me to do it for her.

Every morning Mariela's mother, Consuela, would cook up beans and rice, which filled the apartment with a wonderful, homey cooking smell, not like the strange smell of the seafood stew that Miguel used to make. She insisted I help myself to whatever was on the stove, and more than once I got in trouble for making myself a sandwich when there was rice there for me.

Consuela made the most wonderful rice that always came out perfectly. I hung out in the kitchen one day to learn her secret. She showed me how to heat the oil in a big pot, add the rice, and stir it until every grain was coated in oil. Then she added water and crumbled a stock cube into the pot. When the water was absorbed, she told me to empty out the plastic shopping bag she'd just brought back from the supermarket and hold it out for her. She scooped all the rice out of the pot and into the plastic bag, then tied it up tightly and left it to sweat. That, she told me, was the secret to the perfect rice.

After seeing what her secret was, I regretted having asked for it. I'd been happier eating her wonderful rice before I knew that it had sweated in a plastic bag from Aldi. I tried to block the thought from my mind when it came time for lunch, but after seeing her technique, I was convinced I could taste plastic and other chemicals that I'd never detected before.

On Tuesday afternoons we all got together to clean the apartment, and I became the joke of the house when I admitted that I didn't know how to use a mop. "We don't have them in my country!" was my pathetic excuse, but no one believed me. I also had to learn how to whisk eggs without a whisk and peel carrots without a veggie peeler. The first time I tried, Mariela snatched the poor massacred carrot out of my hands and showed it to the whole house. The Latinas crowded around laughing hysterically at the hacked sliver of carrot. *At least I keep them entertained*, I thought, trying not to take it personally.

We were all poor, but it didn't feel that way. No one behaved like we were poor or complained about money. No one went without anything, either, and the Venezuelans never spent their time talking about beautiful things they couldn't afford. There was no talk of mink-trimmed gloves or Birkin bags.

When I first moved in, I had to buy linen for my bed. I'd never bought sheets or towels before, but I remembered seeing them on Level Six, Manchester. So I went to the big department store in the center of Madrid. I fell in love with the bed on display, which was made up with the most exquisite white linen. But when I added up the price of the sheets, pillowcases, and duvet covers, it came to over seven hundred euro. Seven hundred euro…that was more than a thousand dollars! That was how much it would cost me to make up my bed? How was that possible?

I left the department store and stood at the traffic lights waiting to cross the road, feeling the weight of the world pressing down on me. This was why everyone had been telling me to get an education and a good job. This was why my teachers had shaken their heads when I said I didn't care about money. They knew that pillowcases cost seventy dollars.

By then I was feeling exhausted and overwhelmed by everything. I'd dealt with a lot since arriving in Spain, but if I couldn't afford to buy myself a towel, then maybe it was time for me to give up and go home. I bowed my head and started to cry, right there on the street. Part of me knew I was being ridiculous, but I couldn't help it. I just felt like I wasn't going to get anything right, ever. And now I was going to have to sleep on a bare mattress because I was too broke to buy sheets.

I walked back to the apartment in a whirl of despair. Mariela was in the kitchen, frying banana, and when she saw my face, she asked me what had happened. I told her my sad story, and she stared at me for a moment before she burst out laughing.

That afternoon Mariela and her two girls and Brigita and her sister took me to a store up the road and helped me pick out sheets, blankets, rugs, towels, puffy embroidered cushion covers, curtains, even a cute tissue box cover, all for a hundred euro. The quality wasn't as luxurious as the department store brands, but it was all a beautiful cream color. And we transformed my room into a charming boudoir.

How is it possible, I wondered to myself, *that after years in retail I still don't know how to shop?*

✳

Every Wednesday we all got together for a big family lunch. Mariela's boyfriend would come over, and the Venezuelans made *calimochos*, red wine with Coca-Cola. And by red wine I mean the kind that comes in a box. "That's an Australian invention!" I declared proudly as Mariela took a box out of a shopping bag.

I'd heard that boxed wine was an Australian invention, though I wasn't entirely sure. In the past I've also tried to claim Tupperware and the Bee Gees as Australian and been proven wrong. Boxed wine was the only thing I had left to boast about to Spaniards, who in return could claim things like surrealism, cubism, bolero jackets, submarines, and the polka dot.

I come from a family of wine drinkers. My parents have a glass with almost every meal, and my father is what I would call a wine snob. He's endeavored to teach me about wine ever since I can remember. Before I was allowed to drink, Dad would get me to smell the wine in his glass and identify the different odors. I would put on a little performance at dinner parties and make up things like "the smell of turned earth, of burnt vanilla, a hint of pomegranate, and a swirl of broken dreams."

I thought about that as I helped Mariela mix the *calimochos*. If Dad could see what I was doing, he would be horrified. No daughter of his would drink boxed wine, and mixing it with Coca-Cola would be considered a mortal sin.

It occurred to me that this was the ultimate rebellion against my upbringing. As a child I'd found it so difficult to rebel against my parents. They were the ones who behaved like irresponsible teenagers, and I was always the one who felt like I had to keep everything together. I mediated disputes and turned out lights in empty rooms and tried to advise my parents on how to save money at the supermarket. I even forced my father to sit down and do a blind taste test of the pretentious imported tinned tomatoes he bought from a shop in Haberfield, which had them flown in once a month from Lucca, and the No Frills brand. But he ignored my attempts at economy and told me to relax and act like a teenager, to go out and get piercings and listen to some loud music for a change.

I always felt that my parents were disappointed with my attempts at being a rebellious teenager. It was as if I didn't try hard enough. But now I'd finally found a way to rebel. I sent a text message to my father telling him what I was drinking. I'd barely hit Send when the response came back: YOU'RE DRINKING WHAT???!!! If only I'd thought of this at thirteen, my teenage years could have been so much easier.

※

Though I was happy in my new home, I still had my moments of gloominess when I would shut myself up in my room and stare out at the street, wishing that I was back in Seville. I missed the orange blossoms and the strum of a guitar from an open window. I missed dancing alone in the studio in the dusky evening light, and I missed Enrique. Though we had only had one kiss, it was still the most romantic story of my life. But I knew that it was just a fantasy. I felt like my whole time in Seville had been a dream. I'd been on a wonderful flamenco holiday and hadn't had to deal with real life. Even knowing this, I still couldn't help missing the *toma que toma*. Andy and Mandy played Venezuelan music at full volume in the lounge room, but I wanted to hear a live flamenco guitar.

"Nellie!" Mandy pushed open my door one afternoon while I sat there morosely. "*Estás aquí!*" she squealed, excited to find me home. She grabbed my arm and pulled me up off the bed, dragging me out into the living room where Mariela and Andy were pushing back the couch and rolling up the carpet to make a dance floor.

"*Sabes bailar merengue?*" Mandy asked. I shook my head no, I didn't know how to dance merengue, but Andy showed me the basic steps. There were just two steps, one and two, one and two, kinda like walking to work. But if that sounds easy it was deceptively so, as I found when I tried it and sent everyone into hoots of laughter.

"No, no, no, Nellie!" Little Mandy showed me how to do the steps low to the floor with a swing in her hips. How did a ten-year-old learn to dance like that? I tried again, but everyone only laughed harder.

"*Ay, mami!*" Mariela wailed, clutching the sofa for support as she laughed. I had to stop dancing for a few minutes because Consuela was laughing so hard she couldn't breathe. Then Mariela took my hand and spun me around, telling me to follow her lead. They taught me merengue and salsa, and we danced until my head was so full of Latin beats that I forgot all about my depression. Because it's hard to be sad when you're dancing salsa in your socks on the living room floor.

Although I knew that my new Latin family loved to party, I was still surprised when Mariela came to my room one day and asked me if, instead of paying the rent for the next month, I could spend the money on alcohol for Andy's fifteenth birthday party. Money was tight that month, because Brigita and her sister had gone back to Brazil, and the family hadn't rented out their room yet.

The preparation for the party went on for weeks, and it was all anyone could talk about. It was going to be held at Andy's aunt's bar, which was just up the road from the café where Mariela worked. The family spent everything they had on food and drink and decorations. They wanted it to be a night Andy would remember for the rest of her life.

On the afternoon of the party, I struggled home carrying my own body weight in alcohol, bags full of bottles of rum, whiskey, and gin. The spirits were for the adults, not the children. But Andy already drank *calimochos* at the weekly family lunches. The bags were so heavy that every few steps I had to set them down and give myself a moment to rest and regain my strength.

When I opened the door, I found the living room full of women. Mariela, Consuela, and the girls were there, plus aunts and cousins I hadn't met. Everyone was rushing around getting ready for the party. Mariela used the occasion to practice setting waves in her mother's hair. Andrea already had her long black hair in giant rollers, and another cousin was giving Andy a pedicure while she waited for her mother to blow-dry her hair straight. When they saw me, they all shouted at me to go and get ready because we had to be out the door in less than two hours.

Two hours? Getting ready never took me very long. I didn't have a big enough wardrobe to be able to agonize over what I was going to wear. As I waited for the girls to get ready, I lay down on top of my bed. I'd been working hard all week, and almost as soon as I closed my eyes, I drifted off to sleep.

It was almost midnight when Mariela finally knocked on my door and told me they were ready to go. Everyone had their hair done, either dead straight, bouffant, or in tight ringlets. Their eyes were perfectly outlined with eyeliner and glittered with fake eyelashes. I rubbed the sleep out of mine and quickly touched up my mascara.

We walked together to the bar where the party had already been going on for hours. Salsa music was booming and all the kids were dancing under streamers and a giant Venezuelan flag. One of Mariela's cousins asked me to dance. He was tall and handsome and an excellent dancer.

I found it amazing that I had managed to surround myself with people who lived to dance. Mariela's family had spent every last cent they had on one night of partying, and it was worth it to them. When I asked her how they could afford it, Mariela had just said, "Tomorrow will look after tomorrow."

I'd seen people who had everything: money, time, privilege, a Birkin bag, *and* a Kelly. But I'd never before been around people who lived with such joy. And their secret was that they lived each day as it came and each night for as long as they could make it last.

I wished that I could be like them, but one part of my brain was always reminding me of how little was left in my bank account and how early I'd have to be up on Monday morning. One thing that dancing does, though, is bring you into the present moment. I couldn't drift off while I was dancing *salsa*, because every time I lost concentration I'd miss the beat and step on my poor partner's feet.

I glanced up at the clock on the wall and saw that it was five a.m. "It's already morning!" I said to my partner.

"No," he said, swinging me around so my back was to the clock.

"*Sí!*" I argued back. "I have to get some sleep. I need to be up in the morning!"

He shook his head and smiled. "Tomorrow will look after tomorrow."

THE HAPPY
ENDING

Or
Cheer up, Mary

Before long the inevitable happened. One day in March I went to the bank to take out money to pay for my next week's dance classes and saw the message flash: *Transaction Denied.*

I'm pretty good at calculating how far I can get on a tank of gas, and I'd thought I had enough for one more week of classes. I tried taking out a hundred euro, then eighty, then fifty, but each time the message came up: *Transaction Denied* = No more *toma que toma.* The money I was making teaching English was enough to cover my rent, metro tickets, and food. But now that my Australian savings had been exhausted, how was I going to pay for dance classes?

It was a sad trudge back down the road. I could work more and take on more students, but then I wouldn't have time to dance. The thought of walking away from the Amor de Dios after all I'd done to get there was unbearable, but I could see no alternative. I told myself that it was only temporary, but temporary until when?

I'd come to Spain to study flamenco, and if I couldn't do that, what was the point in carrying on? But how could I go back to Australia so soon? Was I going to head home after just two months, slip in the back door, and hope nobody noticed me? And when people asked, "Hey, aren't you supposed to be living your dream in Spain?" I'd have to look confused and say, "Spain? Oh right! Spain. Yeah, about that…"

I hadn't come all this way to just give up. After all I'd been through—my first nights in the old elevator shaft, shivering under the blankets at Miguel's house, those morning train rides, *jetés* in Jiffies, bursting into tears at the price of towels—was it really going to end like this?

I didn't feel like going back to the apartment, so I wandered, looking for a place to sit for a while. There aren't many parks in Madrid, just busy roads lined with sad, struggling trees that look like the celery you find at the bottom of the crisper when you're cleaning out the fridge, so I stepped into an old stone church. At least I could sit there without having to pay the price of a cup of coffee. I slid into a pew in the darkest corner and sighed.

There were a few people seated in the other pews, and soon two priests came out through the old wooden doors to the side of the altar and started to set up for mass. This was usually my cue to leave, but I wasn't ready to face the world just yet. So I stayed there in my dark corner, hidden behind a wide stone column. And when the service started, the droning monotonous voice of the Spanish priests didn't interrupt my train of thought. The church was steadily filling up with people, and every few minutes or so they would all stand up and mumble something inaudible in Spanish, then sit back down again. But hidden in my corner, I could just sit and stare into space.

I thought about calling my parents, but how could I ask them for money? If they gave it to me, it would probably come with the proviso that I get on a plane back home and into a university course.

In front of me there was a painted statue of a woman in a fabulous flowing gown. She was very beautiful in a silent movie kind of way. Her long auburn hair was arranged in perfect ringlets and her impeccably painted eyebrows were drawn together in an expression of intense emotion. Was it anguish or ecstasy? I remembered reading somewhere once that the difference between the saints and us regular people is that the saints have already seen the happy ending to the story. Perhaps that was what she was looking at. I wished that I could see mine.

The priests stepped down off the altar swinging gold incense burners. *How theatrical*, I thought, and remembered the incense during Semana Santa in Seville. Maybe I should go back there…

Just then, a flamenco guitar began to play. The congregation rose to their feet, and this time I joined them, looking out from behind the column to see where the music was coming from.

A flamenco guitarist was standing at the altar. His head was bowed as he plucked the strings of the guitar. Then he lifted his head and sang to Mary. There were actually five priests at the altar, I saw. They stood with reverently bowed heads listening to the flamenco singer.

And then, as if on cue, the entire congregation sang out with the guitarist the chorus of the song:

Cheer up, Mary.
Don't look so sad, Mary.
Why won't you smile, Mary?

Even the priests had raised their heads and were singing along.

Flamenco-singing priests? Is this what the Spanish do in mass? Every time I'd come into the church, I'd always left before they got started, so I never knew that I was missing the *toma que toma*. And I remembered the tear-streaked face of the old man in the crowded street in Seville during Semana Santa who had told me that Jesus was dancing.

Only in Spain.

Only in Spain could a bloodied and tortured Jesus dance a *bulería* while nailed to a cross. Only in Spain could a congregation sing and clap their hands and tell the Virgin Mary it's not so bad after all.

After the mass I walked back home through the flea market. I passed the old men who sat every day out front of their stores in the sun, clapping *compás* to the flamenco music on the radio. I stepped around old lace fans and castanets and faded postcards of flamenco dancers that were laid out on display on the footpath. It occurred to me that every day I was surrounded by flamenco. I hurried past it every morning on my way to work, and it was always there to greet me as I made my way home. I even had to step over it on the pavement.

I reminded myself of why I had come to Spain. I'd come to live a passionate life. I'd wanted to feel and smell and taste life, and live like that dancer on the stage in Seville, risking that triple turn, never sure she wouldn't spin right off the stage. I'd come because I wanted to learn to live with *toma que toma*, and it seemed that in Spain this was one lesson I couldn't avoid. Even during my darkest night of the soul, when I wanted to sink into the oblivion of self-pity, I'd found myself at the back of a church in the middle of a musical number.

When I reached Mariela's building, I could hear the sound of *salsa* music coming from the second-floor window. I knew what that meant: the couch had been pushed back and there would be a *calimocho* waiting for me. I could use one. I didn't know when I'd be able to afford to go back to dance classes, and I was going to have to take a break until I saved up some money. But there's no time for feeling sorry for yourself in this country. Not even Mary could get away with that.

That night I was woken by the sound of someone singing flamenco. A lone, high voice, it sounded like that of a child. I sat up in bed and leaned across to the window, pulling back the curtains.

A group of teenage boys were walking up the street. They were slim and wore suit jackets and collared shirts. The group clapped *compás* as one boy sang flamenco. I poked my head out the window and watched as they passed beneath the yellow light of the street lamps. The boy threw back his head and belted out his song to the night sky.

"*Olé...*" one of the group said.

They continued down the street, and their voices faded and were replaced by the sound of traffic.

I lay back against the pillow and asked myself: Were they...gypsies?

The boy who had been singing sounded like a gypsy. He had that same high yet raspy voice I was used to hearing on my flamenco CDs. And really, wouldn't you have to be a gypsy to be walking the streets at night singing flamenco?

I lay in bed hoping to hear them come back down the street, but they didn't. *Perhaps they* were *gypsies*, I thought as I eventually drifted off to sleep. *I wonder if they'll let me run away with them...*

THE GYPSIES

Or
Good-for-nothin', gun-totin', bulerías-dancin', polka-dot-wearin'...

I'm one of those people who like to follow the news. Even if it really makes no observable difference to my life how the recent elections in Afghanistan went, or who leaked that embarrassing email to the press back home, I still like to feel informed. But in Spain my news consumption was haphazard at best. I no longer had Radio National to play in the mornings as I did my makeup, and the Latinas didn't have Internet for me to access the English-language press. But now I was glad of that. I wanted to disconnect from the world I had come from and be absorbed into Spanish culture.

So instead I got my info fix from the Spanish TV news that I saw in the cafés where I'd linger between classes. And Spanish news was nothing like the Australian news. Spanish news was full of gypsies. Every day there seemed to be a gypsy story, whether it was an interview with a dark-eyed flamenco artist about their new album or an exposé on life in gypsy ghettos. I would forget my *café con leche* and stare up at the TV in fascination. Each glimpse into the world of the gypsies was like another piece of the puzzle I was putting together in my head.

But the gypsy stories weren't like regular news stories. There was always an element of crazy to them. Like the article I read in a paper someone had left behind on the train about a child wedding in a gypsy compound that was broken up by the police. Apparently thirteen was marrying age in gypsyland, and the gypsies were furious that the Spanish authorities would dare to interfere with their customs.

Then one of my favorite flamenco singers, El Capullo de Jerez, hit the headlines when he was accused of pouring gasoline over the child of a man who owed him money and threatening to set him on fire. You'd think that kind of negative publicity would put me off, but it didn't. Because for every story I heard about those troublesome gypsies, I'd hear another person say that only the gypsies danced *real* flamenco. Of course, if flamenco is, in its essence, pure drama and pure passion, there was no one more dramatic or more passionate than the Spanish gypsies.

I asked my English student Andrés about them. "Gypsies? Bwarf! Where I come from, we say everyone south of Vittoria is a gypsy!" Vittoria is a town near the southern border of the Basque Country. Andrés told me the best way to see gypsy flamenco was to go to a gypsy wedding. Yes, of course—I had to go to a gypsy wedding! But when I asked him how I could get an invite, he just shrugged and said, "Don't ask me, you are the girl from Seville. When you finish with the gypsies, come to Bilbao and I can introduce you to ETA, eh? If you want some more danger!" ETA was the Basque terrorist group who were fighting for independence from Spain.

I asked my other students about gypsies, and from all of them I got the same reaction: "Why do you want to know about the gypsies?" Each one of my students told me the same thing: that the gypsies are nothing but no-good, lying, cheating, gun-toting, knife-wielding, drug-dealing, pimping rascals. Or variations on that theme.

My class at the Ministry of Foreign Affairs went into an uproar when I asked them about the gypsies. They told me that the gypsies used to live in slums in the center of Madrid; then, in an effort to gentrify the area, the government had relocated them to nice new apartments outside the city. The gypsies, my class told me, had gone in and ripped up the carpets, pulled out the air-conditioning units, and sold off all the appliances. They even kept goats, donkeys, and chickens inside the apartments. That I found hard to believe.

I didn't know what to think of all this information. Were the gypsies born artists and the creators and guardians of flamenco, or were they dangerous parasites to be avoided at all costs? Or were they both? Were they gun-toting, knife-wielding, polka-dot–wearing, *bulerías*-dancing, *compás*-clapping rogues? If so, I wanted to meet one. *Maybe I could become a* bulerías-*dancing roguette, I thought, with a polka-dot scarf around my neck and a knife in my garter. I'd live by night to the sound of* compás *and the clicking fingers and tapping feet of the gypsy boys.*

The gypsy boys…those same boys passed underneath my window every night. I could hear the sound of their hands clapping as they approached, and the clear, heartbreaking voices of the young singers. I started to recognize the same boys in the streets around El Rastro. Aged between thirteen and twenty, they dressed like mini Frank Sinatras in suit jackets over jeans, and they always wore sunglasses, even at night.

When I went out in the evening, I'd pass them on the street. Sometimes as I walked past they would be singing and clapping while one of the group danced flamenco. I'd slow down and watch the kids' thin leather shoes dancing on the street and be amazed by how casually they performed steps as complicated as the ones I sweated over in class.

I wished that I could stop and talk to them and get them to teach me to dance the way they did, but the boys never took any notice of me, even when I deliberately circled the block to walk past them two or three times. They were too taken up in their songs to see that I was walking slowly past them, longing to be included in their group. And the fact that they were too busy singing and dancing to see me just made me all the more determined to find a way in.

But how was I going to get into the underground world of gypsy flamenco? My students at the Ministry of Foreign Affairs told me that the gypsies didn't mix with nongypsies. They had communities in Madrid, right in the city, but they still lived according to their own code. They didn't have regular jobs or send their children to school; instead they lived off social benefits and what they made *trapicheando*. That was a new word for me. Antonio wrote it up on the whiteboard and tried to explain its meaning. "They are buying and selling things. Making deals…"

"Like wheeling and dealing?" I suggested. It was the best English equivalent I could come up with. I asked what they dealt in, and the group threw out different examples: gold, weapons, drugs, women.

That evening on my way home from work, I walked down to the corner where I'd seen the gypsy boys dancing that morning. They weren't there, so I walked through the backstreets looking for them, listening for the sound of *palmas* or flamenco singing. I was aware of the fact that I had become a gypsy stalker, but I didn't care. I was a girl on a mission, and my mission was to run away with the gypsies. First, I just had to find them…

I turned a corner, and the street opened out into a square that was full of gypsies. The whole family was out. The old men stood together smoking cigars, their bushy sideburns almost reaching the crisp collars of their shirts. Their wives stood in a group, all dressed in black apart from their heavy gold jewelry and bright lipstick. And in the center under the trees the young gypsies were gathered in a circle around a guitarist who played flamenco.

The night air was cold enough for me to wrap my scarf tightly around my neck, but the gypsy girls were in short skirts and heels so high they made my ankles hurt just to look at them. They stamped their stiletto heels on the pavements and twirled their long, glittery nails through the air.

A gypsy girl sang, her rough voice ringing out over the sound of traffic and the sirens echoing in the distance, and one of the boys stepped forward to dance. He stood tall, his hands held high as he clapped the rhythm. He tossed his long black hair over his shoulders and stamped his fake leather shoes on the old stones of the square.

Olé...

This was the world that I longed to become a part of. I wanted to be able to sing with a raspy voice like the gypsy girls did, and tear up the cobblestoned streets like the boys. And I knew that I could if they let me in. But as I stood there, I might as well have been invisible. I was just another foreigner who'd strayed onto their turf.

LA SOLEÁ

Or
She want marry a gypsy!

Sooo…do gypsies ever marry nongypsies?" I asked my class at the ministry.

"She want marry a gypsy!" Antonio declared to the class.

Everyone started shouting out at once, "No, Nellie! Keep away from gypsies! They are bad for you! We don't want lose our teacher!"

"No!" I said, trying to make myself heard over their protests. "I don't want to marry a gypsy. I'm only curious. And it's *'wants to.'* 'She *wants to* marry a gypsy.' Third-person singular," I said, trying to use grammar to reestablish my authority.

But they weren't buying it. I'd been asking too many questions about gypsies for it to be just idle curiosity. Every class I'd come in with different queries about how and where they lived. My class wasn't stupid. They were on to me.

I had convinced myself that my gypsy stalking was really part of an informal anthropological study I was doing of this intriguing race of people. I was like one of those explorers who discover a tribe in the Amazon and observe their customs. Except that my Amazon was the capital of Spain, the trees were the apartment buildings of my neighborhood, and their huts were rent-controlled apartments in

El Rastro. But who was I kidding? I wasn't happy observing them through my imaginary binoculars and jotting down field notes. I wanted in. I just didn't know how I was going to get there.

That night I walked home slowly through the old part of Madrid. I loved walking back after my last class of the day. I didn't care if it took me an hour or more; each time I tried to take a different route, wandering down little lanes and alleyways. Getting lost is the best way to get to know a city.

Tonight I stumbled upon a street I'd never taken before, and as I walked along the pavement, I heard music coming from inside a bar. I stopped at the doorway where a bouncer stood. I could hear the sound of a guitar and someone singing flamenco.

The sound made my heart skip a beat. Only in Spain could I turn a corner and find myself on the doorstep of a new flamenco adventure. The sign above the door said LA SOLEÁ. I'd heard people talking of this place but hadn't known where it was. The bouncer gestured for me to come inside, so I walked up the worn stone steps, between the iron gates, and into the bar.

The place must have been hundreds of years old, and the low stone ceilings gave it the feeling of a cave. Someone had told me that the old buildings in this historic part of town were originally used as dungeons in the days of the Inquisition. Now the stone walls were covered in black-and-white photos of all the famous flamenco artists who had frequented the bar over the years.

I stepped in through the doorway of the room where the music was coming from. It was filled with low tables and little wooden chairs where people sat over glasses of red wine, watching the musicians in the corner. An old flamenco singer dressed in a suit and a polka-dot tie leaned on a walking stick, which he picked up and banged into the floor every now and again to mark *compás*.

I looked around for a place to sit, but I couldn't see an empty seat.

A waiter with a tray of drinks beckoned me over and pointed to an empty space on a wooden bench next to a man he introduced as Juan. I heard the waiter tell Juan to keep an eye on me. I was confused by this. Did I need someone to look out for me? What kind of place was this? Looking around the crowd, I noticed a lot of long black hair and gold jewelry. Was this a gypsy bar?

The guitarist started to play a *bulería*, and I joined the bar in clapping *compás*. I noticed Juan watching my hands as I clapped. In his early sixties, he had slicked-back gray hair and wore a polo shirt under a leather jacket. I met his eye and he said, "*Muy bien,*" then turned his attention back to the singer.

The waiter brought me a glass of red wine and Juan offered me a cigarette, which I declined. (Though it did occur to me that I might as well smoke my first-ever cigarette, because with the amount of smoke there was in the bar, I would passive-smoke a whole pack by the time I'd finished my drink.)

The singer began a new song in a different style, and I switched *palmas* to match the new *compás*. I caught Juan watching my hands again. He seemed surprised to see a foreign girl who knew her *compás*. When the song came to an end, he ordered me another glass of wine and asked me where I was from and what I was doing in Spain. When I told him that I had come to dance flamenco, he stared at me incredulously. He told me that I didn't look like a flamenco dancer, and I tried not to feel insulted by that.

He asked me where I was studying and looked impressed when I said the Amor de Dios. I didn't mention that I hadn't taken a class in weeks. How could I explain to a stranger that I was broke and living on a diet of white rice and leftover fried banana until I could scrape together enough money to go back to dance class?

I heard the sound of raised voices at the door and looked around to see what the commotion was. The waiter left his tray on the bar and went quickly to join the bouncer at the door. I asked Juan what was going on, and he said it was probably a group of gypsies trying to get in.

"You don't need to worry about this place," Juan told me. "They only let the good gypsies in here." Ha. That was interesting. I looked around again at the crowd. There were dozens of dark-skinned and dark-eyed men in blue jeans and suit jackets. Gold and silver rings glinted in the light as they clapped *compás* for *bulerías*.

So these were the "good gypsies." The respectable gypsies. The well-heeled and well-behaved gypsies… The other gypsies couldn't get in the door. The loud, unpredictable gypsies weren't welcome. So where did they go? I asked Juan and he told me they went to a place called Cardamomo. "Where's that?" I asked. He looked at me a long moment, then told me that Cardamomo was no place for a girl like me.

That was all I needed to hear. As soon as he spoke those words, I knew that I had to find this place called Cardamomo where the bad gypsies went. I wasn't sure what I would do if I did find it. I liked to imagine myself walking in wearing a red dress and ordering a shot of something on fire, but I doubted I would actually have the courage to pull it off. I'd probably be better off setting up gypsy surveillance in a cute café opposite, preferably one that served muffins.

The singer switched to an up-tempo rumba, and the gypsies cried "*Olé!*" and stamped their feet and clapped their hands. Two Spanish girls got up to dance. They twirled their arms above their heads and swished their long hair. I could count the days since I'd last danced flamenco, and a live guitar and a gypsy singer were all I needed. I got to my feet and stamped my boots on the tiled floor and danced until the guitarist strummed the final chords of the song.

I fell in love with La Soleá that first night. It gave me a place to go where I could live flamenco, and it made the loss of my dance classes easier to bear. I started going almost every night, and every time I walked in Juan made space for me on the bench and the waiter would come over with a glass of red wine. Juan and I would sit there until the early hours of the morning, clapping *compás,* and every now and again he would nod his head and say, "*Bien, Australiana.*"

I gradually came to realize that Juan was a gypsy stalker just like me. He chuckled to himself about the way they spoke, trying to translate their idioms to me. He'd discreetly point out a particularly eye-catching pair of pointy-toed loafers with oversize buckles, or a massive solid-gold pendant, or some other eccentric gypsy accessory. It became a game between us to spot the most outrageous gypsy fashion.

So even though I wasn't going to dance class, I was getting a different kind of flamenco education. Juan filled me in on who the singers were and let me know every time an important gypsy walked into the room. And so began a most unexpected friendship. With Juan I laughed more than I had since I'd arrived in Madrid. No matter the day I'd had, if I'd had to wait an hour in the rain for a bus or arrived late to class, I'd forget all about it when he put a glass of *rioja* in my hand and told me a joke that he'd heard from the gypsies.

I put him under strict instructions to call me if any famous flamenco artists showed up in La Soleá when I wasn't there. Sometimes I'd get a call from him past midnight when I was already tucked up in bed. He'd hold up the phone so I could hear what was going on and tell me he was ordering me a drink. I'd be out of bed in a flash and halfway up the street before he'd even hung up.

Every so often someone would walk in off the street and give a performance that I knew I would remember for the rest of my life. It wasn't always something showy, though there was no shortage of show-stealers—gypsies who would jump up and sing their hearts out and dance a *bulería*. But sometimes the moments that gave me goose bumps happened at a quiet time in the early hours of the morning. Like one Friday at three a.m. when a man came in off the street with his boyfriend. The boyfriend was upset about something; perhaps they'd had a fight or an anniversary had been forgotten. To apologize the man sat down next to the guitarist and began to sing a flamenco love song.

I'd never before seen anyone ask forgiveness by stepping off the street into a flamenco bar and singing a love song in front of a crowd of strangers. There wasn't a person in the room who wasn't moved almost to tears, and I sent up a silent prayer to the universe that one day someone would do something that beautiful for me.

Anything could happen at La Soleá. Famous stars could walk in at five in the morning, and often did. This was no incentive for me to get an early night. In Madrid the weekend starts on Thursday afternoon and ends sometime around two p.m. on Monday, so Friday morning is generally a write-off. I'd already learned that teaching English. Often my Friday morning student, an auditing director at an energy company, didn't show up at all, but I still had to go out to his office. Sometimes I slipped his grammar book into my handbag on Thursday nights, so that if flamenco magic did take place, I could stay out all night and get a coffee with the guitarist when he finished work at six a.m. before going straight to the train.

Of course, the body will get the rest it needs whether you like it or not. The sound of the doors closing on the metro was my cue to fall into REM. Somehow my subconscious kept track of the stations I passed and woke me up when it was time to change trains. Falling asleep in class was a bigger problem. It seemed that there was no amount of coffee that would keep me awake through an hour and a half of English grammar. But if you asked me to choose between phrasal verbs and gypsy bars, what kind of a choice is that?

THE VEGAN AFICIONADA

Or
No hay quinto malo

No hay quinto malo. That was the new Spanish expression I'd learned. Literally it means that the fifth one can't be bad. It's bullfighting talk: at every bullfight there are three *toreros* (bullfighters) and six bulls, and the best bull is always number five.

The fifth bull had just run out onto the sand. Even from my spot in the arena I could see he was a big one. I sat forward in my seat as the crowd around me cheered. This was Las Ventas, Madrid's bullring. A huge arena, painted golden yellow and red ocher, the colors of blood on sand.

I never really understood the bullfight. A guy standing in front of a bull, twitching a red cape—it always made me think of cartoons I used to watch as a kid. Anything red would make the cartoon bull go crazy and pitch some unsuspecting person into the air. But it was so quintessentially Spanish that I felt I had to try to understand it. Back in Seville, Enrique once told the class that if you don't like the bullfight, you'll never dance flamenco. In the end it's the same art: the dancer impersonates the *torero*, and the *torero* moves like a dancer. I had been repulsed by the idea. The bullfight had always seemed so barbaric to me. But now I could see that he had been right. The bullfighter positioned himself in front of the bull, like a dancer waiting for his cue. He had the same stance that we had learned—chest raised, shoulders pulled down, chin up. Just watching him made me long to be back in the studio.

The bullfighter took out his red cape now, and a hush descended on the crowd. The bull lowered its horns and pawed the sand. "*Ay!*" the bullfighter yelled. The bull charged and the bullfighter held his position. He dragged the cape over the sand as the bull's horns just missed him. The crowd called out, "*Olé!*"

This fight was part of the Festival of San Isidro, the patron saint of Madrid, held every May. Tickets were virtually impossible to get, but mine had been a gift from one of my English students, Tomás, the director of sales at Andrés's company. The company had season tickets to the bullfights so they could take visiting clients. This particular day he had a spare ticket and he'd given it to me.

Tomás was a bullfight aficionado. Actually, the word "aficionado" originally meant someone who is enthusiastic about bullfighting. Tomás taught me that. In his spare time he wrote articles for a bullfighting magazine, and whenever he had a new piece published, he'd bring it to class and we'd translate sections of it into English.

Mine was a *sombra* ticket, a seat in the shade. Though it was spring and the afternoon sun still wasn't that hot, the tradition of dividing tickets into *sol* (sun) and *sombra* came from the south of Spain where the sun is scorching. The *sombra* tickets were the most expensive and sought after.

I was entranced by the audience as much as by the fight itself. The arena seated twenty-five thousand people, and looking around, I couldn't see an empty seat. The crowd seemed to ripple as thousands of women lazily waved fans. People still dressed up for the bullfight, the men in crisp cotton shirts and blazers, and I saw many polka-dot handkerchiefs poking out of pockets, red carnations on lapels, and little Spanish flag tiepins. The women wore wonderful combs in their hair like the ones the Sevillians wore to the feria.

Sitting in the arena, I remembered a picture I'd once seen of Ava Gardner and Orson Welles watching a bullfight. They were both sucking on cigarettes and looking tanned and rumpled in the afternoon sun, just like two Spaniards. I hoped that I looked Spanish, too. Hmmm, probably not. I was so pale after the winter that Juan had nicknamed me "*La Transparente*." And even with my blue eyes hidden behind my sunglasses, the mop of red hair I tried to keep back in a ponytail was a bit of a giveaway.

The *torero* held out his cape and called to the bull. His weight was forward on the balls of his feet and his arm was outstretched. The bull charged, and the *torero* deftly twitched the cape and turned his torso so that the bull's horns just grazed the gold embroidery of his costume.

Watching him made me remember my classes with Enrique. That was the way he had wanted us to move. It was the distillation of drama in the subtlest movement. I half closed my eyes and felt myself back in the studio in the backstreets of the Macarena. My feet back in my red shoes, and the soft folds of my skirt against my legs. I felt myself lifting up onto one toe, trying to hold my balance as Enrique pressed one finger sharply beneath my rib cage. *Gira*.

What was the passion I felt in those days? That desperate, crazy love that gripped me on the nights when I walked in and out of the bars around the bullring with flamenco in my head and the moon in my eyes? I remembered the night that Zahra and I heard the woman singing in that little bar by the river. "When you fall in love in Seville, you fall in love with Seville." But I hadn't just fallen in love with Seville; I had fallen in love with Spain.

I felt that same passion again as I watched the bullfighter move around the ring like a flamenco dancer. But why? What was my link to this crazy, wonderful country? I couldn't have been more foreign if I tried, so what was I doing, rising to my feet with a crowd of Spaniards, drawing in my breath as the bullfighter spread out his red cape and the bull, lowering his horns, pawed the sand? As it charged, the bullfighter lifted up onto his toes with the balance of a dancer and plunged the sword right between the bull's shoulder blades.

And all around me the crowd cried, "*Olé!*"

❋

I climbed the stairs again, up past the butchers and grocers until the smell of fish and meat was replaced by varnish and cigarette smoke. It was mid-May, and the Amor de Dios was full of activity. Dancers were hurrying up and down the corridors, and girls in long skirts crowded around the notice board, writing down class times. I'd done my sums, and it looked like I'd have enough money by the end of the month to take a class, if I pulled my belt in an extra notch.

I edged my way in to see what classes were up on the board, and as I gazed at all the different possibilities, a young guy squeezed in next to me and pinned up a flyer for a show. "*Qué buscas?*" he asked me. He looked like every other guy at the Amor de Dios, with long black hair and those dark eyes that I was starting to build up resistance to. What choice did I have, when the guy who made my coffee in the morning was a more gorgeous version of Javier Bardem, and the bus driver who took me out to the suburbs to teach was Enrique Iglesias's long-lost twin brother? I'm not even going to talk about the riot police who wander around Madrid in their chic black uniforms. I couldn't get weak at the knees every time I left the house.

"*Qué buscas?*" He asked me again what I was looking for, and I told him that I was trying to choose a dance class. He told me to try his cousin's class. "*Muy gitano,*" he said. Very gypsy. Everyone wants to be "gypsy" in flamenco. Actually, it generally goes that the whiter you are, the more gypsy you want to be… Take me, for example.

The flyer he'd pinned up was for a show; he was the lead dancer, Diego Caballero. He handed me one, and then he mentioned that, if I was up for it, maybe we could go out one night…to a little place called Cardamomo.

I hadn't forgotten the name. That was the place Juan said the bad gypsies went. I took a second look at this boy. Yes, he had those high, sharp cheekbones and that strong nose, and his eyes were even darker than average… I was finally getting picked up by a gypsy.

And he wanted to take me to Cardamomo! When I'd pressed him, Juan had told me stories he'd heard about the fights that went on there. He assured me that every gypsy in the place was armed and that the girls were more dangerous than the boys. All I had to do, Juan warned me, was dance with the wrong guy, and the gypsy girls would be outside waiting for me. He told me about girls who had been disfigured by the gypsies' long acrylic nails. They'd attacked foreign girls before, hacking off their hair and spraying their blue eyes with purse-size hairspray.

If you know what's good for you, he'd told me, you'll keep away from Cardamomo. And I should have remembered his advice as this gypsy boy wrote his number down on the flyer. I should have, but I was too busy thinking about what I was going to wear.

THE LITTLE
BLACK DRESS

Or
What am I going to wear?!

Seriously! I had absolutely no idea. What does one wear on a first date with a gypsy? If anyone should know, it would be me: I'd read every article ever written on date dressing. I knew that beach walk = sundress, Sunday brunch = jeans and cashmere sweater, cocktail party = tailored pants (everyone else will be in party dresses and you'll want to stand out). But what do you wear when your first date is to a notorious gypsy bar?

I cast my mind back to the shots in the *Harper's Bazaar* mag, those tantalizing images that set my imagination on fire. If only I had a fashionably tattered red dress...but then that would be too much. If there's one date rule that applies to all situations, it's to never overdress.

But what was I going to wear?

That phrase repeated itself over and over in my head as I walked back through the streets of Antón Martin, weaving between pedestrians and stopped cars in the eternally congested streets. In my mind I was tipping my suitcase upside down and watching leotard after leotard fall out. That was all I had, apart from the jeans I was wearing and the few semirespectable white shirts I'd bought for work. There was only one thing to do: shop. So instead of walking back to the apartment, I directed my steps to the big department store in the center of town.

You know the one…they are the same in every city in the world. More predictable than airport duty-free shops, and more comforting than Starbucks. As my dusty sneakers tramped up the marble steps, the automatic doors slid open and I was greeted by the smell of Estée Lauder Pleasures spiked with Dior Tender Poison. I let the escalators carry me up to *Señoras*: Women's Fashion.

I'd figured out what I needed: a sexy red top that I could wear with jeans and high heels. That was a look I had labeled in my mind as "understated gypsy." And my budget was twenty euro. More than I could afford, but then it isn't every day you get invited to a dangerous den of vice and sin. As I wandered through the racks and rails, though, I started to feel more and more hopeless. The clothing was drab, to be generous, and I didn't want to rock up at Cardamomo looking like a dental hygienist or the mother of the bride. So I did something I knew I would regret: I went up another flight to High Fashion.

But there are shades of regret. There are things in life that you really do regret, like missing friends' birthdays or mixing beer and wine. And then there are things that fall into the category of mistakes you just had to make. Mistakes that add the exclamation marks to your life. And as the escalator leveled out into the world of designer fashion, I found myself staring at one such mistake.

It was the black dress on the mannequin. Well, it was sold as a dress, but it was really just a piece of black, aerodynamic cling wrap. It was Eurotrash perfection, the kind of dress that was guaranteed to get a girl into trouble. And if it didn't, then the price tag would. I knew as soon as I saw it that I had to have it. I didn't even need to try it on. But I did take a peek at the price tag. Ouch. It was the same amount that I had saved for dance class. I knew that I shouldn't even be thinking about buying it. I should put it back and walk right out of the store. But I'd been given an invitation into the underground world of gypsy flamenco, and wasn't that more important than a few dance classes? If I was ever going to learn to dance authentic flamenco, I had to go to the source. And if there was ever a dress for dancing with gypsies, this was it.

I had to smuggle the dress into the apartment. I knew if Mariela and the girls saw the shopping bag they'd want to see what I'd bought, and how could I explain that the girl who couldn't afford to buy her own olive oil had just blown half a month's rent on a dress?

Once I was safely in my room with the door firmly shut, I took out the dress and tried it on. Yes, it was perfect. And with my one pair of battered heels and the gypsy princess earrings I'd bought from Lola, I had the perfect outfit for a date with a gypsy.

※

Cardamomo is tucked in among a tangle of streets in the center of Madrid, in an area known as Huertas. If it's true that Madrid has the highest concentration of bars per capita in all of Europe—and I have absolutely no reason to doubt that claim—most of them are in Huertas.

After dark on any night of the week, Huertas is busier than the busiest shopping strip in Sydney. There are traffic jams all through the night, and the footpaths are so crowded that to get anywhere you have to weave through the cars.

I tottered down the street with my gypsy earrings jangling, dodging the drunks that stumbled out of bars in front of me and the boys who kept trying to push free drink cards into my hands.

"*Guapa*."

There was Diego, leaning against the wall smoking a cigarette. I suddenly realized just how handsome he was. In the Amor de Dios he was just another young dancer, but standing under the streetlight, his black hair slicked back and his dark eyes sparkling, he could have been one of the boys from that *Harper's* shoot. Yes…I was finally running away with the gypsies.

He pushed open a plain wooden door with no sign. Flamenco music blared out and I got my first glimpse of the infamous Cardamomo. I stepped through the door and into another world. The club was packed with gypsies. Everywhere I looked, long-haired men in black suits were clapping *compás* with lit cigarettes tucked between their fingers, and *gitanas*, gypsy girls, waved fans in front of their faces as they danced.

Within moments we were surrounded by a crowd of young gypsies, and Diego started introducing me to the *primos*, or cousins. "*Mi primo* José." I kissed both cheeks of a gypsy boy with playful eyes. "*Mi primo* Luis." Luis elbowed his cousin out of the way and leaned in to give me two kisses. "*Mi primo* José Luis." Another gypsy boy stepped forward. "*Mi primo* Antonio…*mi primo* Luis Antonio…*mi primo* José…" and on and on it went until I was dizzy from kissing the cheeks of so many dark-eyed boys called either José, Luis, or Antonio.

The *primos* formed a circle around me, clapping *compás* and shouting out, "*Que toma que toma…*" and Diego stepped forward like a bullfighter, clicking his fingers.

One of my favorite songs from the latest Vicente Amigo album came on over the speakers. I'd been listening to this song over and over again on my iPod, trying to figure out the words. I asked Diego, "What is he singing?" He pulled me close and sang in my ear. "*Mi primo Antonio qué bien me baila…*" My cousin Antonio dances so well… Diego explained that the singer was referring to the legendary flamenco dancer Antonio Canales.

It was the first time I'd had a gypsy boy sing flamenco in my ear, and I melted. I melted like a Popsicle on the backseat of a car on a summer day. When Diego pressed a glass of rum into my hands, I knew I shouldn't take it. I'm such a cheap drunk I get tipsy off the pop of a champagne cork. But I thought: *Why don't I? It's not every day that you get the chance to dance till dawn with the gypsies.*

THE PRIMOS

Or
In heaven everyone dances sevillanas

*H*ola!"
　　"*Guapa!*"
"*Estás allí?*" Are you there?

I opened my eyes and yawned, listening to the boys talking on the street beneath my window. "*Está allí?*" "*No lo sé.*" "*Canta algo.*" Is she there? I don't know. Sing something.

"*Solo por tus besos, solo por tus besos…*" Just for your kisses, just for your kisses…

I sat up, leaned over to the window, and pulled back the curtains. The *primos* stood below, looking like my own little gypsy Rat Pack. They'd come to wake me from my siesta. That's right—I'd taken the siesta to the limit, sleeping for an hour between eleven p.m. and midnight. It was the only way I was able to go out dancing with the *primos*, then get up for work in the morning.

"*A dónde vamos?*" I called down. Where are we going?

"El Carda," they said, shrugging as if to say, "Where else?"

Where else was there to go? The gypsies weren't allowed into any other bars in the city, and with a *primo* behind the bar in Cardamomo, the boys could drink for free.

These were the same boys I used to watch dancing on the street corners of my neighborhood. It was only a week ago that I'd rushed to the window whenever I heard them pass to listen to them sing. Now they came by singing to me every night. They were Diego's *primos*. Well, a few of his *primos*. It seemed like every gypsy under the age of twenty-five was his *primo*. And the ones over twenty-five were his *tíos*, or uncles.

Yes, I'd spent both my dance budget and my food budget on the dress, but I didn't care. These boys danced as well as any teacher at the Amor de Dios, and they hadn't taken a dance class in their lives. So though I couldn't go to class, I was learning every day. When I passed the boys on the corner on my way to teach English, they would show me a step. I'd try it a few times on the cobblestones, and when I had it down, I'd hurry off to the metro. I'd practice on the platform and in the reception of the company where I was teaching while I waited for my student to appear. Then on my way home the boys would show me another new step.

I even had my first guitar lesson under the trees in the square where the gypsies all got together in the evenings. I was walking back from work when I saw the *primos* gathered around a stone bench where one of the boys was sitting with an old guitar. They waved me over and asked if I knew how to play. I shook my head, and they sat me down and arranged my fingers over the fretboard, showing me how to strum the introduction to a *soleá*.

When I gave the guitar back to the *primos*, one of the boys played a *bulerías* as another sang and the rest clapped *compás*. I shrugged to myself and said, "We've come a long way from Level Two."

Now it was my midnight wake-up call, and boys were calling up impatiently, "*Venga, niña! Nos vamos de fiesta!*" Come on, girl, we're going out to party!

I slipped out of bed and back into the black dress—after all, I had to wear it as much as possible to get the price-per-wear ratio down. I grabbed my heels, tossed a pair of earrings in my bag, and skipped out of the apartment. As soon as I'd closed the door quietly behind me, I stepped into my shoes and clacked down the stairs to where the gypsies were waiting.

We walked up the street, the boys clapping their hands to the flamenco music in their heads. Every so often one would break out and sing, as the others murmured, "*Así es…*"

People we passed on the street stared at the strange sight of a pale-skinned, red-haired girl and a group of dark-eyed gypsy boys. We walked up a lane that was so narrow the moonlight couldn't even reach us, then turned a corner into a square that was full of gypsies.

The *primos* saw Diego's car parked on the other side of the plaza, so we walked through the throng to where he was standing with a group of long-haired guys singing along to the music playing on his car radio.

I fell for Diego the first time he sang flamenco in my ear in Cardamomo, but each time I heard him sing I fell all over again. I once heard it said of a flamenco singer that he sang "with his heart in his mouth," and that was how Diego sang. With his brows drawn and his eyes closed, the gold rings on his fingers flashing in the lamplight as he threw up his hands. "*Olé…*" And when he opened his eyes, that wicked sparkle returned, and I was under the gypsy spell again.

"*Anda, niña,*" he said, opening the door of his car for me to get in. He climbed into the driver's seat and called out to the *primos* to get behind the car and push as he revved the engine. I stuck my head out the window and watched as a crowd of boys in suit jackets and sunglasses pushed Diego's car up the street until the engine caught.

We drove through the old streets of Madrid with El Cigala playing on the radio. Diego sang along, beating his hands on the steering wheel in time. I leaned back to enjoy my gypsy adventure. It wasn't exactly a painted caravan, but it wasn't too far off, either. They say guys buy sports cars to get girls: Porsches and Mercs never did it for me, but I was a sucker for Diego's gypsy mobile.

The *primos* went out dancing every night. At Cardamomo, Tuesday was no different than Saturday. And it was in the early hours of the morning, when the dancers and musicians who had been performing in flamenco *tablaos* and theaters around town started arriving, that the real show began.

When I complained to Diego about missing my dance classes, he told me to look around. "Who do you want to learn from?" he asked. His *tío* at the bar was Enrique Morente's cousin. The guy who had just walked in with a guitar played with Tomatito, and if that wasn't enough, Tío Joaquín Cortés was standing around looking bored.

"*Anda, niña*," Diego would say. "You don't need the Amor de Dios."

Diego hadn't taken a class since he was thirteen, and he performed all over town. But that was because he learned all he needed to know from *la familia*—the family. Of course, gypsies don't need to go to a dance school because their whole lives are one long dance class. Diego had illustrated this point by showing me videos he'd taken with his phone at his cousin's wedding.

The first video was of his grandmother, who was sitting on a wooden chair surrounded by a group of black-suited musicians. Her wrinkled brown skin and toothless grin made her look like one of those thousand-year-old tortoises. If you can picture that swathed in polka dots, you've got her. She held a walking stick in one hand and pounded it into the floor to mark the *compás*.

She hoisted herself up out of her chair with the help of her walking stick, and then this woman, who was a hundred years old if she was a day, started dancing the sexiest flamenco I had ever seen. I felt my jaw drop. My grandma wouldn't dance if you got half a bottle of dry sherry into her, but this granny made Beyoncé look tame.

Then two more little old ladies got up to join her. These three old women in their cheap cotton dresses were suddenly Diana Ross and the Supremes, doing a fully choreographed hip-swiveling number. "Wow," I murmured.

Then he showed me a video of a girl he said was his ex-girlfriend. She was dancing a *bulería*, and I stared at the tiny screen not really understanding what I was seeing. Yes, she was an incredible dancer, but she was…huge. I mean, really big. She was the kind of girl who, had she dared to come to Level Two looking for new season fashion, would have been met with tight smiles and redirected out of the store to a plus-size boutique. What was skinny-as-a-rake Diego doing with a girl like that?

"You need a good butt to dance flamenco," he said.

I couldn't help taking that as a criticism of my skinniness. *What is wrong with this country?* I wanted to shout. *Why is everything upside down?* I hadn't spent my whole life denying myself a second helping of everything to have a guy show off his size fourteen ex. I was so used to being hungry that I couldn't even imagine how someone could get to that size. I needed an explanation, but I didn't know how to ask for one.

"In Spain you like women who are more…" I faltered, and he finished the sentence off for me with the word *enteras*: complete, whole. So Marina had been right when she'd told me to go down to the market and buy myself a *culo*. She'd known that I was missing something…

Perhaps I've been wrong to deny myself all these years, I thought. It wasn't even a conscious decision that I'd made; it was just that ever since I was fifteen, every time I saw anything that resembled a curve or a bulge on my body, I switched to a diet of carrot sticks until it went back to wherever it came from. But maybe—and I was only prepared to say "maybe"—I could have my cake and eat it, too.

The gypsy girls certainly did, anyway. There were never more than a handful at Cardamomo. The ratio was normally twenty guys to one girl, which suited me just fine, because it made me feel like the star of my very own flamenco extravaganza. As soon as I lifted my arms up to dance, I'd find myself surrounded by dozens of dark eyes and clapping hands.

But Diego would push through them and step forward to dance with me, and I had to admit that no one else danced like he did. There was a style and elegance to his movements that the other boys just didn't have. He wore a white cotton shirt under his black suit jacket, and it was open to reveal a heavy gold medallion with a picture of Jesus's face on it. It was quite possibly the ugliest piece of jewelry I'd ever seen.

"Do you believe in God?" I asked him when the song finished.

"*Sí*," he said.

"And heaven and hell?"

"*Sí*."

"But hell with, like, flames, and devils that poke you with forks?"

He nodded, seriously. I was amazed. I'd never met a person who actually believed in hell before.

"And heaven?" I asked. "What is heaven like?" He told me that in heaven everyone dances *sevillanas*. "I want to go to your heaven!"

In that case, Diego said, I should start praying to the God of Flamenco.

"I will!" I promised. Next time I went to the cathedral I would ask the God of Flamenco to bless my feet and make them fast and wise, and get me back to dance class, and save a place for me in flamenco heaven so I could *toma que toma* until the end of time.

THE GHETTO

Or

Let's see how this kangaroo dances

Having a gypsy boyfriend, I decided, was my ticket to a flamenco lifestyle. It would mean being allowed into their secret world and learning to dance like a real gypsy girl.

I knew that I was getting ahead of myself. I'd only been going out with Diego for a couple of weeks, and I can't say that we had a deep connection. The only thing we had in common was our need to live and breathe flamenco, but that was enough for me. In fact, it was the most important thing. I couldn't imagine going out with a guy who wasn't interested in flamenco. Who didn't drum his fingers on tabletops in *compás*, or know how to dance a *bulería*, or sing flamenco softly in my ear.

I wanted to meet Diego's family. He'd baited the hook when he'd shown me those videos, so when he suggested we stop by his gypsy home the next day, I could barely control my excitement. It was like the Holy Grail of flamenco was just within my reach. But before long, my joy turned to panic. Would they like me? Would they accept me? Would they think me good enough for their son?

I was so desperate to tell someone my news that on my way home I stopped at the salon where Mariela was doing her apprenticeship. She was wrapping an old lady's violet hair in rollers when I walked in.

"*Hola, mamí*," she said over a haze of hairspray. Seeing the excitement on my face, she asked what was going on. When I told her that the guy I was going out with was taking me home to meet the folks, Mariela shrieked in delight. Her cousin came out from the back room to see what was going on, and Mariela told her that Nellie had a new boyfriend.

"*Ay yi yi!*" they both celebrated.

Mariela told me to sit down while she finished her client's wave, so I riffled through the selection of magazines. I love looking at magazines in foreign countries. There's nothing like picking up a gossip mag and flicking through the entire thing without recognizing one face. It always reminds me that the world is much bigger than we realize.

Sifting through past issues of *Hola!*, I uncovered an old fashion mag in English. On the cover was the headline *Meeting His Parents: Four Easy Steps to Wow His Folks.* The article inside was illustrated with one of those stock photos of an aspirational career woman presenting a bottle of chardonnay to a set of silver-haired yacht club parents. *Hmmm,* I thought to myself, *perhaps I should pick up a nice bottle of red on the way over? Or maybe a gourmet basket?*

Step 1: Dress to impress.

"Don't wear bold, aggressive colors like red, but choose soft pastels that will make you appear more approachable."

Pastels…I wasn't sure about that one. From what I'd seen of gypsy girls, leopard-print jumpsuits and thigh-high plastic boots seemed to be more the way to go.

Mariela put the dryer down over her client's head and asked me if I wanted her to straighten my hair for the big date. "No, *gracias*," I said. But I did ask if I could borrow the magazine. And later, back in my room, I tipped out the contents of my suitcase and searched for an outfit that would impress.

I had one gypsyesque skirt, which I'd picked up in a hippie shop for seven euro. I teamed it with a pair of heels and tried the combination on in front of the mirror. Okay, it wasn't *Harper's Bazaar*, but it did have *toma que toma*.

Step 2: Understand their point of view.

"Often parents may feel concerned if you're from a different background. They could worry *that you'll be a bad influence on their son*."

I didn't think there was any chance of me being a bad influence on Diego. He seemed to believe that he was the emperor of Madrid and that he could do whatever he wanted. He left his broken-down car parked wherever he liked and used the parking tickets he got as filters for his cigarettes. Luckily he always seemed to have an entourage of *primos* around to push-start his car.

I had managed to scrape together enough money for a week of classes at the Amor de Dios, and on Tuesday afternoon, after an hour of *bulerías de Jerez*, I changed into my date outfit. I found Diego at reception, leaning against the notice board, jacket slung over one shoulder, flirting with a group of Japanese girls. I don't know how Diego managed to flirt with girls who didn't know the difference between "*sí*" and "*no*," but he did. He could flirt with a pile of bricks and they would follow him home. Just as I followed him, out of the school, down the stairs, through the fish market, and out onto the street where he'd left the gypsy mobile double-parked.

I pulled open the passenger door and climbed in. The car stank like an ashtray and as I wound down the window the handle came off in my hand. Meanwhile, Diego had convinced the fish guys to push the car while he revved the engine. Finally it caught and we were off.

We sped through the city with the cool spring air racing through the car. Diego turned the radio to Radio Olé and sang along in his raspy voice.

Step 3: Don't be intimidated, even if they are Mr. and Mrs. Posh.

We'd left the grungy boho neighborhood of the Amor de Dios and were driving through the big end of town. Flamenco music blaring from the stereo, we whizzed down the grand old avenues, overtaking black BMWs and silver Mercedes. I couldn't help noticing the way everyone stared at us as we passed. "Damn gypsies," they muttered to themselves. As a lifelong mutterer myself, it was nice for once to be the mutteree.

Diego zigzagged down the avenue in his tin-can car, narrowly dodging motorcycles and stray pedestrians. I suddenly realized that I had no idea where he was taking me, so I asked, "Where are we going?"

Diego kept his eyes on the road and snapped, "You always want to know everything, don't you?"

Er…I'm sorry? As I opened my mouth to reply, he turned up the radio and beat the steering wheel with the palms of his hands in time to the music.

Soon the old gray stone buildings and paved roads of central Madrid were replaced with office buildings and glass skyscrapers. This was the business district. Workers in suits and ties were racing back from their coffee breaks clutching briefcases and newspapers.

My phone rang. From the caller ID I saw that it was my father calling from Australia. Before I could answer it, Diego slapped the phone out of my hand. "Ow!" I cried.

His eyes flashed. "You *never* use your phone when you are with me," he said. "Don't you know how disrespectful that is?"

Uh-oh. Who *was* this guy? It was one of those moments when you mentally track back over all those stranger danger rules you learned when you were little. Had I told anyone where I was going, and with whom? No, of course not. I thought about jumping out of the car at the next traffic light, but then he swerved onto an entrance ramp and we were speeding onto a highway, and I'm not really the type to jump and roll.

I suddenly realized how stupid and arrogant I had been for thinking I could just pack up my life and run away with the gypsies. But then, I wasn't running away with the gypsies, was I? I was being taken away. But where to? *Oh Lord*, I thought as I made fervent prayers to a god I didn't really believe in. *I guess this is what I get for reading too many magazines.*

When Diego turned off the highway, we entered a part of the city I hadn't seen in any guidebook. I didn't even know if we were still officially in Madrid. It was a flat expanse of wide concrete streets lined with uniform apartment blocks. Gray washing and dying houseplants hung from square windows. Groups of kids kicked footballs along the gutter. Old women dressed all in black struggled home with groceries, while the old men stood around the corner bars smoking their cigarettes and watching cars pass. I thought back to my class at the Ministry of Foreign Affairs and how my students had told me about the gypsy ghettos outside Madrid, the apartment blocks that the Spanish government had paid the gypsies to go and live in. Oh great. I'd been brought to the ghetto.

Finally, Diego pulled up in a dirt parking lot. The sun had gone down and a crowd of gypsies was standing around a fire burning in an upturned garbage bin. This was the family. Yes, all fifty of them. I knew that for the gypsies the term "family" had a much broader meaning than our two-point-five-children model, but even so, I hadn't expected to meet an entire village.

The *tíos* looked sinister in the firelight with their sideburns and bushy eyebrows. Next to them stood the aunts, the *tías*. Bloated like blowfish and dressed all in black, they wore thick gold earrings that made their earlobes hang out of shape and bright frosted lipstick painted outside their mouths.

Then there were the *primas*, or nieces, who looked supernaturally beautiful. They all had identical doe eyes with Cleopatra eyeliner and sparkly pouting lips, and wore their black hair in tightly wound ringlets.

The *primos*, many of whom I knew, were looking as suave as ever in the gypsy uniform of suit jackets over jeans and fake crocodile-skin shoes. The older boys had carefully trimmed goatees and long black hair that fell straight down their backs. Some had pale skin and jet-black hair, while others were dark-skinned.

In the center of the group, a guy with long hair was playing a beat-up guitar. The gypsies were clapping *compás*, and they dipped in and out of different rhythm patterns and switched from the beat to the offbeat. Every now and again someone broke out and danced. It was one of the boys now. He threw his long hair behind his shoulders and stepped into the middle of the circle with the panache of a bullfighter. As he lifted his arms and clicked his fingers, the family shouted, "*Olé*! *Así es*! *Eso*! *Eso*!"

Diego strode across the parking lot toward the fire. I lagged behind, not wanting to follow him but afraid to be left alone on the street. He grabbed my arm, dragging me with him across the parking lot. "I can walk, you know!" I complained as I skidded over the dusty ground. But he wasn't paying attention to me. By now the family had spotted us. The music stopped, and all eyes were on us. The beloved son had come home…with a white girl.

I was in no way prepared for the sensation I caused. The aunts started shouting at Diego when they saw me. The uncles forgot their cigars and rumbled among themselves. The girls looked me up and down and laughed derisively at my outfit. But the boys smiled shyly, and one even lowered his sunglasses to give me a cheeky wink.

"She's okay," Diego said to the family. "She dances flamenco." At this the shouts turned to laughter. An Australian dancing flamenco?

Impossible! Who did she learn from, the kangaroos? Well, that was one half of the group. The other half wanted someone to explain to them what an "Australia" was.

Diego insisted that I could dance flamenco as well as a gypsy, which I knew wasn't true. I wished there was somewhere I could hide. I even considered making a run for it, but I wouldn't get far in my "meet the parents" heels.

A silver-haired man in a black frock coat stood up and everyone fell silent. His face was dark and leathery. He walked slowly toward us, leaning on a brass-capped cane. When he stopped in front of me, I smelled alcohol on his breath. "*Niña*. You dance flamenco?" he asked.

"*Sí*," I said, trying not to let him stare me down.

He cleared his throat and spat a wad of phlegm into the dirt, then unclasped his frock coat and handed it to Diego. "Let's see how this kangaroo dances."

The old gypsy stepped into the center of the circle, and Diego told me to join him there. When I didn't move, two of the *primas* grabbed me, digging their acrylic nails into my arms, and pushed me into the circle.

After the darkness, the light from the fire was so bright it was almost blinding. Squinting, I saw the guitarist prep the fretboard and strum the opening chords of a *bulería*. Great. No one dances *bulería* like the gypsies. What had I gotten myself into?

I tried to concentrate on the music, moving on instinct. The old man and I held each other's gaze as we circled around the fire. The family were clapping the rhythm. The *primas* sneered and hissed as I moved past them. The *primos* cheered us on, clapping and laughing, their faces appearing in front of me like gargoyles in the firelight.

I don't know what I danced, and I know I couldn't repeat it. All I know is that it felt good. Not just good; crazy good. My feet moved of their own accord, propelling me around the circle. I crossed one leg in front of the other and did the sharp turns that always eluded me in class, and somehow I never lost the beat. I was there, suspended in the moment, until the gypsy dropped his arms and grabbed me around the shoulders. He gave me a kiss on both cheeks and said, "*Mu salá*!"

I had passed the first test. *Mu salá*, or *muy salada* in proper Spanish, can be literally translated as "very salty." This is possibly the highest compliment you can receive from a gypsy. In Spain a woman is like a serving of hot chips—no good without salt.

Step 4: Remember his family's names—and use them!

Okay, whoever wrote that has clearly never dated a gypsy. First Diego introduced me to his *tía* Antonia. Tía Antonia gave me a kiss on each cheek then spun me around to face Tía Maria. Tía Maria gave me two kisses and passed me on to another Tía Antonia. Tía Antonia pinched my cheek and kissed me, and passed me to the next Tía Maria.

When the *tías* were done covering me in their lipstick, they pushed me toward the *tíos*. Tío Antonio grabbed my shoulders to steady me before giving me his two kisses and passing me on to Tío José. After Tío José there was another Tío Antonio, then, just to break it up a little, there was Tío José Antonio. My head was spinning. How could one guy have so many aunts and uncles? And why did they all have the same names?

When the introductions were over, the guitarist strummed another *bulería*, and the family picked up the *compás* again and started clapping and singing. I still had no idea where I was or how I was going to get home, so I asked Diego.

"*Casa*?" he repeated, apparently refusing to understand my meaning. "*Ahora eres mi mujer, y ésta es tu casa.*"

Eh? I didn't understand. That is to say, I did but I didn't. I mean,

I couldn't have. Surely he didn't just say that I was his *wife*? That had to be my bad Spanish.

Diego could be extremely informative when he wanted to be, but it seemed he chose his moments carefully. He now decided it was time to let me know what was going on, so he explained that there's a clause in the unwritten gypsy law that if a gypsy male brings a non-gypsy female onto gypsy territory it means that they are married. So, according to the gypsy law, we were already man and wife.

"*Anda, niña!*" he said. "We'll have twelve kids, half gypsy, half Australian. They'll be Gystralians."

Gystralians? Surely this was all some crazy dream. It couldn't be happening. I looked around the dark parking lot, wondering how I could get away.

Meanwhile, Diego was taking my lack of enthusiasm as a personal insult. "What's wrong with you?" he shouted.

What was wrong with me? Where should I begin? For a start, I'd never imagined that my wedding reception would be held in a dusty parking lot on a Tuesday night. I didn't mean to sound like a snob, but it had simply never occurred to me. Same as it had never occurred to me that I would be challenged to a dance-off by a gypsy patriarch in a frock coat. These were things that my suburban upbringing had not prepared me for.

By now the guitarist had switched to a fast rumba. The beat was infectious, and in spite of myself I started to dance. The boys surrounded me in two seconds flat, clapping their hands and shouting, "*Toma que toma que toma.*" One kid stepped forward to dance with me. He came in close and shimmied his shoulders, lowering his sunglasses to flash his dark eyes at me.

Would you think me crazy if I told you that at this point I was actually considering going along with the whole thing? Wasn't this, after all, what I'd been dreaming of? I'd wanted to run away with the gypsies, and okay, I had been picturing something a little more airbrushed, but I guess that's to be expected when you base your life on fashion spreads in *Harper's*.

The boys were laughing and dancing in the firelight, and the girls joined them, swinging their hips and combing their long acrylic nails through the air. I took a step back and watched them all. Every one of them would belong on a stage, yet none of them had taken a dance class in their lives. Even Diego hadn't set foot in a classroom since he was thirteen, but he toured the world with his very own company. Maybe, just maybe, if I stayed here and lived with these people, I could learn to dance like they did. For the gypsies, singing is as natural as talking, and dancing is as easy as walking.

The stars shone brightly over the parking lot, and the gypsy kids danced rumbas in loafers and stilettos. And I thought, *Maybe this could work.* Maybe, with the help of some fake tan and eyeliner, I could become a gypsy chick.

THE ESCAPE

Or
Put your hands up!

I've heard a lot of stories about dates gone wrong, nights that just go from bad to worse, but if there's a worst-date competition anywhere in the world, I would win it hands down, because I've never heard of a girl going home to meet her date's parents and ending up trapped in a gypsy ghetto at one in the morning with a donkey.

That's right, a donkey.

When the fire died out and the party broke up, Diego took me up a flight of stairs to an apartment where he told me to wait for him while he went to talk "business" with his *primos*. I sat down on a wooden chair beside a table spotted with cigarette burns. It wasn't until Diego had slammed the door behind him and his singing had faded away down the corridor that I heard another sound. A *clop clop clop*.

I turned, slowly, not sure that I wanted to see what was behind me, and there it was: a donkey.

Or at least I assumed it was a donkey. They aren't a regular sight in Sydney. But even so, I was pretty sure that donkeys belonged in barns, not in two-bedroom apartments. I know that was terribly middle class of me, but that's just the way I was raised.

And as I sat there in the cold apartment, tired, hungry, and married, it occurred to me that I had never really appreciated my privileged middle-class upbringing. I had always resented it, just as I had resented growing up in suburbia, with the neat lawns and friendly neighbors and the quaint little fences. But what I would have given to be back there now...

I had known the risk I was taking by choosing to step out of my context and into a culture I knew nothing about. I knew when I chose to dive headfirst into flamenco that it would be sink or swim. But what's the point in being alive if you're not going to be a little wild sometimes? I didn't want to live by the manual. I wanted to do what I loved, even if it did get me into trouble. And I could officially classify this as "trouble."

However, there was one thing I knew for sure: it was time for me to get out of there. The problem was that the donkey was between me and the door, and though I knew in theory that donkeys didn't eat people, this one looked pretty hungry.

The donkey started coming toward me. I yelped and climbed up onto my chair. It went to sniff my feet, so I jumped up onto the table. While the donkey was distracted with sniffing something on the floor, I jumped off the other side of the table and made a dash for the door.

I ran down the stairs, out the front exit, and onto the street. The night air was cold and made me shiver. My sense of direction isn't generally that good, but by the way the wind was blowing and the position of the North Star, and the fact that I was in a gypsy ghetto, I made a pretty accurate estimate that I was in the middle of nowhere.

I started walking down the dark street. There was nothing on either side of me but identical apartment blocks. Most of the windows were bare, but some were covered with newspaper in place of curtains. In one of the apartments an old man was singing flamenco.

What a voice! It ripped through the silence. I couldn't pause to listen, but kept on walking in the hope that I might turn a corner and see a bus stop, or a metro station, or some other sign of modern society.

I had to keep moving to stay warm, but which way should I go? How far would I have to walk to find a landmark? Each time a car came past I didn't know whether I should flag it down or hide behind a pile of garbage till it was out of sight. I thought about calling someone, but I was out of credit, and as I tried dialing Juan's number, all I got was an extremely unhelpful recorded message advising me to recharge my phone.

As I stood there trying to decide which way to go, I heard another car coming down the street, flamenco music blaring on the radio. Uh-oh. Gypsies. Where could I hide? I ducked behind a garbage can, which did little to hide me, but at least it got me off the street. Fortunately, the car sped past, and the music faded into the distance.

I picked right and walked as fast as I could down the street. A dog was sniffing around in the gutter up ahead. *Maybe I'll end up mauled by wild dogs*, I thought. *That'd be a classy way to end the evening.*

I kept on walking, my heels clacking on the pavement. There was a boy coming toward me, singing a song to the night in a sweet young voice. He would have been about eleven or twelve years old. As we passed each other, he looked me up and down and said, "*Guapa.*" Then I felt him pinch my butt. The little brat! I turned around, but he had already disappeared into the darkness.

When I turned the next corner, my heart jumped. I'd found a main road. At least, it looked like a main road. There were no cars, but it had freshly painted lane markings, a sign that someone cared. I looked both ways and wondered which way led to Madrid. It was hard to tell. There was nothing but suburban wasteland for as far as the eye could see. Once again, I picked a direction and started walking. A cold wind had picked up, and my ankles were killing me. I considered taking off my shoes and walking barefoot, but the broken glass and random syringes on the street convinced me that was a bad idea.

I was hit by a wave of exhaustion and with a pang of regret realized I had made a huge mistake. Sascha had been right all along. I should have bought that Kelly bag. If I'd bought that bag, I wouldn't be here. Because let's face it, girls with Kelly bags don't have to dance for their lives with gypsy patriarchs. Girls with Kelly bags don't have to run away from donkeys, or hide behind garbage cans, or walk back to town after a date gone wrong. Girls with Birkin bags, perhaps, but not girls with Kellys. And I wondered whether I'd ever set foot in another Hermès boutique again.

I heard the sound of a car coming. "Thank you!" I said out loud to the universe. I imagined that it was being driven by a nice young couple who had also lost their way; maybe they'd be friendly Brits or Americans. They'd let me hop in, and I'd joke with them about the night I'd had while we drove around until we miraculously found ourselves back in Madrid. I'd show my appreciation by treating them to an early breakfast in an all-night pancake house. Mmm, pancakes with maple syrup…

As the car came closer, I heard the music coming from the stereo. The beat was unmistakable. After living with the Latinas, I could pick up Puerto Rican hip-hop a mile off. As the car came closer and the music got louder, my fantasies of the charmingly helpful young couple disappeared like smoke rings in a gust of wind.

I don't do car models, but I can say that these guys had clearly seen *Fast and Furious* one too many times. The car was so low that it could clean the gum off the street, and the picture was completed by a glow-in-the-dark dashboard Jesus with outstretched arms.

As the car approached, it slowed down. I wasn't sure if this was a good thing or a very, very bad thing. The guys were leaning out the windows, as guys tend to do when the highlight of their night is driving up and down empty streets.

The driver grinned at me, flashing a set of gold teeth, and said, "*Hola, preciosa.*" He was wearing a tight white tank top that showed off his multicolored tats. There were four guys in the car, all dressed in shell suits with bandanas and baseball caps pulled on sideways. They hung halfway out of the car, leering at me like ghouls in a ghost train.

There are some situations in life where whatever decision you make sends shivers down your spine. At this moment I was faced with two choices: hitch a ride in a homeymobile, or keep on walking down a deserted road through the ghetto. Which one of these two options was less likely to result in me being left for dead by the side of the road? That's really not the kind of question that you ever want to have to put to yourself. I took a deep breath and asked them if they were going to the city.

"*Sí,*" the driver said, and one of the guys in the back opened the door and stepped out. He gave me a kiss on each cheek and introduced himself as Julio, then held open the door, gesturing graciously for me to get in.

I hesitated for a moment, and thought about all those hours I'd spent in the cathedral over the last month. I hoped that some of that Jesus magic had rubbed off on me. Maybe if I just tried to see the happy ending, everything would be okay...

I climbed into the middle of the backseat, and Julio followed me in, squashing me between himself and a guy called Juanito on the other side. Julio slammed the door, and we drove off.

The whole car was reverberating with the stereo bass. The driver caught my eye in the rearview mirror and introduced himself as Mauri. He asked me where I was from, and when I said, "Australia," they all nodded and said, "*Síí?*" in that way that people in Spain always do when they have no idea where Australia is.

Mauri ejected the reggaeton CD and put in a new disc. It was, of course, the patron saint of guys in shell suits: Fifty Cent. He pumped up the volume and the guys sang along with their hands in the air, "Hands up. Put 'em up, put 'em up, put 'em up!" Julio nudged me with his elbow, so I obediently raised my hands and danced along with the boys. Mauri had taken his hands off the wheel and was driving with his knees. He tapped his foot on the clutch, making the car bounce down the street. I felt like I was in a cheap hip-hop video.

Then we pulled onto a highway on-ramp. As we drove up the ramp I could see the lights of Madrid glimmering in the distance. I almost shrieked with glee.

"There it is! Madrid!" Julio said. It had been a long day. I settled back into my seat, thankful that soon I would be tucked up in my own bed.

❊

But my night wasn't over yet. The boys weren't interested in taking me home. They wanted to go to a bar run by a friend of theirs in the south of Madrid. "*Vamos a bailar*," they said. And I didn't know how to explain to them that for once in my life, dancing was the absolute last thing I felt like doing.

Mauri pulled up in front of the bar, and we all tumbled out of the car. From the curb I could hear the reggaeton blasting inside. I hate reggaeton, but I'd prefer to listen to it all night than be back in that room with the donkey.

"Ledis first," Juanito said, holding the door to the bar open for me. I stepped inside and was surprised to see that it was actually a cool Latino club. Juanito offered me his hand for the next dance, and before I could accept he'd pulled me onto the dance floor. "*Sabes bailar merengue?*" Of course I knew how to dance *merengue*. I told him that I lived with Venezuelans.

When the song ended, we joined Mauri and the boys at a table. The music switched to a hip-hop beat. It was Mauri's favorite song, Snoop Dogg's "Drop It Like It's Hot." He looked at me and asked me again what the name of my country was.

"Uh, Australia."

He asked if we spoke English in my country, and if so, did I understand the lyrics of the song? I told him I didn't understand all of it, but I got the main bit.

"Drop it." I picked up the ashtray from the table and let it fall from my hand. "This is to drop."

The boys nodded. "Ah, *caer*?"

"Good, Julio! And hot. Who knows what hot means?"

"*Caliente*," Mauri offered.

"Good! So the phrase is 'drop it like it's hot.'"

"Drop like hot?" Julio echoed, confused.

Hmmm…I racked my tired brain for an easy way of explaining it. "Okay, so. You're baking a potato. You know potato?"

"*Patatas, sí.*" They nodded together.

"So you take the potato," I continued, miming the action for them. "But it's *hot*! So what do you do?"

"Ah! *La dejas caer!*"

I gave Mauri my disappointed teacher look. "Say it in English. You drop it like it's…"

"Hot!" the boys answered together.

"Good! So, Mauri, what's the line?"

Mauri said proudly, "Dropping like it's hot."

"Okay, good. But this is a command—so we use the…"

"*Imperativo!*" Juanito interjected.

"Excellent, Juanito! Which is?"

"Drop."

"So the line is?"

The boys repeated together, "Drop it like it's hot."

It was moments like that I wished I had a pack of chocolate bars.

The guys wanted to know what a girl like me was doing wandering the streets all by myself in the early hours of the morning, so I told them the story of Diego and the *primos*, and dancing with the patriarch.

They listened with horrified expressions, then exchanged glances and said it was time for me to go home to bed. Mauri took off his jacket and draped it over my shoulders as we walked back out to the car. I settled into the backseat and they drove me home. *So much for thugs*, I thought as I let my head rest against the seat and my eyes close. My mother always said there are angels everywhere. She was right.

THE DARK NIGHT
OF THE SOUL

Or
Me, myself, and other reflexive pronouns

I called the English academy as soon as it opened. "Can you cancel my morning class?" I said to the receptionist. "I was kidnapped by gypsies last night and there's no way I'll make it."

There was a pause on the line before the receptionist said, "Okay… I'll just tell them you're sick."

After hanging up, I lay back exhausted against the pillows. I was physically, mentally, emotionally, and even spiritually exhausted. *What on earth am I doing here?* I asked myself. Here, on this bed, in this room overlooking this market, in this city full of gypsies in this country called Spain? I'd tried to dance at the Amor de Dios and I'd failed. I'd tried to dance with the gypsies and failed spectacularly. This whole trip was one big fat failure.

What had possessed me to come to Spain to be a flamenco dancer? Of all the stupid ideas circulating in the ethers of this great universe, how did I manage to pull down the stupidest? Running away with the gypsies might make a good tagline for a fashion shoot, but it's a bad lifestyle choice.

I pulled out a notebook that I'd been using as a kind of diary. It was full of scribbled notes, Spanish words, song lyrics, ideas, CDs to buy. I found the page where, sitting in that abandoned elevator shaft/ hostel room, I had written my New Year's resolutions:

- *DANCE FLAMENCO*
- *LEARN BALLET*
- *RUN AWAY WITH THE GYPSIES*
- *FALL IN LOVE*
- *WEAR POLKA DOTS*
- *TOMA QUE TOMA*

I stared at that list for a good long while. *No wonder I'm in this situation*, I thought, *with goals like that.* It had to be the most nonsensical list of aspirations ever put to paper. It was exactly the kind of list that would lead to having to hide behind garbage bins in a gypsy ghetto in the early hours of a Wednesday morning.

I closed my eyes and slept again until the midmorning sun fell on my face, then dragged myself off to shower and to try to get the stink of smoke and donkey out of my hair before going to teach at the Ministry of Foreign Affairs.

Today I walked quickly through the gypsy-infested streets, never more conscious of the fact that I was on their territory. But I didn't see any on the quick walk. It was too early for them to be out.

The class was assembled by the time I got to the office. When I walked in and saw them, I was suddenly overwhelmed with the joy of being alive. "Guys!" I said. "I thought I'd never see you again!" I wanted to hug and kiss each one of them. My beautiful, beautiful students. They sat there staring at me, wondering what on earth was going on. "I think I need to sit down," I said, collapsing into a chair.

"Are you okay?" Paloma asked.

"Yes," I said. "I just haven't slept."

"Why? What happened with you?"

I thought about explaining to them the night I'd had. I imagined their reaction, how they would cluck and scold and tell me I was an idiot. They had warned me, after all.

"Teacher? Are you okay?"

"Yes, I'm fine," I said, getting up out of the chair. "Let's have a look at your homework."

❋

That week I avoided the gypsies as much as I could, but it wasn't easy when I was still living in their neighborhood. When the boys sang at my window, I ignored them, and even when they sang my favorite songs I didn't weaken. I was mad. I took Diego's outrageous behavior as an insult from the whole gypsy race. I considered tipping a bucket of water on them but decided it would be better to let them think I wasn't home. So I kept the window firmly shut until they gave up and moved on.

I've heard it said that one should never settle for second best, and after trotting over shards of broken glass on unlit streets in the small hours of the morning in "meet the parents" heels, that no longer seemed like an empty platitude. I didn't have a lot of experience in the relationship sector, but it didn't take an expert to tell me that Diego had exhibited enough red flag behavior to give a bull a panic attack. But even so, twelve long-stemmed roses delivered to my door might have made me put it all behind me. I am, after all, a hopeless romantic. A nice card with tickets to a flamenco show tucked inside could have made me see the whole episode as a charming, if quirky, anecdote we could tell our *bulerías*-dancing Gystralian children about in years to come.

Long-stemmed roses? Theater tickets? A card?

Go ahead, laugh. I was still that delusional. I hadn't fully come to the realization of what dating a gypsy from the ghetto truly meant.

There would be no apologies. Diego called a few times that week, and after ignoring him a couple of times, I picked up. But instead of the smooth, charming voice that had won me over in Cardamomo, I got an earful of indignant rage. How dare I leave him! Walk out like that, making him the laughing stock of the ghetto.

And as for the donkey…

"What donkey?" he snapped back at me.

Er…the one that tried to eat my skirt?

"*Tu estás loca,*" he said. You're crazy.

He called a few more times over the next few days, then stopped. I was relieved, and also slightly miffed that he wasn't prepared to fight for our marriage. I imagined that he'd found another clueless foreign girl who'd fall for the old "take a girl to the ghetto and make her dance with your frock-coat-wearing uncle, then tell her she's your wife" trick.

I did wonder briefly whether that marriage was in any way legally binding. For all I knew, traditional gypsy law was recognized by the state. I was beyond the point where anything in Spain could surprise me. The government had just passed a law giving human rights to chimpanzees, so that made me think anything was possible.

As all these thoughts circulated in my head, I couldn't get that list of New Year's resolutions out of my mind. I'd never realized before just how stupid I was capable of being. *Toma que toma* is not a resolution. It's not even a sentence. The more I thought about it, the more I came to realize that it was time for me to get my act together. I hadn't totally thrown my life away yet. I still had a chance to go home and enroll in university. I'd see if I could get a place in law. Perhaps human rights law. Then I could fight for the rights of ethnic minorities… Except that would include gypsies.

Forget that plan.

Well, maybe some other kind of law. One that involved wearing skirt suits and defending big business from the people who drink the water they put chemical waste into. Yes, it would mean swallowing my pride and admitting that I'd made a mistake in coming to Spain, but I told myself that would be character building. And anyway, I didn't need to go home just yet. I could tell the academy I was prepared to take on more English classes. Then I could save up and go home with some money in my pocket. That would make a nice change from being perpetually broke. And with my next paycheck I'd go to Zara and buy myself a suit so that I looked like a real teacher. On top of that, I should probably learn some of what I was teaching.

So when I got home, I pulled one of the grammar textbooks the academy had given me out from under my bed, blew the dust bunnies off it, and settled in for a night of gerunds and collocations. *Anyway*, I said to myself, *who needs gypsies when you've got Saxon genitives?*

I started to read a lesson.

Prepositional phrases. Hmmm...

My phone rang. I checked the caller ID—Juan. It was past eleven, so he was either in La Soleá or on his way there. I knew that if I answered the phone Juan would talk me into going out, and that was the last thing I wanted to do. I'd had my Madrid flamenco experience. And what more could I gain from nights out in flamenco bars? Only more trouble. So I let the phone ring out as I read the example in the grammar book.

Some verbs are commonly followed by dependent prepositions. Really? How interesting...

My phone rang again. I stared at Juan's name flashing on the screen, took a deep breath, and pressed Reject.

These verb + preposition combinations can have specific meanings...

"Yes, I see," I said, nodding at the examples in the book. That could make a good class for Andrés. Though each time I'd brought the grammar book to class, he'd pushed it away and enticed me into a conversation about Basques, gypsies, surfers, or anything else he could come up with to distract me from the task of teaching English. And he'd kept on pushing the textbook aside, gradually nudging it with his elbow until it fell to the floor.

A message alert flashed on my phone. **Where are you hiding, lamparilla?**

Lamparilla was Juan's nickname for me. It literally meant "little lamp," but the gypsies used it all the time to mean "thing." The bill was a *lamparilla*, a new verse in a *bulería* was a *lamparilla*, the waiter in La Soleá was a *lamparilla*. "*Oyé, lamparilla!*" the gypsies would call out when they wanted to get his attention.

I stared at the message and wondered what I should do.

Prepositional phrases usually begin with a preposition...

I replied to Juan, telling him that I was tired and having an early night. The phone rang again, and this time I had to pick up or he would know I was deliberately avoiding his calls.

"*Hola?*" I said. All I could hear was a flamenco guitar and a singer. Even over the phone the sound of the voice gave me goose bumps.

Dammit, Juan.

"*Lamparilla!*" He told me he'd ordered me a glass of wine and hung up. I put down the phone and looked back at the open grammar book in my lap.

Examples:

a) Lucy arrived with impeccable timing.

"Oh, who cares?" I said, snapping the book shut. Who cares how Lucy arrived? She could arrive with perfect timing, impeccable timing, immaculate timing, or transcendental timing for all I cared. It didn't change the fact that I had to go out and face the gypsies again.

I stepped into my boots and pulled on a jacket. "Dammit, Juan," I repeated as I left the apartment.

As I walked up the stone steps to the entrance of La Soleá, I could hear the strum of the guitar and the voice of the singer. It was a rough and broken voice that carried out into the street. From the doorway I saw the waiter standing watching the singer with a tray of drinks in his hands. I'd never seen him so transfixed by a flamenco artist.

Walking farther in, I saw him, an old gypsy man with wrinkled skin so dark he was almost black. I sat down next to Juan, who put the waiting glass of wine into my hands. "El Aborigine," Juan whispered. Juan had told me about this singer before. He was a famous flamenco artist who used to come often to La Soleá, but he suffered from addictions that had taken their toll on his body and mind—though not, it seemed, on his voice.

The singer sang with his eyes closed, then slowly lifted himself to his feet. He stood, swaying ever so slightly as he sang. His legs didn't look strong enough to support him; perhaps it was the power of his voice that held him up. Then, with a stamp of his foot, he began to dance. He shuffled a *bulerías* around the room, and everyone jumped to their feet, shouting "*Olé*!" and clapping *compás*. Even the waiter put down the drinks tray and clapped his hands. Juan looked at me and raised one eyebrow, as if to say, "And you wanted an early night."

I knew then that the mistake I'd made was thinking that flamenco was something I needed to chase. I'd been trying to hunt it down, when in fact all I needed to do was allow myself to live it.

Flamenco didn't belong to the gypsies any more than it belonged to anyone else, though I knew the *primos* would argue that with me. But I was past caring what they thought. Here I was having an unforgettable flamenco experience with Juan, who was almost as white as I was. And all I could say was "*Olé*."

THE STRANGER

Or
Wouldn't it be nice?

There he was, walking up the street toward me. The sun had gone down an hour earlier, and the old lamps bathed the street in a golden light. I'd seen him before, in the café in the square, his brow furrowed handsomely over the morning papers, and I'd seen him sitting out in the evenings with a drink and a book. You don't often see people in Madrid sitting alone with a book. I'd stared at him a moment too long, and his eyes had lifted just in time to catch mine.

And here he was again, walking toward me. As our eyes met he said, "*Hola.*" My heart jumped to my throat and I mumbled something that ended in "la," dropping my eyes as though the cobblestones I was stepping over were the most interesting things I'd seen that week.

As he passed by and I walked on up the street, I let out a sigh. It was the middle of spring, but it was already hot like Sydney summer. I'd been warned that in Madrid it's either cold or hot, and there's nothing in between. Now only a couple of weeks after shivering in the ghetto, I was walking around in a tank top and flip-flops. And there's nothing like warm weather to make you want to get out and share it with someone.

It would be so nice to have someone to enjoy the sun with. It didn't have to be Mr. Tall, Dark, and Handsome, though that would most definitely be nice. There was something about him that had attracted my attention the first time I saw him. A seriousness in his jaw, a kindness in his eyes. He didn't look like the kind of guy who would make me dance with his frock-coat-wearing uncle. He didn't look like the kind of guy who would *have* a frock-coat-wearing uncle.

Tonight I was walking up to La Soleá, where I knew that Juan would be waiting for me with my usual glass of red wine. This was what my life had become. I was living from *bulería* to *bulería* and *rioja* to *rioja*. But wouldn't it be nice…to have someone to be with, to talk to, to call, and someone who would call me, too? Someone to complain about my day with over coffee, or open a bottle of wine with, or just do nothing at all with.

Juan only ever sang one song, and he only ever sang it early in the night before the real flamenco artists arrived. He had learned to play flamenco guitar in his fifties and didn't like to play in front of the professionals. I never asked him why he had decided to take up guitar. I suppose it never occurred to me to. I knew what it was to fall in love with flamenco.

I never felt the need to ask him questions, though I really didn't know anything about him. In turn he offered very little information, except for a reference he once made to an ex-wife who couldn't understand his love for the guitar, and two grown-up children he would occasionally speak of proudly. I didn't know what he did in the real world, but we weren't friends in the real world. We were friends in the world of La Soleá. Two wannabe gypsies united by an absurd love of flamenco.

Every so often Juan would poke me in the ribs and tell me that it was my turn to sing. In La Soleá everyone took a turn at singing. People came in off the street and sat down next to the guitarist and told him what song they wanted to sing. I was always amazed by how good they were. They were people who had regular lives and families. They were bankers, grocers, secretaries, bus drivers, lawyers, nurses, but whatever it was they did during the day it was forgotten when they stepped into La Soleá.

Each time Juan tried to convince me to sing, I shook my head. I wished I could sing. I loved the way the women sang with rough gypsy voices. I'd tried many times in my bedroom to sing along with my favorite flamenco artists and do that hoarse, broken thing they do with their voices, but I just sounded like Snow White with a bad cough. I guess I just wasn't meant to sing like that.

✳

There he was again! It was Friday night and I was walking to La Soleá, and once more he was walking dowsn the street toward me. Could he have been more handsome? In the glow of the street lamps he looked like the leading man in a Hollywood romance. *This time I'll meet his gaze*, I told myself. *This time I'll be confident and smile and say,* "Hola." *This time…*

But as he came closer and our paths were about to cross, I dropped my eyes again, and he passed by without saying hello. *How is it*, I asked myself, *that I can run away and dance flamenco with gypsies, but I'm too much of a 'fraidy cat to say hello to a man in the street?*

When I walked into La Soleá, a woman in a gold-tasseled shawl was belting out a *tangos*. She balled up her fist and scrunched up her brow as she sang. As I sat down, Juan said in a low voice, "Tonight you're singing, *lamparilla*."

The woman in the gold *mantón* started to dance, and the gypsies jumped to their feet and cheered her on. "*Olé!*"

Once she'd sat down again, Juan called out to the guitarist that I wanted to sing. I could have killed him. "No, no, no, no, no!" I said, but it was too late. The guitarist had already got up and was coming to sit down next to me. I tried to tell him that I couldn't sing flamenco and I didn't know any Spanish songs, but Juan told him I was lying. The guitarist strummed the introductions to a few different songs he thought I might know, but each time I shook my head.

Then he strummed a melody I recognized. It was Peggy Lee's "Perhaps," one of my favorite songs of all time. He saw the recognition in my face and started over, playing the introduction slowly. But I just couldn't do it. Everyone in the bar was watching me, and the sound stuck in my throat.

Juan helped me out by singing the first line in Spanish, then I took over in English. The guitarist picked up the rhythm and the woman in the gold *mantón* joined in, her gravelly voice a full octave below mine. Around the room the gypsies started to clap *compás*.

The guitarist started the second verse in a rumba rhythm, and the gypsies in the bar called out, "*Olé! Así es!*" A girl got up to dance. She twirled her arms above her head and shimmied her hips, and a gypsy man jumped up and stamped his foot, crying, "*Que toma, toma toma!*"

The song came to an end with the crowd shouting, "*Olé!*"

Juan nodded and said, "*Bien, lamparilla. Muy bien.*"

It was nine o'clock on Saturday night and I was walking again to La Soleá. The street was already filling up with people who had gone from a late lunch to beers in a sunny outdoor café to wine and tapas. And as the old road curved around to La Soleá, I saw the handsome stranger again. But this time he looked different. He was standing in the doorway of a restaurant next to La Soleá in a white chef's tunic.

I'd walked past that restaurant dozens of times, but I'd never paid any attention to it. I can be very observant with some things. Sascha had taught me how to spot a fake Birkin bag at twenty paces, and it was a skill I still practiced on the streets of Madrid, where fakes outnumbered the real thing a thousand to one. I always examined people's shoes on the metro; as my father says, you can always tell a person by their shoes. Generally, though, I only noticed things that interested me. I might totally miss the giant service station that took up most of a block, but I could orient myself by the poky wig shop on the corner, or the bar that played flamenco music, or the Italian hosiery boutique.

So even though I'd spent almost every night for two months in La Soleá, I'd never noticed the restaurant with its grand entrance and stylish exposed stonework, and the big windows that gave a tantalizing view into the elegant dining room. Of course, there were no gypsies dancing on the tabletops, so how would I have noticed it? But now that I knew it was the domain of Mr. Tall, Dark, and Handsome, it suddenly became noteworthy.

"*Hola*," he said as he saw me.

"*Hola*," I said, smiling shyly and blushing till I was sure my face must be the color of my hair. Why was it that I could be confident in some situations and so hopeless in others? Luckily for me the Spanish are very social people, and the handsome chef was already leaning forward to give me a kiss on each cheek. I still hadn't come to terms with the European custom of cheek-kissing. I'm a staunch defender of personal space, and I find the idea of kissing the cheeks of a stranger unnecessary at best. But this was one occasion in which I didn't mind at all.

He told me his name was Iñaki and we made standard small talk—Where are you from? How long have you been in Madrid?—but I didn't think about the questions or the answers I gave, just allowed myself to get lost in his deep brown eyes as I thought, *Wouldn't it be nice?*

He invited me into the restaurant for a glass of wine, and of course I accepted. I followed him inside to where the staff was setting up for dinner. A waiter in a crisp white shirt and long black apron was moving from table to table, carefully laying silver cutlery on the white tablecloths. A waitress followed him, placing flower arrangements in the center of each table, and another waitress was carefully folding white napkins and setting them on top of the plates.

Iñaki told me to take a seat at the bar while he opened a bottle of wine. I picked up a menu and was surprised to see that there was only one thing to choose from—meat. The appetizers included *jamón*, cured Spanish ham, and a sort of fried sausage popular in the Basque Country called *chistorra*, and for dessert there was fat from heaven—*tocino del cielo*, a dessert made from egg yolks and sugar syrup.

It was tough being vegan in a country where the word doesn't even exist. I was breaking my rules on an almost daily basis, with *cafés con leche* and toast with butter. But I was still trying not to eat meat.

Iñaki came back from the kitchen with a plate of thinly sliced *jamón*. Seeing the food reminded me that I hadn't had lunch. He poured two glasses of wine and we clinked glasses. "*Salud*," he said.

I was very conflicted about the idea of eating meat. I believed that it was wrong, and I knew that Gandhi would have starved to death before taking the life of another sentient being. But as much as I wished I had the strength of his convictions, I was aware of my own weakness, and now, even with this handsome chef in front of me, it was hard to take my eyes off the *jamón*.

Didn't the Buddha eat meat? I reasoned. He never questioned what was placed in his alms bowl; he just recognized that it was all an illusion. So this *jamón* must be an illusion too.

Iñaki pushed the plate toward me, and I took a piece of bread and one of the thin slices of ham. *It doesn't really exist*, I thought. But for an illusion it sure was good, and one slice just wasn't enough.

I had another sip of wine, and then after an appropriate pause I took a second slice of ham. I asked Iñaki about the restaurant and he told me that it was a traditional Basque *asador*, or grill. In his native Basque Country, it's the men who do the cooking; in fact, women aren't even allowed in the kitchen. Iñaki told me they have men-only societies where the men get together and cook. His father was a chef and owned a restaurant in their village where Iñaki's younger brother worked, and his older brother had another *asador* in Madrid.

I listened, fascinated, and helped myself to another slice of ham and some more bread. The more I ate the hungrier I felt. I asked him about the lack of nonmeat products on the menu—salads, vegetables, sides. "We have *pimientos*." he said. *Pimientos* are little red peppers that are caramelized and eaten with meat. I must have missed them on the menu, I said, taking another piece of ham.

"Would you like to try the steak?" he asked.

"No, thank you," I said. "I don't eat meat." Iñaki looked down at the big empty plate that moments before had held enough ham for a whole table. "Very often," I added.

At about nine thirty the first customers of the evening walked in, so Iñaki excused himself and asked if he could take me out to dinner on his night off. "I'll choose a nice…vegetarian restaurant," he said, with a hint of a smile on his lips.

Yes, I thought as I stepped back out onto the street. *It would be so nice…*

THE FIRST DATE

Or

Ay, mamí!

*A*y, mamí!" Mariela shrieked when I told her about my date with the handsome stranger. He had called that afternoon to invite me out for dinner. "He's not another gypsy, is he?" she asked, her hands on her hips. The family had forbidden me from going out with any more gypsies, and I had no desire to break their rule.

"No!" I told her he was tall and handsome and looked like Hugh Jackman.

"*Quién?*" Mariela asked.

"Hugh Jackman," I repeated. "Wolverine."

"*Ay!*" she shrieked, then shouted for the others to come quick, Nellie had a date with Wolverine.

Everyone came running. Andy and Mandy left their homework on the bed and rushed into the living room. Andrea came out of her room in a pink robe, and Consuela left the pot of beans bubbling on the stove.

"*Quién?*" Consuela asked. Mariela explained to her mother that I was going out to dinner "*con* Jack Hughman!"

"No," I said. "Hugh Jackman."

"Hugh Hackman?" Close enough. Everyone was asking me questions at once, and I tried to give the right answer to the right asker.

"Where is he from?"

"What does he do?"

"How old is he?"

"How did you meet?"

"Is he good-looking?"

"Does he have a cute brother?"

"Where is he taking you?"

"What are you going to wear?"

I told them all that I knew, that he was from the north of Spain, a chef, thirty-one years old, and that I didn't really know anything else…except that I liked him.

"Awww…" they all said in unison.

Mariela told the girls to grab a hairdressing mag each and find a look for me for the night. I wasn't used to doing my hair. I had three looks: hair out, in a ponytail, and up in a clip. But Mariela was not going to let me out of the house without a do. She stopped at a picture of Posh Spice with a sharp, asymmetrical bob.

"No!" I said. She shrugged and kept flipping.

Consuela held up a picture of a girl with glossy curls piled on top of her head, and everyone oohed and aahed. Meanwhile, little ten-year-old Mandy was running around the house gathering up every bottle of nail polish she could find. She presented them all to me to pick a color for my pedicure. I chose a deep red, and she insisted, with a pout and puppy-dog eyes, that I cover it with a coat of sparkles. How could I say no?

Mariela looked at her watch. "*Ay, mami!*" she said again. There were only three hours left before my date. She slapped my arm with one of the magazines and told me off for not getting started earlier, then instructed Andy to get a pot of water on the boil for my facial and pushed me into the bathroom to wash my hair.

The women shook their heads and clucked their tongues. I should have been waxing and steaming and tweezing and plumping the night before, not at five p.m. on the big day. But there was nothing they could do. They were going to have to give me the express treatment and hope for the best. And although my regular hair-care routine consisted of rinse and repeat, I knew that I was going to have to give in and allow myself to be made over. I just hoped that I would recognize myself at the end of it.

❋

"There he is!" Mandy shrieked, running into the living room. The women all raced to the window to see him, and I followed.

"Don't be so obvious!" I begged, afraid that he would look up and see all my roommates staring at him.

There he was, standing in the lamplight, looking as handsome as ever. He was wearing a brown corduroy sports jacket over a black shirt and a pair of jeans. He was effortlessly elegant, and I was sure he was completely unaware of the fact. Mariela shook up the can of Nelly and gave me one last blast of hairspray to keep my carefully sculpted ringlets in place. Then they all wished me luck and told me to get out there and not keep such a good-looking man waiting or some other girl would walk past and snatch him up.

As soon as I was in the stairwell, I pulled the pins out of my hair and tried to break up those lacquered curls into a more natural wave. I wiped off some of the lip gloss they'd gooped onto my mouth and used the back of my hands to rub off any extra blush. Feeling more like myself again, I walked down the last flight and pushed open the door to where the handsome stranger was waiting for me.

Iñaki had made a reservation in a little restaurant just up the street from his own. It had only a dozen tables and a bar displaying the thickest, fattest tortilla I had ever seen. Once we were seated, the waiter brought us two glasses of champagne. We clinked glasses and Iñaki made a toast: "*Para nosotros.*" To us.

We sat there, facing each other, and I tried to hide my embarrassment behind my champagne.

What was I going to say?

Awkward pauses in conversation can normally be filled by witty remarks about the happenings of the day. But faced with this charming man I was so eager to impress, I realized that I literally couldn't string two words together.

My Spanish had improved since I'd arrived in Madrid. I'd had to learn to get by. But I'd been picking it up in a very random fashion. I had vocabulary to open a bank account, buy a metro pass, and understand a flamenco teacher shouting directions across a crowded dance studio. But for first date small talk I had nothing.

I took another gulp of champagne. Iñaki didn't speak any English, but he wasn't fazed by my silence. He moved a little forward in his chair, tilting his head toward mine, and asked me very slow questions about my life in Australia. I stumbled over my words at first, but with a little more champagne, and his gentle encouragement, I became more and more animated. As I spoke, I realized that it was the first time I'd really talked to someone since I'd left home. Communication had been about survival, but now I was actually able to talk to someone about who I was, where I'd come from, and the journey I was on. And Iñaki related to a lot of what I said about being away from home. He had gone on a journey of his own, leaving his home in the Basque Country and moving down to Madrid to run the family restaurant. He was fascinated by the idea of Australia, a land so far away and so different to his own. He filled up my glass as I talked about the things I missed from home and the things I loved about Spain. He gave me space to tell my story, and to confess for the first time that things hadn't been as easy as I'd thought they would be.

The more I got to know him, the more I saw a boy from the mountains. His warm brown eyes were calm, yet always alert, taking in everything that happened around us. I could imagine him at peace in the forest. Beneath all his urban sophistication, he seemed like the kind of guy who would know how to rub sticks together to make a fire, and be able to tell by the wind which way was north and which was south. I was right. When I asked him what he missed most about his home he told me it was his mountain. There was a mountain in his village called Uzterre that he climbed every time he went home. I'd never climbed a mountain before. I wondered if girls with Basque boyfriends have to climb mountains. I wondered how high it was…

My train of thought was derailed by the arrival of the tortilla. And oh my goodness, what a tortilla! It's hard to be elegant when you're eating Spanish food. A big, fat Spanish omelet is messy business, especially a good one. A good Spanish omelet should be three inches high and barely cooked in the middle. It should be just potato and egg held together by the collective Spanish fantasy, against all laws of gravity, and it should melt in your mouth in a kind of "Oh my God, where's my napkin?" moment of sinful food bliss. And this one did. I said good-bye to my lipstick and let Iñaki pour me another glass of red wine.

After dinner we wandered out of the restaurant, tipsy on champagne and wine. It was warm enough for us to sling our jackets over our arms and enjoy the night air. Iñaki walked me through the little yellow-lit streets back to my apartment.

As we turned onto my street, I could see three of the *primos* standing under my window, calling up to see if I was out or just sleeping. "Are they waiting for you?" Iñaki asked.

"Er…I don't think so," I said. The *primos* saw us coming up the street and headed off in the opposite direction. I noticed Iñaki watching them as they walked away.

THE BASQUE

Or
Ardo pixkat

A Basque!" Andrés said, his eyes bulging. "First the gypsies, then the Basques. You like to live dangerous! From where is he in the País Vasco?" "País Vasco" is Spanish for Basque Country, though Andrés told me that the Basques prefer their own name, "Euskadi."

"Um…" I tried to remember the name of Iñaki's village. "Tolosa."

"Tolosa! *Un guipuzcoano*? *Bwarf*!" He shook his head and looked at me with a mixture of horror and delight. "The worst! They are mountain people!" Andrés was originally from Bilbao, the economic and industrial capital of the region. "The *guipuzcoanos* frighten even me! They are *etarras*." *Etarras* was the Spanish word for members of the terrorist group ETA.

But then he laughed and told me not to worry. The Basques, he said, would kill me with food before they got me with a bomb. "First," Andrés told me, "when you go to his village, he will take you out for *zuritos*. This will be at about eleven o'clock."

"What are *zur*…"

"*Zuritos*? Little glasses of beer. You will drink, oh…three of these, maybe with any fried…er…shrimp. Then you go to a different bar and have *txakoli*."

Txakoli? Andrés wrote the word down for me and explained that in Basque they use the "tx" instead of "ch."

"*Txakoli* is a typical Basque wine. Good to have with *pintxos*—like tapas, but much, much better! You have maybe a little steak with peppers, or fish or duck…all this before lunch, eh. With *pintxos* you must to drink *txikitos*."

"Okay," I told him, "you're making these words up."

"No, no!" he protested, crossing his heart. "This is Euskera, the oldest language in the world! You must to learn it, because your children will be Basque." He tore a piece of paper out of his notepad and started writing down some words for me. "When someone says to you, '*Kaixo, zer moduz?*'—'Hello, how are you?'—you must to say, '*Oso ondo.* Very well.' And if they ask you any question, you just must to say, '*Ardo pixkat.*'"

"What does that mean?" I asked.

"It means 'a little wine.' Normally they will be asking what you want to drink. The Basque men are much more dangerous than the gypsies. You know what will happen? He will take you to the mountains and lock you up in a *caserío*, a country house." Andrés shook his head regretfully. "You will not come back. You will be alone up there in the mountains, one poor Australian girl with twelve little Basque children, all talking Euskera so you don't understand."

I laughed at that image. "What makes you think he's going to invite me to his village?"

"He will." Andrés looked at me sadly. "I will be losing my English teacher."

Since I'd met Iñaki there wasn't a day that he didn't call. I didn't notice it at first because he did it in such a gracious way. He called to invite me for dinner, then he called to say he'd had a lovely time, then every day he'd call to offer to be of some assistance. He'd call to ask if I was interested in going to see a new flamenco show, or to let me know about a free concert that was on somewhere, or just to say hello.

One afternoon I came home from work tired and hungry only to find that there was nothing to eat in the kitchen, and all I had left was half a packet of spaghetti. Not long after, he called me. "What are you doing?" he asked.

"I'm eating," I said.

"What are you eating?"

"Spaghetti."

"Spaghetti with what?"

"With…spaghetti."

"With oil and garlic?"

"No, I don't have any oil or garlic."

"With salt?"

"I can't find the salt."

There was a pause. "You're eating just spaghetti."

"Yyyeees…" I said. "I'm hungry."

"Come over here and I'll make you lunch," he said.

"But I just made spaghetti!" I protested.

"Bring the spaghetti," was all he said.

So I put a tea towel over the strainer and carried my spaghetti over to Iñaki's place, which was only a couple of blocks from Mariela's. By the time I got there it had already formed a gluggy mass.

"*Qué tal?*" How are you? he asked, giving me a kiss and whisking the strainer out of my hands. On a board in the kitchen I could see that he already had diced onion and pancetta. He heated up some oil in the pan and put the onions on to soften. It would have been easy for him to put on a fresh pot of pasta that would come out perfectly al dente, but he had graciously accepted my attachment to my poor spaghetti.

In no time the apartment was filled with the smell of caramelized onion and pancetta. Iñaki asked me what I'd like to drink, and I said, "*Ardo pixkat.*"

He stepped out of the kitchen and said, "What?"

"*Ardo pixkat,*" I repeated, hoping I'd got it right and that I wasn't saying something offensive. I wouldn't put it past Andrés to set me up.

Iñaki stared at me for a long moment, then he said, "*Oso ondo,*" and selected a bottle of wine from a rack in the kitchen.

Olé, I said to myself. *Thank you, Andrés.*

"Can I help?" I asked, feeling a bit guilty that I was just lazing on the couch doing nothing while he prepared lunch.

"You've already made the pasta." He placed a salad on the table and served the spaghetti into two bowls. "*Ardo?*" he asked, offering to top up my wine.

"Cheers," I said.

✳

Andrés was right. It was only a month later, in June, that Iñaki told me he had to go up to his village for a wedding and asked if I wanted to go with him. Since the day I'd told Andrés that I was going out with one of his countrymen, our classes had switched from English lessons for him to Basque lessons for me. I felt a little irresponsible, given that I was being paid to teach him English, but Andrés didn't care. He was already CEO of a multinational company and had had his picture taken with the king. His attitude to English was that if someone didn't understand him, he just had to speak louder.

"You know how are these Basque wedding? You will needs a lot of stamina. First you will have *zuritos* and *pintxos* before the church, then at the restaurant a cocktail." The Spanish have taken the English word "cocktail" to mean drinks and nibbles. "Then you have the lunch. In Euskadi the lunch is the most important thing. You don't give a gift at a wedding; you give money. So the people think they are paying for the lunch. The lunch should be first a salad. A Basque salad, not your green shit. A salad of seafood, and maybe duck. Then fish. Then meat. Then another meat! Then dessert—must be two desserts; if not, it is not a Basque wedding. And cake. Cake is not a real dessert, it is—how you say?—an extra. Then gin tonic and cigars. You smoke cigars?"

I shook my head.

"You will have to learn. Don't inhale! Like this." Andrés mimed puffing on a cigar. "Then you are drinking, drinking, drinking, and dancing. You know what is the traditional Basque dance? It is like this, with a drink in one hand and a cigarette in other." Andrés mimed dancing holding a glass and a cigarette. "Then you have dinner. More food, *bwarf!* Then drinking, drinking, drinking until six, maybe seven in the morning. Then breakfast. *Bwarf!* Fried egg and *chistorra*."

"That's impossible," I said, shocked.

Andrés grinned. "It is not only possible, it is your future. This is what happen if you have a boyfriend from Tolosa."

"He's not my boyfriend," I protested.

"You are going with him to his village, to a wedding where will be all his family. I think you must to, how you say? Face the music? I love this expression! Face the music. You have a boyfriend."

✳

The following Friday night, Iñaki picked me up after he'd finished work at midnight to drive up to his village. I was looking forward to seeing the north of Spain. From the tales Andrés told, I imagined the Basques spent their days drinking *txakoli* and lobbing firebombs at each other, though Iñaki told me that if I expected to see any Molotov cocktails I was in for a disappointment.

We drove out beyond the bright lights of the city and on to the highway. We passed groves of olive trees and vineyards, and went through the rolling plains of Castilla–La Mancha, the land where Don Quixote once traveled jousting windmills with his friend Sancho Panza.

I fell asleep as we were driving past fields of grapevines, and when I woke up, we were traveling through the mountains of northern Spain. Up ahead I could see flashing lights signaling drivers to stop at the boom gates. I asked, half asleep, "Is this the border?"

"No," Iñaki said, his eyes on the road. "But it should be." I had quizzed Iñaki about his politics, excited by the idea that I might be dating a separatist. But he had explained that he was a nationalist, meaning that he believed in protecting and promoting Basque culture, but he didn't think that the Basque Country should become an independent state.

We passed through the last tollbooth between central Spain and the Basque Country. I closed my eyes and fell back to sleep.

When I woke up again, we had arrived at Iñaki's home. The radio was on and a man was crooning in a strange language that I assumed must be Euskera. Fresh mountain air rushed into the car as Iñaki opened the door. We pulled our bags out of the back, and I could just see the outline of the mountains through the early morning mist.

We carried our bags up the stairs to the top floor. Big glass doors opened out onto a balcony from which we could see mountain peaks. I sat down on the bed, yawning and rubbing my eyes, while Iñaki went to the kitchen to see what there was to eat.

He came back minutes later with two steaming cups of tea, a block of dark chocolate, and a packet of sliced chorizo sausage. I took my cup of tea and watched as Iñaki broke off a piece of chocolate and wrapped it in a thin slice of chorizo. I'd seen some pretty weird stuff in Spain, starting out with the fried pig's skin I was served for breakfast in Seville, but chorizo with chocolate?

Iñaki offered me a piece, but I said no thanks. "I don't really feel like chocolate and chorizo."

"But this chorizo comes from Pamplona," he said.

"Er…even so, I'll just have tea."

Iñaki shrugged and said it was my loss, and I was happy to agree.

I sat up with him, drinking my tea until I couldn't keep my eyes open any longer. Then we pulled back the bed covers, switched off the lights, and fell asleep, breathing clean mountain air.

THE WEDDING

Or

I thought you said you could surf?

"Every time I come here I swim out to that island," Iñaki said, looking out across the sea to a little island about a half a mile from the shore. Surf was crashing onto the beach, waves three and four feet high. There was only a lone surfer in the water. "*Vamos*?" Iñaki asked, pulling off his shirt.

I had expected a wimpy Spanish beach, not pounding waves, and I hesitated. The sea looked too rough for me.

"I thought you said you could surf?" Iñaki said.

Yes, well, about that. I didn't exactly tell him I could surf. Spanish people have this idea in their heads that all Australians surf, so I just went along with it. He made the assumption that I could surf, and I didn't tell him otherwise. But standing on the sand, I realized that I should have.

The truth was, I hadn't expected to be called on my surfing prowess. Spain didn't seem to me to have a beach culture, and I rather enjoyed being seen as the exotic mermaid from Down Under who is most at home being buffeted by the waves, when the reality is that I hate getting water up my nose.

And now Iñaki was expecting me to run into the surf like a

volunteer lifesaver on Bondi Beach, and that was not going to happen. I still carried the trauma from the swimming lessons I was forced to do in primary school. But this was not the moment to explain that to Iñaki. He had already stripped down to his swimmers and was ready to run into the water.

Here's another thing that I hadn't anticipated—in his spare time, Iñaki was also a triathlete. Of course. Not only was he big-screen gorgeous, a celebrated chef, kind, and considerate, he was also an Iron Man. So there would be no faking it, I realized as I pulled my T-shirt over my head. As soon as we hit the water, he would realize that I was a lousy swimmer.

But I was an even lousier poker player, and Iñaki had already seen through my bluff. "Don't be afraid," he said. "I've got you." And before I had time to protest, he grabbed my hand and ran with me into the water.

The first wave came and lifted me clear off my feet, but I held on to him. I kicked out, trying to swim to get past the breakers. Iñaki pulled me along with him. The next wave almost pulled me away, but he held on to my wrist and we kept swimming.

I came up for air and saw that we had made it out past the surf. The island was only about a third of a mile away. Only, ha! I tried to tell myself that it wasn't that far. A third of a mile is a stroll to the milk bar. *You've run farther in heels to get to the bus stop*, I told myself. I tried swimming my strongest stroke—breaststroke—but Iñaki was powering ahead with freestyle. So I tried to do that too. Stroke, stroke, stroke—gasp and splutter. Stroke, stroke, stroke—come up for air and see how far I've come…but after traveling only a few yards I went back to breaststroke.

We reached the tiny island and sat up on the rocks, enjoying the sun and looking back at the shore. It was past one, and Iñaki decided that it was time for lunch. He suggested that we go and eat with some old friends of his, so we climbed back down off the rocks and swam back to shore.

Iñaki's "old friends" were Juan Mari Arzak and his sister, who run the famous Basque restaurant Arzak where Iñaki received his chef training. Juan Mari met us at the doorway with hugs and kisses and told Iñaki off for taking so long to come back and visit. He asked if we had come for lunch, and though it was almost impossible to get a reservation, he said that something could be arranged. But before we ate, Iñaki wanted to show me around.

First we went into the laboratory where Iñaki's old friends were working as food scientists, investigating and designing new dishes. A young chef who had done his apprenticeship with Iñaki took us into the climate-controlled spice room, where every imaginable spice, seed, and aromatic leaf was categorized and stored in little jars. I gazed at the wall dedicated to spices from Australia. The chef opened some of the little jars and held them up for me to smell. I closed my eyes and let the aromas transport me back to our garden back home.

But there was no time to get homesick. Our next stop was the laboratory where a food scientist was experimenting with dry ice for a spectacular frothing chocolate dessert. He showed us how they would be presenting the new dish on the table, with cascading bubbles flowing from an elegant crystal glass. The house sommelier, another old friend of Iñaki's, then took us to the wine cellar, where he proudly showed me their collection of Australian wines.

They set up a special little table for us in the kitchen where we ate while we watched the dishes being prepared around us. Large white plates with tiny delicacies were brought to us, each with its own story and an accompanying glass of wine selected by Iñaki's friend in the wine cellar.

After lunch we drove up the winding road around the coast, into fairy-tale mountains dotted with old stone houses. These were the *caseríos* that Andrés had told me I would end up in.

Iñaki gazed out at them and told me that his ambition was to buy an old *caserío* and do it up. I asked him if he wanted to have children. Yes, he told me. Twelve. "Twelve?" I repeated. What is the Spanish obsession with having twelve children? "It's to have a football team," Iñaki explained. "Eleven on the field and one reserve."

After our two-hundred-course lunch I couldn't even think about eating again, but Iñaki insisted on taking me to a local cider house for dinner. It was in an old stone *caserío* off a mountain road. Inside were rows of giant cider barrels and little wooden tables to rest your glasses on. We were given a glass each. A man stood beside the barrels; he took a toothpick out of a tiny hole in the side of one, releasing a thin spurt of cider. Iñaki showed me how to catch the cider so that it broke against the side of the glass, giving it just the right amount of fizz. He told me to drink it straight down before the bubbles disappeared.

Iñaki ordered the traditional fare: fried green peppers, codfish, and a prawn omelet followed by cheese with quince paste and a basket of walnuts.

There were no chairs because in a cider house everyone eats standing up. It's more friendly, Iñaki said, easier for people to move around and talk to each other. He picked up a walnut and placed it on the side of the table under his knuckle, then brought his other hand down on it, cracking the hard shell. It was a cool trick. I tried to copy it but only managed to hurt my hand; the shell was unharmed. So I let Iñaki crack the walnuts, while I ate cheese and watched the Basques catching cider in their glasses as it flew through the air.

The wedding was the next day. It was Iñaki's cousin who was getting married, so just as Andrés had predicted, I was being thrown into a huge family event. The ceremony was in a little stone church up in the mountains. Iñaki parked the car nearby, but instead of heading to the church, we went to a little bar around the corner where the guests were drinking cups of hot broth and eating fried *chistorra*.

Iñaki's father was at the bar drinking vermouth and talking loudly in Euskera to a group of big, ruddy-faced Basques. Andrés had told me that all I would understand when the Basques spoke in Euskera was the swearing. For some reason the Basques never invented their own curses, so they have to swear in Spanish. When I listened to the men speak, all I heard was: "(weird sounds) *Hostia*! (more weird sounds) *Hijo de puta*! (really weird sounds) *Me cago en Dios*!"

Spanish swearing is colorful and imaginative and does sound rather curious when it's translated into English. *Hostia* means "the Host," while *hijo de puta* means "son of the whore." But the Spanish particularly like to talk about shitting on things: on your grandma, on your dead, in the milk, and, of course, on God himself. This last one was Iñaki's father's favorite expression. "*Me cago en Dios*!" he repeated. "*Me cago en Dios y en todos sus santos*!" I shit on God and on all of his saints.

Iñaki introduced me to his father, who looked me up and down then said something to me in Basque. I took a deep breath and said, "*Ardo pixkat*." This made everyone laugh, and Iñaki's father shouted to the bartender to get me a glass of wine.

After our *aperitivo* we made our way to the church. At the front was a group of musicians and dancers all dressed up in traditional Basque costume. The women wore white shirts and red skirts with black waistcoats and white scarves over their heads, and the men wore white shirts and pants with red berets and red kerchiefs around their necks. When the bride arrived on the arm of her father, the musicians played folk music on flutes, accompanied by a slow drumbeat, and the dancers jumped and did graceful high kicks.

After the ceremony we drove to a restaurant for the reception. After an array of seemingly endless *pinxtos* that just kept getting more and more extravagant, we were seated for lunch. Again, Andrés was proved right: the food kept coming. After the third course I had to pass my plates over to Iñaki. This kind of eating, I was learning, takes years of training, and the Basques have been at it from birth. After we had finished the final dessert course, it was time for gin and tonics, and cigars.

After the first round of cigars had been stubbed out in empty glasses, the music started and the bride and groom got up to dance their first dance as a married couple. The DJ played all the wedding classics, as well as some that I would never have expected, like a Spanish version of the chicken dance, which had everyone from grandma down to the flower girls flapping their arms and twisting their hips. And of course, what Basque wedding would be complete without…the "YMCA"? The whole family became the Village People. Iñaki's father stuck his cigar between his lips and together we formed the letters with our arms.

So this is my life, I thought to myself. I had come all the way from Sydney to the mountains of the north of Spain to dance the "YMCA" with a roomful of cigar-smoking Basques. Well…why not?

❋

That night as we lay in bed, Iñaki rolled over and bundled me up in his arms. He whispered in my ear, "*Te quiero*."

There it was. The moment I'd been waiting for my entire life, when my handsome prince would take me in his arms and say those three magic words: I love you.

When I was young, I had envisioned this moment in so many ways: on a bridge in Paris in the rain, under the neon lights of some grungy diner on a busy street in New York, or on the beach in my hometown. I had never imagined it in the mountains of the Basque Country. But neither had I dared to imagine that those words would come from a man as perfect as Iñaki.

"*Te quiero*," he whispered.

There was just one small problem: I didn't understand him. The words sounded familiar—I'd probably heard them before in a song or something. But instead of looking at him, tears welling up in my eyes, and telling him that I loved him too, as I had always imagined that I would, I said what I said every time I didn't understand him, "*Sí, sí.*" And I closed my eyes and went back to sleep, not knowing that the man I was falling in love with had just told me he felt the same way.

THE DOCTOR'S ORDERS

Or
What language are we speaking?

I'd often meet up with Iñaki after he finished work at midnight, but then I'd have to be up again at six in the morning to get to work. My accumulated exhaustion kept growing because I didn't even get to rest on the weekends; instead I'd go out with Juan to listen to flamenco all night, or when Iñaki could take a weekend off, we'd go up to his village.

My body reached a point where it refused to cooperate. Some days I couldn't even walk to my English classes; I had to climb into a taxi for a two-minute ride from the metro to the company. One day I even had to sit down at the foot of the stairs in the Ministry of Foreign Affairs because I didn't know how I was going to make it up the three flights.

I got a shock one afternoon when I left Iñaki's apartment to go to class. Iñaki lived on the fifth floor of a building with no elevator. We'd just had lunch and I had to go off to my class at the ministry. I was walking down the stairs when I tripped and fell, hitting my eye on the banister and somehow going head over heels to land with the back of my head hitting the wall.

The neighbors came up to see what had happened, and Iñaki

came racing down. I lay in a crumpled heap in the stairwell, not wanting to move ever again.

After that I knew I couldn't keep on living the way I was living, but it was too late. A couple of days later I came down with a fever. It descended over me like a mist, and I was unable to move the whole night. In the morning I had just enough energy to reach for my phone to cancel all my classes, then I lay on my bed, my body aching, drifting in and out of consciousness.

Iñaki called in the afternoon, and when he heard the sound of my voice, he told me he'd be there straightaway. When he saw me, I could see from the expression on his face that I was worse than I'd realized. He sat with me until he had to go back to work. Mariela told him not to worry, they were making me soup and chamomile tea, but he said that as soon as he could escape from the kitchen he'd come back to see how I was.

I lay in bed with fever for three days, maybe four, getting worse and worse. I couldn't tell the difference between my waking hours and dreams. When Iñaki came to see me on the fourth day, I was so frightened I had tears streaming down my face. He tried to calm me down as I rambled deliriously about home, about my dreams, about the gypsies that came past my window singing. I didn't want to die, but I was losing the little strength I had left. I closed my eyes and went to sleep.

✳

When I opened my eyes, I had no idea where I was. *Am I in my bedroom in Sydney? What time is it?* I wondered. *Am I late for work?* Then I remembered that I had gone to Seville to dance flamenco. Maybe I was in my room in Inés's apartment. I closed my eyes again and reopened them, and my memory started to come back. *I went to Madrid*, I thought. But where was I now? I was moving. There were bright lights flashing by. What was I lying on? I touched leather. I was in the backseat of a car.

I could hear a man's deep voice speaking in a language I couldn't understand. *Where am I?* I propped myself up on one elbow. A man was driving and talking on a mobile phone. I looked at the back of his head. His hair was brown. Who is that? Something told me I knew him. He looked at me in the rearview mirror. It was Iñaki. It all came back to me. I sank back into the seat. I didn't know where he was taking me, and I didn't care. I just wanted to sleep.

❋

I had to walk from the car, but it was so far and I didn't think I could make it. Iñaki held me up, and I concentrated on putting one foot in front of the other. The lights shone brightly ahead of me. "*Vamos, cariño.*" Come on, darling, he said. I just had to make it to the doors and I could sit down again.

The cool air started to bring me around. "Where are we?" I asked. Then I realized I was speaking in English. I searched my brain for the equivalent in Spanish. "*Dónde estamos?*"

Iñaki gave me a concerned look. "*Estamos en el hospital.*"

A man in a green smock came toward us pushing a wheelchair. "I can walk," I said, though it came out as a murmur.

"I know you can walk," the man said with a smile. "But it's more fun this way."

I sat down in the wheelchair and felt all the energy drain out of my body. It took all my strength to keep my head from lolling on my shoulders.

We traveled down the corridor of the hospital and into the elevator. "Where are you from?" the man asked.

"Sydney," I said, my voice little more than a whisper.

"Sydney? I want to go to Sydney. It is a beautiful city. What are you doing in Spain?"

I didn't want to answer his questions, I just wanted to sleep. But it occurred to me that he was probably trying to keep me conscious, so I made an effort. "Dancing flamenco."

"Wow, flamenco," he said.

I wondered what language we were speaking. It felt like English, but I couldn't be sure. "Where are you from?" I asked him.

"I'm from Romania." The elevator doors opened and he wheeled me out into another long white corridor.

"Do you speak English?" I asked him.

"Yes, I do. We're speaking English right now."

"Really?" I said, my eyelids closing heavily. "That's nice. I like English. I teach English…" but I wasn't sure if I was saying that out loud or only in my head.

He wheeled me into a room and helped me climb up onto a big, high bed. My eyelids dropped as if they were weighed down with heavy stones. I felt someone take my arm and a needle prick my skin, and I heard the sound of someone tearing off a strip of tape. But I didn't really care what they were doing. I just closed my eyes and fell asleep.

✳

"Give me your arm."

I opened my eyes. There was a nun in a white habit standing over me. She took my arm and wrapped a strap around it. She told me to make a fist, which required all my strength, then took a needle and pushed it into my vein. I closed my eyes as the syringe filled up with blood.

What's wrong with me? I wondered. *Why are they taking all my blood? What happened?* I looked down at my arm and saw that I was hooked up to an IV. *Am I dying?* But it was simply curiosity. I didn't really care. So long as I didn't have to move or talk or open my eyes, it didn't really matter.

When I finally woke up, I didn't know how long I'd been asleep. A night, a day, two days. I had lost all concept of time. When I tried to move, pain coursed through my body, so I stayed still, soaking up whatever dosage of painkillers they were pumping through my veins.

I looked around at the room. It was painted white with great high ceilings. On the opposite wall there was a Christ on the cross, and next to him a framed picture of Mary looking weepy. It was a huge room with a sofa and glass sliding doors that led out onto a sunny balcony. *This is sooooo much nicer than my apartment*, I thought as I looked around.

Then, finally, I started to panic. I was in a fancy private hospital in a foreign country. What on earth must this be costing? I didn't even have travel insurance. Oh my God, I'm going to be in debt for the rest of my life. Maybe I'll have to skip the country and start a new life in Morocco.

There was a knock at the door and I was surprised to see Juan poke his head in. His gray hair was combed back and he wore a suit and tie. He looked like a different person, so serious and businesslike, not like my friend from La Soleá.

"*Lamparilla!*" He walked in, picked up the clipboard at the foot of my bed, and flipped through the pages. "Iñaki called to tell me you're not well. What's happened?"

"What are you doing here?" I asked, confused.

"What am I doing here? This is my hospital. What are you doing here?" Juan pulled up a chair next to me and placed a box of chocolates on my bedside table. He explained to me that in his life outside of La Soleá, he was the president of one of the biggest medical insurance companies in Spain. So he told me not to worry about a thing, all I needed to do was rest.

There was another knock at the door and Iñaki walked in carrying a bunch of flowers. "*Hola, Iñaki,*" Juan said, standing up. He took the clipboard and explained my situation to Iñaki in Spanish, then said he was going out to smoke a cigarette. Iñaki sat down next to my bed and took my hand.

"I'm not going to die?" I asked him.

Iñaki smiled and shook his head. "You're fine," he said, stroking my hair. "You have a fever, but you're going to be okay."

The nurse came in with a tray of food. She put it down on my bedside table. "I'm not hungry," I said as Iñaki took the lid off a dish of vegetable puree. But he placed the spoon in my hand and watched like an anxious parent as I put a spoonful of puree into my mouth. The taste of food replaced the medicinal taste in my mouth from the drugs, and as I started to eat, I realized that I was hungry after all. I finished off the puree and ate the little fruit salad provided for dessert.

Then I let my head fall back on the pillow. I was tired again, but I didn't want Iñaki to leave. It was starting to hit me what had happened. I was in a Spanish hospital. How was that possible? Never in all my dreaming and planning about moving to Spain had I once entertained the idea that I would end up in hospital. What a disaster.

A tear ran down my cheek. "No, no, no," Iñaki said, wiping the tear off with his finger. I didn't have the energy to try to explain to him why I was crying. I was such a failure. It was all a complete and utter disaster. I hadn't even been able to look after myself. I was so lucky that I had Juan and Iñaki to look after me; I dreaded to think what could have happened to me if they hadn't been there.

Iñaki unzipped his backpack and took out my copy of *Harry Potter and the Sorcerer's Stone* in Spanish. He asked if I wanted him to read to me, and I nodded. I pulled the blankets up around me and settled back into my bed as he began. Before he'd finished the second page I was asleep.

They kept me in the hospital for three days. I decided not to tell my parents where I was. There was nothing they could do except worry, and there was no need for that. Each day Iñaki came straight from the restaurant after lunch, bringing food. He'd gotten approval from my doctor to bring me fresh fish cooked on the grill with olive oil and garlic, and vegetable soups and crunchy bread. He'd set up the meals on my little table, and while I ate the food from his restaurant, he'd eat my hospital meals.

Every night after dinner he would come back to the hospital and read to me until I fell asleep, then he'd make himself up a bed on the couch so that he'd be there if I needed anything during the night.

When the doctor came in with my results, I found out just how bad my condition was. Apart from the savage virus I'd caught, I was suffering from serious anemia and many other deficiencies. The doctor warned me that if I didn't start looking after myself, I'd soon be back in the hospital. And that meant I had to sleep and eat. And by eating he meant red meat.

"Don't worry," Iñaki said. "I'll make sure of that."

That afternoon Iñaki took me home, and after I'd had a few days to recover, he brought me to the restaurant for my first steak. I'd broken my veganism on many occasions since leaving Sydney, but each time I was only flirting with meat. But this was the real deal.

He put the plate in front of me, and there was an island of red meat surrounded by caramelized red peppers. I looked down at it and said, "There's no way I can eat that."

"Uh!" Iñaki said, raising a finger. "Doctor's orders." Doctor's orders indeed…only a Spanish doctor would prescribe this.

I cut into the thick steak and put a small piece in my mouth.

Okay…I've eaten a lot of good things in my life, but nothing could compare to this. It was perfection, and I understood why most people aren't vegan or vegetarian, because this is what we're missing out on. I felt my whole body respond to the nourishing protein, so I ate a little more.

It didn't change my mind about the ethics of eating meat, but I was able to say thank you to the world for feeding me and looking after me at this time when I really needed it. And when Iñaki was satisfied that I'd eaten enough, he whisked away the plate and replaced it with a bowl of rice pudding. "But—" I tried to protest.

"Nell…" he said in a warning voice.

"I know," I mumbled. "Doctor's orders."

THE HAPPILY EVER AFTER

Or
Vivan los novios!

The church bells in the tall steeple rang out over the green hills of Italian Switzerland. The crowd of guests around the door cheered as the newly married couple stepped out of the church.

"*Toma que toma*!" Zahra called to me as she walked out on the arm of her new husband, Mario. Around us Swiss bankers and bankerettes threw rose petals over the couple as they made their way to the waiting Rolls-Royce.

"*Vivan los novios*!" Iñaki shouted. Long live the bride and groom!

Zahra was the ultimate flamenco bride in a white dress with a long ruffled train. Her hair was gathered up on top of her head, covered with a flowing lace mantilla and held in place with an elaborate comb carved out of mother-of-pearl. In her hand she held a white lace fan that she waved in front of her face as she and Mario ducked under the shower of petals.

I loved that dress. Zahra had had it made in Seville at a famous bridal boutique. "I wanted a real *toma que toma* flamenco dress!" she said, telling me that she'd gone through every style in the designer's book until she came to one that fulfilled her flamenco dreams.

As a prewedding present, I had bought Zahra a set of jewelry from my favorite flamenco shop in Madrid. The earrings, the necklace, the bracelets, and the combs were all inlaid with little red stones. It was just like the sets we had drooled over in Seville and promised each other that we would come back for.

A month before the wedding, Iñaki and I had traveled down to Seville to spend a couple of days with Zahra and Mario while she had her final fitting. Mario was Italian Swiss, softly spoken, and a perfect gentleman, and he was head over heels in love with Zahra.

"And he loves meat!" Zahra had said when I told her that Iñaki would be cooking for us that evening. He'd brought wine and *jamón* and steak from the restaurant to cook on the barbecue on the terrace of the apartment where we were staying for the weekend. Iñaki and Mario immediately bonded over food, which left Zahra and me to the more important matter of the dress.

Zahra stood in front of the bridal store mirror in her white lace dress with its ruffled skirt and train. Her eyes darted to each imperfection, each wrinkle, and every inch of slack fabric. It made me think back to standing with her in the busy dress shop for the fitting of her flamenco costume days before the feria.

Two years had passed since that day. Zahra caught my eye in the mirror. She seemed to be thinking the same thing, and when the tailor hurried off to get more pins, she said, "Do you remember that night in *Sevilla*? That magic night on the bridge when we made a wish?" Of course I remembered. "I wished to get married and to move to Geneva and manage a bank."

"And I wished that I could live in Spain."

"And you see?" Zahra said. "Our wishes have come true."

She was right; our wishes had come true. Standing on the bridge that night, I had wished to be able to live with the joy that I had found dancing flamenco in Seville. It had been a hard road to get here. I'd gone down a couple of dead ends, and I'd learned a few lessons along the way. Yet somehow, in spite of all my recklessness, I'd managed to fall into my place in the world. And that's the only way I can describe it. I don't think it would be right to say that I had "found" it. Maybe it found me.

Living with Iñaki was a joy that grew with every day we spent together. It was quite possible, I sometimes mused, that we were actually made for each other. I tried to find some flaw, something wrong with him or with us, but I couldn't.

Even Juan agreed. He invited us around for lunch one day in the lavish new house he was decorating in Madrid's most exclusive suburb. We sat in the garden on deck chairs, enjoying the midday sun as Iñaki swam laps in Juan's new swimming pool. "He's a good man, *lamparilla*," Juan said. "You got lucky."

Zahra approved too. When I'd originally received my invitation to the wedding, I'd called her and asked if I could bring a date. There was a pause on the line before she said, "It is not some gypsy, *ey, chica*? You know this is a stylish wedding." When she met him in Seville, she looked at him and said approvingly, "*Muchísimos ojos!*"

And stylish wedding was right. By the time we arrived at the reception, for which we had to cross the border into Italy to get to a palatial villa on Lake Como, I was feeling like the poor cousin. All the other women had changed after the ceremony and were arriving in spectacular evening gowns. I was still in the only evening dress that I owned, a light silk bias-cut dress covered in red roses. I'd bought it with my mother years ago on sale and never worn it; I'd only put it in my suitcase to take to Madrid on Mum's insistence, because she said that you never know when you might need something special.

The tables in the dining room were all named according to places that had a special significance to Zahra and Mario, and I was delighted to see that Iñaki and I were seated at Seville. At the table with us was a young banker and his girlfriend. He was the child of

Swiss foreign diplomats and had been born in Argentina, raised in the United States, educated in England, then worked in Brussels before moving to Geneva.

"How many passports do you have?" I asked.

"Three," he said.

"Awww…" I was disappointed to be beaten at "count my passports." "I've only got two. I want three!"

He gave me a diplomatic Swiss smile and said, "You have time."

"What's the third one going to be?" his girlfriend asked.

Iñaki leaned forward and said, "It will be Basque."

After dinner, Iñaki and I wandered down to the lake. He'd taken two weeks off work so that we could turn the trip into a holiday. We'd just spent a week swimming and sunbathing on the Ligurian coast, and it was hard to think about going back to work.

I would be starting a new job when we got back. Iñaki had introduced me to a friend of his who worked as an English teacher, and he had passed on my CV to his academy. A week later they called me for an interview, and I got the job. The pay was three times what I'd been making, all my classes were in the center of Madrid, and I insisted on nothing before ten a.m. With my new salary and reduced workload, I could easily pick up two dance classes a day, and in a year's time, who knew?

I was sad about leaving my students at the old academy, especially my group at the Ministry of Foreign Affairs. On the day of our last class, they took me out for a farewell lunch. They'd bought me a present: a flamenco CD and a book about Spain.

When I looked at them all gathered at the long table, talking and laughing, I felt so sad to think that I had to say good-bye. I remembered how I'd started out that class with only two students, who both intimidated me to the point that I couldn't even hold up the sheet of paper I was reading off because my hands were trembling, and then every week after that a new student had arrived. And here we were, a group of more than twenty. Looking at them digging into their desserts and joking in Spanish, I felt tears well up in my eyes. I would have loved to continue teaching them, even if I wasn't paid for it, but the academy had already reassigned the class.

We carried our glasses of champagne into the ballroom for the bridal waltz. Iñaki slipped his hand into mine as we watched Mario and Zahra sweep across the marble floor, their eyes locked, blissful smiles on their faces.

I wondered in that moment if I could ever do that. And by "that" I don't mean the waltz; I mean the other bit, getting married. If I did, it wouldn't be in a palace, and I couldn't imagine that I'd have a hundred bankers in attendance. And I really didn't see myself flying to Seville for my dress and Milan for makeup tests. But perhaps a small church, with a flamenco guitarist...

Just as I was drifting off into a daydream, Zahra's voice jolted me back into the present moment. "*Chica*!" Mario cued up a CD of *sevillanas*. Oh dear...

Zahra beckoned to me to join her in the center of the dance floor. This was one day when I couldn't deny her a *sevillanas*. Though I'd never expected to be dancing it in front of a crowd of Swiss bankers with cameras.

Mario restarted the song from the beginning, and Zahra and I stood facing each other. We reached our arms slowly out and up, and I watched my hands as they twirled above me. We'd come a long way from Bar Andaluz.

I thought about flamenco and how it had swept into my life and turned everything upside down. I remembered that day in the lunchroom when I saw the ad in the classifieds and just knew that I had to dial the number. But I could never have guessed the journey it would take me on.

Flamenco took me out of that narrow world where success was equated with the value of your handbag on eBay, your boyfriend's taxable income, and how close you were to buying that waterfront property, and showed me joy in *compás*, in a *calimocho*, a bowl of olives, warm sun on my cheek, and the smell of orange blossoms. With its special brand of *toma que toma* magic, it whisked me out of that world of piped music and muted colors and showed me a life that is outrageous and covered in polka dots. Where red is the new black and everyone can wear orange, but not Hermès orange. Brighter.

With flamenco I was transported into a world where everyone is beautiful, because beauty is in everything, the glorious and the ugly; because flamenco celebrates living, through the cries of pain and the cries of joy, the symmetry of a young face and the character of an old face. A young dancer is applauded for displays of dizzying technique, and an old dancer is celebrated for saying the same thing with a flick of the hip and a twirl of the wrist.

And when each stage of life is celebrated and expressed through art, it is impossible to be afraid of life. Perhaps that was flamenco's biggest gift. It taught me not to be afraid. Whether it was the fear of death by secondhand smoke in a bar in Seville, of making it to the end of the week with only five euro to my name, of escaping from a gypsy ghetto in the middle of the night, or of falling in love, flamenco taught me to take that fear and crush it under the heel of my shoe and move on, because life is too important to be missed by worrying.

Okay, I may not have totally mastered that lesson, because I was starting to worry that I couldn't remember all the steps of *sevillanas*. It had been a long time since our nights out in Seville. I might just have to make something up. Stay close, flamenco. I'll be needing you…

And why do I get the feeling you're not done with me yet? What other adventures do you have in store for me? No, actually, don't tell me. I don't think I want to know.

"*Olé*!" Zahra cried as the first *copla* started up. We stepped toward each other, and then back. Forward and back, and I heard in my mind my first partner at Bar Andaluz saying, "*Pasa*! *Gira*! *Pasa*!"

The ballroom was filled with the flash of cameras, like the light of the fire in the gypsy ghetto. And I heard that old familiar voice in my ear, whispering: *Why don't you...ride off into the sunset in a painted caravan?*

Why not?

THE NEW
BEGINNING

Or

Vamos, chica!

This one is fantastic!" Alejandro cried, turning up the car stereo. He tried to translate the lyrics for me. "My love has no…*fronteras*?"

"Borders," I helped him.

Alejandro was one of my English students in Madrid, but now we were driving together across Spain. I needed to travel this weekend, but every train and bus and goat cart heading south had been booked out for weeks. Alejandro was going to his village for the long weekend, and when I'd mentioned I was looking at flights, he insisted I come with him. And as we drove over the mountains, he treated me to his personal collection of all-time greatest love songs.

"This song! This song is *lo mejor*, the best!" I cringed at the opening strains of "My Heart Will Go On" from *Titanic*. I knew Alejandro was planning to spend his weekend dancing *sevillanas*, so why wouldn't he play some flamenco? But he could see that I wasn't myself, and he was trying to cheer me up. And I was grateful.

I was still reeling from what I'd done. With four simple words my life had been turned upside down. It was a conversation that started when Iñaki and I went to bed, and went on for hours as we drifted in and out of sleep. At three o'clock in the morning the beautiful, wonderful man of my life asked me the question that I had been avoiding for too long: "What do you want?"

I had looked at the man lying next to me, the man I had slept alongside every night for three years. I loved him so much that it was impossible to bear. I loved him before I even knew him, and the more I knew him the more I loved him. At the beginning our communication was stilted at best, but with time, as I picked up more and more Spanish, we became closer and closer. He was the kindest, gentlest man I had ever known. And yet…I wasn't happy.

I wasn't happy with the life I was leading. It was a beautiful life. We had a beautiful home, with a lovely little rooftop terrace where I had an herb garden, and a block of wood I could practice my flamenco footwork on while gazing out over the Madrid skyline. During the days we both went off to work, then we'd meet for a beer in a sunny outdoor café in the afternoon. On Iñaki's nights off we'd go out to dinner, then wander home through the cobblestoned streets of old Madrid. It was idyllic and romantic and everything I had ever wanted. So what the hell what wrong with me???

That was the question that plagued me. I could feel the restlessness building inside of me. I wanted another adventure. I wanted to see more of the world and experience other ways of living. But Iñaki had found everything he wanted, and he couldn't understand why I didn't feel the same way. Now we were talking about getting married. He wanted children, and I didn't know what I wanted. But if I was going to have twelve, it was time to get started.

Sensing that I was awake, he stirred and pulled me to him. "What do you want?" he asked, his voice heavy with sleep.

Good question. What did I want? I needed to find that out. But I was starting to realize what I didn't want. I didn't want to settle down and start a family. I knew that I still had a few more good escapades in me.

I whispered, "I don't want this." And so, at exactly three oh two a.m. on March 17, moments before drifting into sleep, I said the words that ended the most beautiful love story of my life.

I'll never get over this, I thought. Maybe there are some things in life we just aren't meant to get over. Just breathe, I told myself. Perhaps I shouldn't expect to ever be free of this pain; I should just hope for little victories. One whole day without tears, for example. To dance again. To learn to enjoy life's little moments without needing to share them with him.

A big green sign up ahead told us we were about to cross over into *Andalucía*. "*Ay! Estamos llegando!*" We're almost there! Alejandro yelped in excitement.

Wait for it, wait for it…

The sign grew bigger and bigger, and as we sped past it Alejandro threw back his head and sang, "*Olé, olé, Olé!*" Gone was the smooth professional I used to visit once a week in his Madrid office. Alejandro was home now, and he could forget about primary catchment areas and the summer marketing campaign. He was thinking about his sofa, his remote control, and his mother's cooking.

But I still had another sixty miles to go. Alejandro pulled up outside the train station and we went in to see if there was any way I could travel that night. He scanned the board. "There is a train that leaves in five minutes." We raced to the ticket window, and I handed over my ID and credit card, signed without even looking at what I was signing, and, ticket in hand, raced to the platform.

The train was waiting, and the staff were greeting passengers and helping them find their seats. Alejandro took my bags from my hands and tossed them through the security X-ray. As someone scanned my ticket, I shouted good-bye.

My carriage was at the far end of the platform and I ran to it, swinging myself onboard just before the doors closed. I found my place and fell into the plush chair with relief.

All around me people were dressed up for the feria. Men walked up and down the aisle in their best suits, and women were peering into compact mirrors as they painted on red lips. In front of me a group of teenage girls were applying eyeliner, swapping earrings and high heels, and going over the plans for the festivities.

The train pulled away from the station, and I leaned back in my seat for the smooth forty-minute ride. I was going back to where my story began. I had one weekend to make some sense of my life. Four years ago I stood by the river in the moonlight and made a wish. It was time to wish again.

❋

There's nowhere more beautiful than Seville. Well, not for me. It's not just about the palm trees that line the river or the low white-washed buildings; Seville is beautiful to me because I remember the nights that I wandered through its streets with the moon in my eyes.

It all came back to me as I walked those streets again, past the old marketplace, under the orange trees, and to the little café where I used to go for my morning *café con leche*. I walked in and once again breathed a sigh of relief. Nothing had changed. Seville had remained in a time capsule for me. The same gruff waiter was serving the same strong coffee for the same price; the same crowd were lining up for their heart starters and lighting up their morning cigarettes.

The only thing that had changed was me. Or so I thought. The waiter set down in front of me a glass with a shot of espresso coffee, then filled it to the brim with hot milk. He flicked his eyes up at me, raised one shaggy eyebrow, and said, "*Cuánto tiempo.*" It's been awhile.

So it had. It had been four years almost to the day since I'd last stood in that café, and I couldn't believe that the waiter remembered me. "So what, you been busy?" he asked casually.

My phone beeped. A new message: Chica, I'm at the airport. How's the weather?

I didn't expect my old friend to be wearing a white gold Rolex studded with rubies. I should have expected it, but I didn't. After all, wasn't it only yesterday that we were counting out our few euro to pay for tapas in El Rinconcillo? But many things had changed in Zahra's life since those days. She'd gotten married, of course—a fact that was demonstrated by the heavy diamond rings that shone like flashlights on her finger. And she had become second in charge of a Swiss bank. But as we walked again down our favorite streets, it was as if nothing had changed.

"Remember how we used to walk?" She linked her arm through mine and sang with each step, "*Toma que toma que toma que toma.*"

I laughed and sang with her, "*Que toma que toma que toma que toma!*"

We went back to El Rinconcillo for vegetarian meat and vino. "*Chica*, listen!" One of our favorite songs was playing on the radio, and before I knew it I was crying. "You know," Zahra said, "sometimes what you want most in the world does not make you happy." She was right, and I knew it.

"I just don't know what I want anymore."

Zahra searched my face with her beautiful eyes and said, "You are changing. You are growing up. But you know…be patient. Because when you change, the world will change with you."

Music was coming from the street outside. We looked out the window and saw a man walking down the road playing *rumbas* on an old guitar, and a dozen people following him, all singing and dancing.

"*Vamos, chica!*" Zahra said. "Let's go dance!"

We ran out of the café and joined the crowd dancing in the street.

I forgot my tears and allowed myself to be swallowed up once again in another spring night in Seville.

The next morning I went back to the same café for my morning coffee. Rain fell lightly as I walked up to the Alameda. It was that beautiful spring rain, *txirimiri*, as they call it in Basque.

I asked myself again as I stirred my coffee why I'd done what I'd done. It was the same question I asked myself a thousand times a day. And a response came to me through my sorrow: "You're not ready to stop yet."

I knew that Madrid wasn't my final destination. I didn't know what was ahead of me, but I couldn't help feeling that this was the beginning of my journey, not the end. *Perhaps I'm just not the marrying kind*, I thought with a sigh. *Or at least, not the marrying and having twelve children kind.*

As I wandered back through the streets, the rain came down harder, and then suddenly the skies opened and I found myself beneath a Sevillian spring downpour. People dashed into doorways to escape it, only to be splashed by the cars that drove through the flooded streets.

I didn't care about getting wet, and the raindrops disguised the tears on my cheeks. I had no plans for my future beyond this weekend in Seville. I didn't know what I was going to do or where I was going to go. But I knew that I would always love Iñaki. It was as if the love I felt for him had opened up a place in my heart that hadn't existed before, and it would travel with me as I stepped into the darkness of my own uncertainty.

The rain got stronger and stronger until I had to run to the nearest awning to take cover. As I wiped the water from my face, I saw that I was in front of a travel agency.

Paris, Miami, Cairo…

I felt something stir inside me that I hadn't felt in a long time. A longing for a new adventure, a journey into the unknown. I could go south, where life is hotter and wilder. I could ride a camel across the Sahara and see the sun rise over the pyramids.

Calcutta, Mumbai…

Or drink chai on the streets of India and wrap myself in silks and whirl like a dervish.

Lima, Santiago, Buenos Aires…

Or dance in red shoes in an underground tango bar.

And just think of all the trouble I could get into in Marrakesh! Marauding through the Medina, or rocking the Kasbahs.

And an old familiar voice whispered softly, *Why don't you…?*

ACKNOWLEDGMENTS

I'd like to thank all the people who made this book happen: the amazing Daniel Lazar and the Writers House team, and everyone at Sourcebooks, in particular my wonderful editorial manager, Shana Drehs, and my divine editor, Anna Klenke, for turning my manuscript into such a beautiful book. Thank you!

I'd also like to thank my Australian publisher, Annette Barlow, and the team at Allen & Unwin, in particular my editors Vanessa Pellatt and Clara Finlay. And, of course, Catherine Milne, who first envisioned this book and dared to say, *"Why don't you?"*

I want to thank all the people who fill these pages. In writing this book it's been important to me to respect the privacy of the extraordinary people who've shared my journey. To that end, some names have been changed and some characters have been merged.

And finally, I would like to thank my agent, Fran Moore, and everyone at Curtis Brown for your support, wisdom, and guidance. I can't thank you enough, but I'm going to try: thank you, thank you, thank you!

ABOUT THE AUTHOR

Nellie Bennett grew up in Sydney, Australia. After completing high school, she worked as a shopgirl in a department store, mastering the art of ironing silk and pleating tissue paper. In her early twenties Nellie discovered flamenco dance and traveled to

Photo by Fernando López Coloma

Spain to further her studies in the birthplace of flamenco, Seville. She soon fell in love with all things Spanish and moved to Madrid, where she learned to dance from the neighborhood gypsies. Nellie has worked as a screenwriter in both Australia and Bollywood and contributed feature articles to the *Australian* and the *Sydney Morning Herald*. Her interests include eating, drinking, daydreaming, wandering aimlessly, and dancing till dawn.